OSCILLATE WILDLY

Also by Peter Hitchcock

Dialogics of the Oppressed
Working-Class Fiction in Theory and Practice

OSCILLATE WILDLY

SPACE, BODY, AND SPIRIT OF MILLENNIAL MATERIALISM

PETER HITCHCOCK

FOREWORD BY STEPHEN E. CULLENBERG

University of Minnesota Press

Minneapolis

London

Published by the University of Minnesota Press
111 Third Avenue South, Suite 290
Minneapolis, MN 55401-2520
http://www.upress.umn.edu

Printed in the United States of America on acid-free paper

The University of Minnesota is an equal-opportunity educator and employer.

Library of Congress Cataloging-in-Publication Data

Hitchcock, Peter.
    Oscillate wildly : space, body, and spirit of millennial
materialism / Peter Hitchcock ; foreword by Stephen E. Cullenberg.
        p.   cm.
    Includes bibliographical references.
    ISBN 0-8166-3149-2 (hardcover). – ISBN 0-8166-3150-6
    1. Materialism.   2. Philosophy, Modern – 20th century.   I. Title.
B825.H64   1999
146'.3 – DC21   98–36588

10 09 08 07 06 05 04 03 02 01 00 99   10 9 8 7 6 5 4 3 2 1

For my mother

What is mind but motion in the intellectual sphere?

— Oscar Wilde

CONTENTS

FOREWORD

Stephen E. Cullenberg

It would be tempting to concede Marxism's defeat at the end of the long, tortuous journey through the course of the twentieth century, both as ideology and political practice. The signs are all here: the collapse of worldwide communism after 1989, the increased globalization of capitalism's hegemony, the uncertain cultural challenge of postmodernism to the certain materialist discourses that guided oppositional politics throughout this troubled century. Yet, in the face of these transformative millennial moments, Peter Hitchcock reminds us that one of the profound lessons of history is oscillation. And, as he brilliantly performs throughout his book, we shouldn't just oscillate theoretically and politically in the current period — we need to oscillate wildly.

For Hitchcock, oscillation is not just a metaphor but also a theoretical concept, a concept that will help us come to terms with the tumultuous and tremulous changes facing the world today. Oscillation has epistemic meaning as well, as it allows for new articulations and complex combinatorics of older materialisms with various new "cultural" discourses. This new materialism, what Hitchcock calls "millennial materialism," builds from the materialism of Marx (indeed, one might equally refer to millennial materialism as millennial Marxism), while also refusing to submerge all that has traditionally been effaced in traditional Marxism. One example is the body, which feminist theorists have explained is too often represented by Marxism as simply masculine, a stick-figured *Homo economicus*, unaware of its sexed, gendered, raced, and ironically, even classed manifestations. *Oscillate Wildly* takes us through a number of other oscillations of materialist critique — ideology, space, body, fetishism, and spirit — and deftly (re)values some of the work of Deleuze and Guattari, Spivak, Foucault, and Derrida, among others, finding "value" in these putatively nonmaterialist authors.

It is arguable that materialism's first major oscillation occurred 150 years ago with the publication of the *Communist Manifesto*. Materialist theory in the hands of Marx and Engels breathed powerful life into the political movements of Europe. Just weeks after the *Manifesto*'s appearance, the uprising of French workers in the Paris Commune inaugurated the century and a half of challenges to and oscillations of Marxian theory and practice. Indeed, today, as the new millennium nears, one can see the oscillations of materialism's genealogy, where it has been elaborated, transformed, and renewed many more times, and in many more ways than often understood. Interestingly, one of the most profound oscillations of the current period is the fact that not only the text of Marxian discourse but also its discursive form are being transformed rapidly in the current period. Marx's *Capital* can now be purchased as a multimedia CD-ROM, and much of Marx and Engels's work can be accessed and searched over the Internet. The Internet itself has become an important site for Left and Marxist organizing, as many web sites announce conferences, provide electronic versions of published articles, present multimedia versions of political and cultural events before unavailable easily and inexpensively, and support worldwide dialogue and discussion about important political issues through chat rooms and listserves. Recently, a new, "slick" version of the *Manifesto* has been produced and will be prominently marketed in Barnes and Nobles superstores, among other places. All this has contributed to a rapidly changing Left culture, one that might be dubbed a culture of CyberMarx, and has created new challenges and opportunities for a renewed Marxian and Left global dialogue.

This virtual oscillation brings to materialism new contingent possibilities, yet the initial vision articulated by Marx and Engels still speaks powerfully to the wanton destruction and widespread injustices associated with the development of capitalism and, therefore, for the liberatory dreams of peoples and movements the world over. Marx and Engels in 1848 already recognized the incipient forces of globalization, and in today's world, where instant communication and footloose corporations seem to imbricate themselves into every dimension of our economy and culture, this materialist presence, where all that is solid melts into air, marks yet a new materialist oscillation. Hitchcock beautifully elaborates this with reference to the chronotope of the shoe, the articulation of culture and class located in the sensate imaginary of the commodity. The material conditions of the Indonesian Nike worker and the culture of affect and desire of the Western consumer are both constitutive of millennial materialism, a contemporary oscillation mirrored long ago by Marx's analysis of commodity fetishism.

The greatest challenge of materialism's current oscillations is one that involves the discovery and opening of new political spaces. The presence of new political identities and subjects, sometimes referred to as "new social movements," seems to confound any spectral politics based on the self-confident class identities of previous periods. Anticapitalist oscillations have lost their grounding in the once clear opposition between capitalism and socialism since the "Fall" in 1989. Postmodernist and poststructural insights have ruptured the once hegemonic suturing of the social space around the materialist or even class axis. The theoretical accomplishment of Hitchcock's millennial materialism is that it recognizes the oscillation of political subjects, an oscillation both in the world and in theory, and thus one that reverberates between them. It is these contingent, but nevertheless real, reverberations that a millennial materialist practice must confront.

ACKNOWLEDGMENTS

The progress of this book has been somewhat tortuous, both for its author and for others who have had to live with this manuscript in one way or another. Like most books, its direction has changed in the act of writing itself, but I never intended its creation to follow the principle of oscillation in the very form of its composition. Because of the nature of the metatheory that is at its heart, I've sometimes felt like "Oscillating Ozio" in *Primary Colors*, a parody of the Cuomo who is unable to take the next big step. As I try to elaborate in this work, the task is not to find virtue in hesitancy, but to come to terms with the material constraints on theoretical vacillation themselves. This, indeed, has left its mark on the question of intent in the book that follows, even as the primary color remains red.

I have many people to thank for keeping me oscillating wildly while assuring that my text did not dance away from me. First, the ideas in this book have been tried out at various venues: at the Graduate Center of CUNY, where many years ago I problematized the politics of multiculturalism; at Duke (twice), where I discussed the odd journey of cultural materialism and then the principle of "moving" theory itself; at McGill, where I had the great pleasure of debating the transatlantic trade in theory with Darko Suvin, Marc Angenot, and the inestimable Robert Barsky (the latter's work on Chomsky is a tribute to an *agent oscillatoire*); at the American Studies Association meeting in Kansas, where I linked the process of the production and consumption of athletic shoes to late capital via an interpretation of Bakhtin's sense of chronotope (developed in chapter 4 of the present work); at the University of Western Ontario, in an event graciously hosted by Clive Thomson, where I told a materialist ghost story (reworked and reincarnated at a *Rethinking Marxism* conference in Amherst in 1996); and finally, at Bakhtinian events in Moscow and Cerisy-la-Salle, where I attempted to show how the body of labor gets emptied out by representational aesthetics (the difference in the Russian and French intellectual reactions to my papers is itself a measure of the international division of labor after the collapse of "actually existing socialism"). Obviously I am concerned with movements much greater than the mask of Bacchus in the breeze.

Fellow oscillators in the reading process are numerous. Amitava Kumar knows a good specter (and spectacle) when he sees one and provided an important critical account of the manuscript in its entirety. So too did Richard Dienst, who has helped me to "read the shape of the world" in productive ways. Without their careful criticism I could not have got this project to its current state (although they are clearly not responsible for my misinterpretations of their advice). Lawrence Venuti has shown immense patience with my extravagant materialist musings and has taught me how to edit a thought without compromising it. Two anonymous readers also contributed greatly to this process, and while this is not the book they envisaged, they may yet see better for its appearance.

Some friends and colleagues have provided less formal but inspiring advice. Tim Brennan may not always be at home in the world of my prose, but he has nevertheless understood the particular political implications of this text. Laura Kipnis discussed a Marxian carbuncle or two over coffee as well as making me understand how the materiality of the body provides its own oscillation as feminist intervention. Françoise Lionnet offered crucial encouragement for my analysis of Glissant and Caribbean discourse, although my discussion falls short of her work on *métissage,* which provides a benchmark for the theorization of Caribbean and African aesthetics. Jeff Kerr Ritchie is a more recent victim of my paean to oscillatory practice, and as a historian he knows that the "hurt" of history has a theoretical provenance. Thank you all.

Steve Cullenberg deserves a special note of thanks. Not only has he read my work judiciously, but as a self-professed postmodern Marxist economist he has readily thought through the connections and disjunctions between my theory and his. Indeed, I take his foreword not just as a personal favor but as an act of solidarity among Leftist economists and cultural theorists in general, however marginal that constituency is and must necessarily remain.

The folks at the University of Minnesota Press have supported my work for some years. Lisa Freeman, in particular, gave the present tome her strong professional support. My editor, William Murphy, has been enthusiastic all the way, even when he didn't have to be. His assistant, Robin A. Moir, has kept me up-to-date with the paperwork — an important task, since publishing has its own version of chaos theory. While other academic publishers have made significant contributions to the world of cultural theory, Minnesota stands out in its commitment and has undeniably changed the landscape of theoretical inquiry in the last twenty years. I would also like to thank Hank Schlau for his copyediting, which, given the metatheory of the current work, was a Herculean labor to be sure.

The Left, in all its new configurations, continues to need theory. Theory need not keep people from the barricades; it can teach us to build barricades or cross them when necessary. Whether this is some paradoxical luxury of lassitude the reader must decide.

William Blake once opined that without "contraries" there would be no progression. Of course, now we forbid such progressivist discourse (!), but surely the progress of a book could not occur without friends and colleagues? My social being has been nurtured by Baruch College and the Graduate School of the City University of New York, whose professors, students, and staff have lifted my spirits at key moments in the writing of this book. In particular, Tuzyline Jita Allan, Carmel Jordan, Bill McClellan, Tom Hayes, Gary Hentzi, John Todd, and Connie Terrero performed this miracle at Baruch, while Bill Kelly, Anne Humpherys, Alyosha Goldstein, Sarah Relyea, Lopamudra Basu, Jung-wan Yu, Jennifer Starbuck, and a wild oscillator *avant la lettre,* Clarence Robertson, did the same at the Graduate School. Friends who have kept me going include Eric Mendelsohn (the most underrated Melvillean in town), Isabelle Lorenz, Kris Torgeson, Xiao Qiang, Obioma Nnaemeka, Vince Cheng, and the elusive Lawrence Haddad (where are you now?).

Oscillate Wildly? Of course, it is Oscar, and my thanks to Morrissey and *The Smiths* for getting me to dance to a pun at the end of the twentieth century. Music is "louder than bombs." My favorite dance partner is Amy Dooling, who not only lives my wild oscillations, but loves them. The feeling is mutual.

AN INTRODUCTORY OSCILLATION

[E]verything changes when you grasp base-and-superstructure not as a full-fledged theory in its own right, but rather as the name for a problem, whose solution is always a unique, ad hoc invention. — FREDRIC JAMESON

My own hunch is to base our utopistics on the inherent lack of long-term equilibria in any phenomena — physical, biological, or social. — IMMANUEL WALLERSTEIN

The wealth of theory in which oscillation prevails appears as a monstrous collection of contradictions; an individual theoretical contradiction appears as its elementary form. Oscillation? By rewriting Marx's opening of *Capital* under the sign of "oscillation" I hope to implicate several materialist insights more forcefully in the present. This book is an analysis of what oscillation can mean for materialist theory bound by specific contradictions in space, in the body, and in spirit. Obviously, such statements are too concise, and indeed it has taken a book to bring them into more explanatory focus. That a crisis is implied by my use of oscillation (as a metaphor and as a concept) will come as no surprise to materialists, especially those who have pondered the turbulent collapse and/or rearticulation of "actually existing socialism" and the uneven acceleration of globalization and transnationalism. Concomitantly, there has been a sustained challenge to materialist metanarratives formerly buttressed by the axiological stability of "history" as a concept. The storm this has caused has been intense and has often divided Leftist thinkers according to the relative status of history for their intellectual projects. To my mind, the vitality of a good many of materialism's propositions is in danger of being quashed by an orthodoxy whose historicism ironically suppresses Marx's analysis of historical process. Things fall apart in materialism's history for good materialist reasons.

For some materialists, my introduction of an oscillatory paradigm will sound scandalous, a symptom of that crude ambivalence that displaces anticapitalism onto myriad degrees of culturalism. Yet, in effect, the following chapters are no more than a reply to the basic call (variously expressed by, say, Terry Eagleton in *The Illusions of Postmodernism,* Fredric Jameson in *The Seeds of Time,* or a number of essays in the Callari/Ruccio collection, *Postmodern Materialism and the Future of Marxist Theory*) to understand anew the material constraints on materialism at the turn of the millennium. Millennial materialism is a name for this reply. It is a form of practice that begins with the "bad new things" of the material world today, even as it risks some difficult paths of metatheory in order to negotiate them. My only hope is that those who believe in more just, egalitarian forms of society are inspired to stay the course by my critique of materialist theory's role in that process.

But oscillation? Oscillation here is a basic metaphor for a particular mode of theory, materialism — both oscillation within materialism and materialism's oscillation with respect to competing orders of knowledge. The use of metaphor in this endeavor is not new, or unproblematic. For instance, both Perry Anderson's notion of "a zone of engagement" and Martin Jay's use of "force fields" deploy provocative spatial metaphors as organizational tools in materialist argumentation.[1] Oscillation, however, describes space *and* time relations and, more importantly, is an *active* and not simply a descriptive metaphor of materialist inquiry from Marx to the present. It is not just a label for a theoretical position *but is intrinsic* to the logic of various forms of materialist analysis. This does not make oscillation a transhistorical essence as such because the nature of its dynamic expression is precisely dependent on historical flux — that which works its potential into a material force. To study oscillation now is to analyze the necessity for such logic in materialism at a moment when its tenets are otherwise brusquely dismissed as effete and the conditions of its material force appear critically disengaged. That such a move entails the terrors or errors of metaphoricity must remain a constitutive risk for a materialist polemic. The argument must acknowledge the function of tenor and vehicle for a social analytic.

So oscillation is a metaphor. One can say more, however, about the varying parameters of this metaphorical embrace. I use oscillation to refer simultaneously to movement within and between bodies of theory, within theories of the body, and within and between institutions and institutional spaces in which such theory is taken up. Yet if oscillation is seen only as a principle of movement, then it cancels through almost any theory and institution that one could think of and would be about as rewarding as the discovery of death in human existence. No. I will argue that oscillation is a particular form and expression of materialist politics in theory, one that is, on the one hand, newly autocritical regarding its own formulations and, on the other, conspicuously tactical in its treatment of others. It is a form of politics that shares something of the legacy of historical materialism but whose greatest promise (*and* weakness) lies in its development within and beyond the conceptual range of cultural materialism.[2] Indeed, if one takes seriously the concept of oscillation for materialism, it allows a critical perspective on the key divisions within materialist thought as symptomatic of both its dynamism and dead-ends at specific moments in history. It is both a descriptive device for the state of materialism and a critical tool for a polemic about what materialism can do at this juncture — a moment in which various forms of materialism incessantly wonder about their status in the great wake of materialist practice once known as socialist revolution.[3]

The chapters that follow will show how oscillation works within and on key components of materialist theory, and on some that should be. Obviously, materialism provides several competing paradigms that seek to explain material reality — for instance, the reality of integration and fragmentation on a world scale within capitalism — but the magnitude of their differences, their agitated condition, defines the way that materialist theory must address the otherwise unimaginable time/space regimes that seek hegemony in the world system. The degree of intensity is actually the ground of possibility for materialism to move beyond the detritus that marks its historically determined formations. David Simpson once suggested that materialism must be the Oliver Twist of theory — it must always ask for more, more of its objectivist and subjectivist modes of understanding.[4] There is a nice movement from quantity to quality in this formulation, but it does not quite capture the para-dialectics I have in mind (perhaps a composite of the ghosts in "A Christmas Carol" would be more appropriate given the question of time and spirit that animates a later chapter).

One of the subthemes that runs throughout this study is that oscillation invokes not only a restless inquiry but also an attendant danger for materialist politics: that is, oscillation is simultaneously vacillation — a moment of doubt, of hesitation, of wavering. Such a danger might seem to offer an inhibiting and compromised political practice, one that could eat away at even the most steadfast convictions. Yet most progressive forms of materialism promote a radical skepticism both toward the objects of their critique (the bourgeois liberal state, the transnational corporation, or mutations of oppressive ideology) and toward materialism's founding principles themselves. The moment of doubt is also one of autocritique. In addition, and just as importantly, the hesitation in oscillation may be symptomatic of a theoretical aporia, an impasse produced by the nature of a formulation according to the new contexts in which it finds itself (certainly we will see evidence of this in my own and Balibar's reading of Marx). In general, I will argue that the double entendre of oscillation is what must be risked if materialism is to articulate a radical politics apposite with the tremendous dislocations of contemporary social orders. Oscillation means embracing the dynamic changes of the present, the specific intensities of globalization or the aftermath of imploding socialist states for instance, but with the attendant hazard of vacillation. At the conscious and unconscious levels of intellectual inquiry it now presents itself as a *determinate condition of materialism*.[5] This is precisely how the assuredness (and masculinism) of traditional forms of materialism are being shaken out of their ossified practices. Terry Eagleton, of course, mistrusts this maneuver almost as much as he despises CEOs and religious heads of various persuasions. No doubt what I am suggesting is perilously indicative of "a cult of ambiguity and indeterminacy" instead of more "aggressive" modes of opposition that get cracking by ripping up capitalism's brute realities of everyday existence.[6] Yet it is a mistake on Eagleton's part to believe that every moment of indeterminacy is simply the ruse of some whimsical or vacuous "postmodern" thinking. Indeed, Eagleton's attack on "postmodern" ambiguity runs counter to his own beliefs in the mutability of the materialist project, which has frequently, as his book on the aesthetic clearly shows, had to turn to its ambiguous, liminal being between the imagination and the real. One cannot turn one's back on that history. One of its lessons is that to oscillate wildly might just keep the deadwood in materialism from seeming otherwise.

The prospect of a materialism dogged by the risk of oscillation as vacillation provides little comfort, especially to those whose materialisms have recently foundered on the shattered contradiction between the state and communism. Yet it might contribute to an explanation for this hiatus, when communism must come to exist in other forms than those that banalized its greater aims. For those who now suffer under the largesse of financialization and transnationalism, wavering might seem fatal, if not fatalistic. Certainly a politics that appears to trip over its heels does not offer a particularly alluring model of confrontation with the speed and hyperreality of contemporary regimes of capital. Here two points must be emphasized (their elaboration is in evidence in the chapters below): first, the moment of pause is also one of reflexivity — it must precede any viable rearticulation of the problem at hand; second, the moment of doubt is a more general function of the era: it certainly permeates the apparently fluid operations of capital and its adherents — political victories, however, accrue only to those who better understand its logic.

To interpret oscillation as vacillation is in part to recall and reinterpret Adorno's elaboration of homeostasis in *Aesthetic Theory*.[7] Briefly, Adorno presents a concept of art that is not immutable, but is open to dialectical change. A concept of art can only appear momentarily as "a fragile balance," but "disturbances continually upset the balance, keeping the process in motion." This leads Adorno to suggest that "every work of art is an instant; every great work of art is a stoppage of the process, a momentary standing still, whereas a persistent eye sees only the process" (9). We can observe the process of art but only conceptualize its possibility in the moment of a fragile balance. This equilibrium is not significant in itself — it only gains importance in light of the tensions that produced it. As Adorno comments later, "the beautiful" is itself a "homeostasis of tensions" that, once apprehended within its totality, is "sucked into an eddy" (78). Similarly, the pause in oscillation cannot be properly understood outside the system of tensions or alternating variations that are its genesis. If the movement implied in oscillation simultaneously provides a laudable and lamentable dynamism, then its momentary stasis marks the truth of that disturbance. The pause in oscillation is the mean of its corollary in movement.

For Adorno, homeostasis in art was a portent of crisis, and one of particularly modernist inclinations where crisis is linked to the paradoxical status of art as autonomous:

> The notion of homeostasis denotes an equilibrium which comes to pass only in the totality of the work of art. It probably occurs at a point in time when the art work becomes discernibly autonomous. It is then that homeostasis, if it does not fully realize itself, becomes at least an imminent possibility. This casts a shadow of doubt on homeostasis, which in turn reflects a more general crisis of this concept in modern art. Precisely at the point when the work of art deems itself autonomous — being certain of itself as an inherently consistent particular — it ceases to be consistent because the very achievement of autonomy entails reification, divesting it of its openness which too is part of its concept. (409)[8]

Adorno used homeostasis in other ways, particularly in analyzing the relationship between subject and object that is integral to both his discussion of the work of art and the present interest in the function of pause for theory (oscillation is assured, to a great degree, by the asymmetry of subject and object). The difficulty throughout is understanding that stasis is not being valorized as a goal in itself: it is the paradox of homeostasis that is at issue; it is a moment of fragile equilibrium in a sea of movement that is its very possibility. Theory's relationship to this is in turn paradoxical. Adorno, for instance, realized in *Aesthetic Theory* that aesthetics demands a solution to a problem that cannot be delivered in the medium of theory itself. Jameson comments that "we cannot think the form and the content of a given concept simultaneously or in the same way," but nevertheless he suggests that Adorno's dialectics provides just this "stereoscopic thinking."[9] Similarly, oscillation addresses this paradox of theory, but for materialism in particular. If materialist theory becomes the name or form of praxis, then praxis itself folds back into a philosophical void from which materialism seeks to salvage it. There are many lessons to be learned from the mistakes of various theoreticians of the state, and one is that materialist praxis is social not theoretical qua theory. Thus, the pause for theory in oscillation simultaneously reminds us of theory's potential for reification and its inscription in forms of the social that seek to transcend it.

We are at the end of a low, dishonest century. It began with the promise of scientific and technological progress and ends with the specter of ecological and social disaster. The world was rocked by socialist revolution, and now is rocked to sleep by capitalist triumphalism. The century began with a "great" war to end ethnic exterminism and ends with forms of ethnic exterminism that mark the utter failure of the nation-state to arbitrate social strife within and without its borders. Materialism has answers to every aspect of this sordid history (Hobsbawm's *The Age of Extremes* is a good example),[10] but not always to its own contributions in making it. I am, however, interested less in apportioning blame than in understanding how culpability structures the contradictory logic I have invoked. On one level this registers the masquerade of the critical endeavor, as if theory could ever stand outside the world it helped create; yet it also underlines the importance of responsibility in theoretical work. For all the playful exuberance that one may witness in the study that follows, oscillation is not a language game, not a philosopher's game, not an academic game in the negative sense: it proceeds from a desire to make materialism matter still more than it did in the twentieth century.

Oscillation is not simply a metaphor but a concept, and one that I hope to imbue with a specific materialist outlook. This concept does not lie behind the word or the metaphor, as if we might scrape through to it like some palimpsest. Oscillation here emerges out of a set of philosophical and political problems in which it is the modus operandi. It does not deliver us from evil (as Deleuze and Guattari note, "There is no heaven for concepts")[11] but provides a working out of the processes of knowledge formation and confrontation. To understand oscillation's function as a concept is to come to terms with a process of becoming. In *What Is Philosophy?* Deleuze and Guattari elaborate this sense of becoming in several ways (some of which will return, in ghostly fashion, later in this book), including a consideration of the concept that precedes the understanding of what they call "the other person" for philosophy. The recognition of the other person by a subject presents or makes possible a world, a possible world. This much is true of several traditions of philosophy, psychology, and social thought where the other person may make possible subjecthood, desire, or a particular form of power structure. Here the concept of oscillation brushes the concept of the other person in positive and negative ways. For Deleuze and Guattari, the other person expresses a possible world — a "perceptual field" that leads to a reconsideration and reevaluation of what is integral to that field. The terms of this modification themselves define an oscillating field for philosophy: "No longer being either subject of the field or object in the field, the other person will become the condition under which not only subject and object are redistributed but also figure and ground, margins and center, moving object and reference point, transitive and substantial, length and depth" (18). Thus, the concept of the other person begins to disturb, or reconceptualize, a whole array of components within the possible world. Here the concept of the other person needs the concept of oscillation without ever being reducible to it. But, to comment on Deleuze and Guattari's approach further, they realize that oscillation is not sufficient if the possible world of the concept remains unarticulated within the world in which its possibility is manifest. In this regard, they see a difference between the concept and the modal logic of propositions and suggest that, in their example, "even when Wittgenstein envisages propositions of fear or pain, he does not see them as modalities that can be expressed in a position of the other person because he leaves the other person oscillating between another subject and a special object" (17–18). This, then, is the promise and precipice of oscillation for philosophical inquiry. On the one hand, Deleuze and Guattari identify a concept whose dynamism guarantees a refiguring of the perceptual field; on the other, the same principle of dynamism can leave a concept unattached or undertheorized as a proposition. Not all concepts function in this way, but the more Deleuze and Guattari explain the logic of the concept, the more a concept *for* the concept recommends itself. In contrast to the rigidity and authority of the abstract idea, they opine: "There is no reason why concepts should cohere.... Even bridges from one concept to another are still junctions, or detours, which do not define any discursive whole. They are movable bridges. From this point of view, philosophy can be seen as being in a perpetual state of digression or digressiveness" (23).

But for oscillation to be a concept it must have explanatory and not just descriptive or digressive power. Oscillation is not the means to survey various spatiotemporal coordinates so much as a way to put them to work, to draw out or produce their implications for complementary and conflicting fields of knowledge. Oscillation is a concept in the sense that Deleuze and Guattari describe it because "it renders components *inseparable within itself*" (19; emphasis added). It resonates with other concepts rather than coheres and is relational rather than uniform. One must beware of this slippery register, however, for what may seem an appreciable openness to various conceptual fields can often turn into mere voluntarism, opportunism, or the cancer of all dialectical thought, relativism. The motor for oscillation as a concept is provided by the relational zone among its theoretical components. These components are not simply interchangeable according to individual will or volition: they are produced by specific conditions of possibility. Similarly, the intensity of interaction within the relational zone is not primarily an effect of pure thought (although this too has a history within Enlightenment philosophy) but is overdetermined by a reality to which it must respond. To be operative *as* a concept demands this response, and it is only within the terms of that response (and responsibility) that oscillation can have any use for materialism. Clearly, any old oscillation will not do.

We have moved rather quickly from the principle of oscillation to its concept, and much of the present work will elaborate that shift as a theoretical necessity. But isn't oscillation just a code word for something that has been materialist for some time: the dialectic? While I do not believe that the wheel needs to be reinvented where the dialectic is concerned, oscillation's relationship to the dialectic is unavoidably ambivalent. This is not the convenience of the term, but it is immanent to its status as a concept. To clarify this relationship, therefore, is to begin to register the portent of oscillation as a rhetorical figure and theoretical compunction. If one thinks of the major original theoretical contributions of Marx to materialism (on the nature of the commodity, on value, on historical contradiction, on ideology, on accumulation, etc.), the nature of the dialectic remains a major organizing principle. Certainly, this was Engels's interpretation in his later works, where the dialectic is formalized into a "science of the general laws of motion and development of nature, human society and thought."[12] These "laws of motion and development" are avowedly progressivist and have been isolated and attacked as part of a general debunking of nineteenth-century social thought. Despite my comments on the twentieth century that such thought helped produce, the dialectic of progress is only superficially the villain of scientific philosophy. For one thing, dialectics takes several forms (the theoretical solution of Hegel, the practical solution of Marx, and, more recently for example, the realist solution of Bhaskar), all of which makes summary evaluations highly suspect. Moreover, as Balibar argues, Marx's concept of the dialectic was itself internally ambivalent and included components that are not easily or logically reconcilable. Can one, for example, subscribe to a certain teleology of emancipatory aims while at the same time subordinating that prescribed historical evolution to the logic of materially determined and historically specific social contradictions? History records that when one simply reads the second formulation as an epiphenomenon of the first the political consequences can be disastrous, particularly in the formation of state ideologies. This is the contradiction conjured by Walter Benjamin in his image of the angel of history propelled forward by the storm called "progress" so that the angel no longer sees the pile of debris that "progress" produces. But of course, such contradictions are not the monopoly of the Marxist dialectic (Fukuyama's absurd refiguring of its Hegelian counterpart replays this aporia as an end of history while Rome, or, let us say, many a Sarajevo, burns).

The nature of oscillation as a concept speaks to the ambivalence of the dialectic without casting itself as a dialectic. It is not a gloss on Marxist principles but a tool for understanding their internal logic within current contingencies. More than that, however, as a concept *of* materialism, oscillation names "a problem, whose solution is always a unique, ad hoc invention," as Jameson puts it. The problematic determinism of base/superstructure arguments is not solved simply by reversing the polarity (as some semioticians and culturalists have attempted in the wake of structuralism) but by understanding the alternating dynamic between the two. Jameson, or a Jamesonian approach at least, would aver that this makes oscillation immanent to the materialist dialectic, and indeed its conceptual integrity may depend on it. But I want to push the notion that oscillation cannot be subsumed within a conventional mode of scientificity, however much the dialectic unlocks the truth claims of science within the social. As a concept, oscillation deemphasizes the propositional in social processes and accentuates a combinatory potential, or *chiffre*, in the sense that Deleuze and Guattari use it. The *chiffre* is not an adding together of components but an articulation of the otherwise indiscernible in their interaction. It is a knowledge *of* materialism *for* science and not *as* science. It is in the dialectic of materialism, but also, as a concept, between the dialectic and other explanatory models of the social.

A brief example may clarify the immanence and imbrication of oscillation as concept. For instance, oscillation is simultaneously implied in the dialectic and the dialogic. Rather than think of the dialectic and the dialogic as mutually exclusive (this is, indeed, Bakhtin's reaction, but this cannot be adequately assessed outside the moment of his particular interpretation of the dialectic available — dialectical materialism or *diamat*),[13] the concept of oscillation traces a contact zone between them, one that is reducible neither to one nor to the other. The dialogic has always entailed a cognitive risk, that the social might be reduced to the semiotic. This, we might say, is the bad side of the dialogic, and one that has often found favor within humanist hermeneutics (the point with which I began, the aestheticization of the social). But the good side of the dialogic proceeds along an alternative vector, one that attends to the social construction of meaning as a creative possibility within the social; thus "dialogues" (an unfortunate word that too often restricts dialogism to "conversation") are not simply reactions to the social, but are also the tissue of its material reality. The implications of this aspect of the dialogic for the dialectic are not immediately clear (except perhaps as knee-jerk generalizations), and that becomes a point of oscillation, a point for oscillation, in materialist critique. Oscillation analyzes the relation and autonomy of such conceptual spaces.

But oscillation, as I have suggested, is not only a concept; it is also a reference point, a symptom if you will, of particular forms of theoretical impasse. This may seem to overload the term as a critical device, but the intention is to think these significations simultaneously but not synonymously. As a rhetorical figure, oscillation crops up all over the theoretical map as an expression of problematic irresolution or undecidability (this also, by the way, speaks to the function of "thirdness" in the dialogic and social transformation in the materialist dialectic — the intimation of deconstruction is, of course, not unintentional). Thus, in addition to the conceptual space marked as oscillation, my study will also attend to the irruptions of oscillation in the discourse of others. Again the oscillation, or vacillation, can be a productive hesitation in my schema, as well as a moment that marks the limits of a theoretical model to overcome the problems that it has set itself or that subsequently confront it. These examples, I will contend, enhance and augment the conceptual weight of oscillation within and between the forms of materialism that are now possible. They constitute much of the evidence for the theoretical interregnum materialism must confront.

The problem of materialist theory today is one not just of conceptual space but also of geographical and institutional space. There is nothing particularly novel in this view within the history of materialism (Raymond Williams's *The Country and the City*, Henri Lefebvre's *The Production of Space*, and Walter Benjamin's *Passagen-Werk* immediately come to mind as critiques that work through this realization albeit in very different ways), but I believe it has taken a specific and complex valence in relation to the forms of the social at the end of the millennium. Without preempting my specific argument about the geographical imagination (as Derek Gregory terms it),[14] it is clear that spatial metaphors have been intrinsic to the language of materialism, but not always to its conceptual logic. This has tended to valorize a false division between what Neil Smith has described as "metaphorical space" and "material space," a division that, while problematic for cartographic discourse in general, is critically disabling for a discourse like Marxism that seeks to understand and transform the production of space itself.[15] Furthermore, if certain forms of geography have labored under oppressive powers of observation, materialism has found a correlative in the suppression of space — a suppression that is insistent in its historicist declensions.

In many respects, materialist geography now provides the theoretical model that answers time's more rigidly teleological modes, but it is not quite the architectonic approach that I have in mind. Oscillation is indeed a spatial metaphor that is simultaneously a phenomenon of material space: at its most basic, we could ask whether there can be a theory of matter outside the materiality of oscillation in space. In addition, or at least paratactic to this formulation, the concept of oscillation explores the shifting registers of the location and locution of theory in the institution. In a sense, institution *means* the instantiation of theory, but the physical and conceptual movement of theory requires an understanding of institutional "flow" (a word whose problematic meanings will be taken up in a later chapter). An architectonic of oscillation must come to terms with the movement of real theory in real space between and in real institutions, yet, of course, this can only be expressed as a conceptual space, as an imaginary map. This is how chapter 3 will try to elaborate the Atlantic, as a "zone of engagement" crisscrossed by competing logics of theoretical discourse — a movement itself that cannot be imagined outside the concrete production of the Atlantic in history.

Just in case this strikes the reader as an overly fanciful theorization of oceanic space, I should add that this spatial imagination is not far removed from the nonlinear modeling of contemporary oceanography and climate studies. A good example is the phenomenon now known as ENSO — El Niño–Southern Oscillation — a large-scale climatic fluctuation of the Pacific Ocean. El Niño is the name for a warm surface current that appears off the Pacific coast of South America around December of each year. Every few years, however, the current remains for up to eighteen months and produces an ENSO, which has multiple and far-reaching effects: terrible fishing off the coast of South America, more rain in the Gulf of Mexico, droughts in Australasia and Indonesia, and huge coastal storms in the western United States. More recently, scientists have been evaluating the possibility of a North Atlantic Oscillation (NAO) that ties the unstable currents of the Atlantic to a disruptive series of climatic anomalies around the Atlantic rim. I will return to the chaos theory that "grounds" these analyses in the conclusion, but these are precisely the approaches that Immanuel Wallerstein has in mind when rethinking the materialism of "utopistics" noted in one of the epigraphs above.[16] While the oscillation I discuss may not appear to be a key to the catastrophic on the physical scale, it often *is* on the social "map" — witness Paul Gilroy's analysis of imperialism, colonialism, and racism in *The Black Atlantic*.[17] The ideologies of theory are never far from the tracks of barbarism across the globe. If the origins of an ENSO as a "natural" phenomenon remain difficult to articulate, we should at least be able to integrate theoretical oscillation in the social construction of global space.

To the extent to which capitalism has always been a space of representations, Marxism stands or falls according to the logic of spatial critique. The problem has been that this requirement is not easily reconcilable with the analysis of historical process. While many forms of thinking confront such a contradiction, it is the materialist tradition that so obviously epitomizes the intractable but imperative interrelation of space and time. In one sense, oscillation may name that aporia in its spatial and temporal dimensions, but this is not enough. The fungible, tactical range of oscillatory practice does not come to rest finally on the abstract rearticulation of a founding contradiction. This would tend to leave space as an abstraction (which, for instance, was ever the object of Lefebvre's criticism),[18] whereas a politics of space can only emerge in its concretization in movement. Conversely, the alienating production of abstract time is not remedied simply by resort to spatial metaphors; its political transformation depends on the ability to apprehend it cognitively and expressively at those moments when it appears to congeal, to distill into a historical sublation (or negation of the negation in dialectical parlance). Without essentializing either coordinate, the time/space relations of the present require a chronotopic imagination — an oscillographic approach to theoretical issues that otherwise so easily devolve into idealist abstractions or metaphysical binaries.[19]

One of the many lessons of materialist geography is that space, or "deep space" in Neil Smith's terminology, is an operative logic of disciplinary breakdown and reformulation. The elaboration of social space has been crucial to the ways in which various branches of knowledge, particularly those of the social sciences, have come to terms with the conceptual explosions of modernity. The analysis of urban space, for instance, is not just a description of the changing face of city life, but is a core critique of the functions and dysfunctions of the modern state — something that has methodological implications across several competing and usually incommensurate disciplines. The study of social space is simultaneously a lesson for how that space is organized and interpreted at the disciplinary level. Of course, it is possible to assess the bounds of academic inquiry without reference to space (Pierre Bourdieu's *Homo academicus* is the most stunning recent example), but I would contend that "deep space" necessitates "deep theory," one that more forcefully embroils social space with the politics of knowledge production itself. The main problem for materialist theory has been whether spatial critique informs its will to scientificity or negates it, whether indeed it undermines materialism's desire to transform social space by giving the lie to its founding tenets or laws. But this masks or detracts from a still greater challenge: What if the genuflections of materialist theory were merely a rational barometer of the status quo represented by the university? For all the revolutionary zeal of theoretical production, if the interrogation of space cannot fundamentally challenge a primary site of its negotiation, then the politics of materialism are not just compromised; they are effectively inconsequential.

As a brief example of a counter tendency, consider the case of cultural studies. If materialism does indeed oscillate with respect to the university, then it has found its wildest home in cultural studies, whose impression on institutional knowledge has a parallel in the hegemonic transactions of theoretical discourse across geographical space alluded to earlier. The politics of space of and in cultural studies are highly contradictory but serve to throw into relief the fundamental importance of spatial awareness in specific concepts of culture (as Manthia Diawara pithily puts it, "Birmingham,

Alabama, is not Birmingham, England").[20] The plethora of definitions for cultural studies now available are certainly symptomatic of oscillation, but the degree of pause in institutional reorganization is not an obvious indication of radical import in its operations. Cultural studies in the United States, for instance, has rapidly become an institutional cyber-salon where anthropologists, literary critics, sociologists, art historians, and ethnographers (among others) have struggled to understand the different conceptual terrains of their analyses (not least around the word "culture" itself). The oscillations in knowledge produced cannot be separated from the logic of the university. It is quite possible, therefore, that a university could predicate the formation of a cultural studies program or department on the "downsizing" or "re-engineering" that many colleges, flush with corporate ideology, tout as the only way to face the economic and social realities of the present. This is not far-fetched if one considers how otherwise progressive institutional developments, like those of ethnic and women's studies programs, have fostered a politics of recognition only to have such knowledge bracketed in terms of institutional reorganization as a whole. Cultural studies focuses the ambivalence of the power/knowledge nexus by emphasizing the aporia between what grounds its knowledge and the logic of the academy that more literally provides the site for its operations. And this is why one finds that behind a cultural studies program there is often an oscillating materialist or *agent oscillatoire*.

Yet the main force of cultural studies derives from its conceptualization of the space of politics and culture. This is a highly charged process that has drawn systematic and often justified criticism. For many materialists, the idea of a cultural politics at all seems to provoke the theoretical equivalent of severe abdominal pain. While we are studying hairstyles and on-the-job sabotage as resistance rituals, what happens to the structures of organized opposition (parties, unions, etc.) that enlightened knowledge used to foster? The question has been repeated in various forms in Leftist journals for at least the last thirty years. The responses are not always satisfactory, but radical critics cannot understand (or indeed promote) the social change from below envisaged without more thoroughgoing and innovative studies of the everyday of their chief constituencies. One of the major achievements of cultural studies in its short history is not that it has masked culture as a preeminent form of politics but that it has significantly broadened the available knowledge about how culture is a ground of the political, and not just its passive effect. The instability of this relationship has an oscillatory potential, but this itself cannot be exorcised from analysis of the production of that knowledge, including the site of the university and the position of the intellectual. And in that respect, cultural studies cannot simply adjudicate the complex politics that defines its very possibility. That dilemma, at least for the purposes of the present study, is another story.

The production of space, in all its signification, is central to a radical materialist politics. But if oscillation is only a somewhat natural disposition in theoretical and practical work, then we lose sense of the meaning of its dynamic architectonic for materialism. I use oscillation not just to underline the dynamism of materialism, the fluidity of its conceptual sway, but to accentuate the weakening of its objectivist paradigms. This is a dangerous proposition only if one believes that the resistance to positivism is a rejection of truth claims altogether. Part of the precarious balance or homeostasis of materialism depends upon how it addresses the burden of its own failures. An openness to historical determination suggests that elements of one moment's rational kernel can become another moment's mystical shell. This does not imply reinverting Hegel (who by now has been turned on his head so many times his feet appear to have eyes and ears), but it does draw attention to how even privileged concepts get rewritten. To this degree, oscillation is a referent for that process.

So far I have attempted to indicate how a rhetorical figure might be reconfigured as a concept for materialist theory, one with implications for its internal dynamic, its institutional and geopolitical import, and its disciplinary purview. Yet the linchpin of oscillation's cognitive power rests in its approach to the conditions of socialization themselves where the principle of movement is concretized, embodied. Marx begins his reinvention of materialism by thinking through the "species-being" of humans, a consideration of the body's sensate life that, as Eagleton reminds us, makes Marx an aesthetician in Alexander Baumgarten's interpretation of the word.[21] Whether one believes in an epistemological break in Marx's work or not, the discourse of the body is submerged in Marx's writing only to reappear with an intimately material vengeance in the production of *Capital* itself. I will address that specific condition of emergence in a chapter below, but the point is that the suppression of body politics in materialism has a determinate history in the same way as the elision of space. On this occasion, however, what has oscillated the body in the material space of theory is feminism, for it is feminism that has persistently materialized the body as an active terrain of the political. Indeed, much feminist theory has drawn attention to the systematic suppression of the body as both a conceptual and actual site of resistance and change in otherwise radical "bodies" of thought.[22] The masculinism of Marx and Marxism, and the often hegemonic patriarchal and antifeminist modes of their interpretation, have surely contributed to the "spacing-out" of the body, to the exclusion of the body as a classed, sexed, gendered, and raced manifestation of the social. Contemporary cultural theory continues to explicate the oscillatory potential of the body in the space between feminism and philosophy. In one chapter below I will consider this conceptual space, but as a specific set of theoretical and practical problems within materialism and feminist materialism in particular. In addition, I will provide a detailed example of how the body is being de- and recorporealized within the space of contemporary transnational capitalism (a mode of accumulation that now interpellates the woman's body as a primary site of superexploitation). Gayatri Chakravorty Spivak, commenting on Mahasweta Devi's narrative of women's bonded labor in India ("Douloti the Bountiful"), has suggested that "douloti is all over the globe."[23] One would have to examine Spivak's strategy of catechresis in some detail to substantiate this claim (to which I will provide a gloss in chapter 2), but few would doubt that "capitalist integration" is currently a massive incorporation (and a concomitant decorporealization) of women's labor on a world scale.

The body productively oscillates within materialism both because of the profound politicization of the body by feminism and because the materiality of the body is a primary force of theory in general. The biological functions of the body are not usually the main focus (even though the human heart is an oscillating organ par excellence), but how the body is situated, worked upon, works, and transgresses are now mainstays of theoretical production. How the body is used and used up, how it is integrated into global circuits of capital exchange and communication, are key areas of investigation. Certainly, Marxism has attended to this under the general rubric of commodification and alienation. But the new narratives of the body push these critiques further by challenging the philosophical and political assumptions about why the body matters for materialism. My own inclination is to explore the materialization of late capitalist bodies through a globalization of desire that "replicates" (a regulation of the body as well as a symptom of simulacra, prosthetics, and cyborganics) and mutates older sedimented discourses on fetishism. Consumerism in some societies has been so naturalized that fetishism forms the text, not just the texture, of the commodity's presence. Here oscillation reflects its psychological cognates, at least in the aura of doubt it invokes. The anxiety of the body's identification with the commodity crisscrosses the fictional and factual narratives of late capitalism with such rapidity that it constitutes a "nervous system" (in Michael Taussig's idiosyncratic interpretation): a consumerist ontology founded on a primary contradiction — the deracination and/or sublimation of Being. It is this oscillation that materializes the body at or beyond the borders of its perception. Thus, in my prime example, an Indonesian woman worker is not just transmogrified by late capitalism (this has ever been the fate of the worker under laws of commodification) but disavowed within a circuit of desire that works geopolitically to exclude workers, particularly women workers, from a consumerist fantasy even as it must use up their labor. And, as yet, there is no form of politics that can systematically short-circuit this global nexus of appropriation and disavowal.[24]

To reprise the discourse of fetishism is to refigure its operations as a (dis)appropriate object of inquiry. Fetishism is not an illusion, the *méconnaissance* of a subject as consumer duped by the fever of possession. Marx noted from the outset of his commodity critique that the riddle of the commodity is articulated by a profound oscillation between the sensuousness of the thing and its suprasensible aura. The "magic" of the commodity is the *interdependence* of the two, not simply the mystique that accrues to the latter. The problem for a viable politics of anticapitalism has been whether it could take account of the desire for objects within a social order in a way that did not transparently reproduce the objectification of capitalist exploitation as a matter of course. Once more, the ambivalence of subject/object relations is pivotal in developing regimes of desire that do not objectify under the law of subjection. To the extent that commodity fetishism must always seek a generalized equivalence in the circuits of value and exchange, a counterdiscourse must always emphasize difference — a difference that is less an identifiable opposite but more a dissolution of the commodity's central logic.

The worker, within the objectified presence of capital, keeps coming back, but not in the form that revolution desires (that is, as the angel who tears asunder the crass machinery of expropriation). The history of materialism has so wanted this subject of transformation that in many a forlorn socialist state it has incarnated it as the monument to a presence it could barely embody. It is not that there have been no worker revolutionaries, although various cultures have systematically attempted to verify this as fiction, but that the worker as agent, the proletarian, was, on the one hand, far too differentiated for the narrative of change she was called upon to enact and, on the other, constituted in a geopolitical structure that still forbids the delinking and socialization she represents. Even as I emphasize the prescience of oscillation as figure and process for a form of the political, it is a politics that cannot in itself undo the knot between worker difference and the Being the worker is forbidden to be within the hegemonic economic order. But rather than pass the buck to the agent of the hour (the proletarian, the refugee, the subaltern, the postcolonial), I do want to maintain metatheory's culpability and responsibility in oscillatory practice. This is not some vague recourse to humanist empathy but a strategic imbrication of the philosophical with the practical.

Mindful of Marx's eleventh thesis on Feuerbach, chapter 5 will discuss the return not of philosophical interpretation (although it is as ubiquitous in the United States as the analytic modus operandi) but of materialism itself as a ghostly presence in philosophical discourse. Derrida's *Specters of Marx* provides a crucial if obvious example here, if only because it eloquently conjures the ghostly metaphors that haunt Marx's writing. But I will use the lessons of Derrida's spectral philosophy to animate the spirits that wander in and between the words of several philosophers of recent notoriety, including Nancy, Deleuze, Guattari, Negri, and Balibar. I am less interested in rescuing their individual positions for materialism (which in some cases would make the labors of Sisyphus look easy) than in seeing how, even with the perspicuous and omnipresent danger of wordplay this invites, materialism keeps coming back to them. Here oscillation is both wavering and hovering, as if materialism is both the paranormal and paranormative to the otherwise abnormative prose of specific philosophers. But just as Feuerbach was Marx's foil for a politics yet to be, so contemporary philosophy often provides the inclination and the indication of the forms of opposition possible. My intention is to provide a radical contrast between the necessity of this spirit and the negation of the spirit that capitalism provides in the form of the worker (incarnated, of course, in the commodity). Materialist oscillation is in this sense not the reconciliation of the irreconcilable but a paratactic alignment of unlikely but necessary alliances.

Before summarizing the theses, ghostly or not, that propel the following chapters, I should explain the arrangement of chapter titles, which seem to eschew the parataxis invoked above for some form of subordination. I have decided to use *of* as an undecidable in the breakup (and not breakdown) of the clauses listed. What makes *of* so tremulous is probably the influence of the French *de* as a genitive substitute that has blended and yet remained separate from its Old English counterpart in surprising ways. I will not list the over sixty variations of *of* that the *OED* provides, but I would like to acknowledge their relevance to the concept of oscillation at issue. *Of* often indicates motion or direction away from something (in fact it could be used as an imperative in this regard, which is preserved in expressions like "Be off with you!" — where "off" itself has come to replace its cognate). It can indicate a point of time, but also the process of time. Interestingly, it can also signify a situation, condition, or state. *Of* can introduce a cause or reason, but also signify an agent, a doer, or an author. The two principal ways I appear to be using *of* in my titles are as a form of "about" and as the means to connect two subjects (although, in effect, *of* splits the connotative from the denotative). Perhaps, however, like the parentheses that internally disturb each title, the *of* can be read as a point of emphasis. On the one hand, this means that not all aspects of each subject are here offered for consideration; on the other, *of* registers a semantic disturbance about how much of the denotative is in the connotative and vice versa. No doubt there are better ways to indicate the condition of oscillation that informs this inquiry (right down to the empty parentheses where materialism could be in the title of chapter 5), but I hope that *of* keeps this sense of tremor alive, if not its adequate articulation.

I have begun to suggest why oscillation is a keyword in the materialism of the present. We will see that as a metaphor and a concept it can illuminate and facilitate an understanding of the crucial components of materialism at this time in a number of provocative ways. That materialism itself speaks to vital questions of ideology, space, body, fetishism, and spirit is not surprising: the problem is how to link conceptually these levels of inquiry without sacrificing the specificity of each. Oscillation is useful in this regard, but as I have indicated, it comes with a certain liability on which, nevertheless, it must depend. The ambivalence of oscillation is not its own reward, but is symptomatic of the danger in materialism's dynamism. At the risk, however, of offering a formula for a process that appears to deny it, let me piece together the comments above in terms of this book's objectives.

1. Oscillation is a motor of this text in two ways: as a metaphor and as a concept. As a metaphor, it provides insight into the complex relationship between the macrological politics of economics and culture in the world system and their correlatives in materialist theory. As a concept, oscillation develops the notion that dynamism of this kind is a specific constituent logic of opposition and disarticulation. The movement between these levels is itself oscillatory, which will tend to weaken their autonomy while strengthening their mutual integrity.

2. Although I will have cause to mention oscillation's cognates in the physical sciences (without which, for instance, we would have no measure for time, no principle for electricity, and nothing as luxurious as radar), it is its metaphorical possibilities that have proved more suggestive for the meta-theory of the present work. In this regard, oscillation often appears as a theoretical descriptor in materialist critique where no solution or sublation seems readily available or indeed possible. Part of what I do here is to draw out these references from a variety of theoretical sources and integrate them into a nontotalizable materialist apparatus. Given my comments on the dialectic, this may seem an anti-Marxist or otherwise heretical move, but one of the lessons of oscillation is that one may be able to think the totality in specific ways without being able to represent it (except as a movement between two poles that oscillation cannot guarantee). Rather than see this as an absolute break from classical forms of materialism, particularly historical materialism, oscillation (as aporia, as hesitation about a constitutive outside) is something that has been the motor of most radical materialism all along. A millennial materialism must now bring this to the fore not because the materialist might wish it but because the contingent possibilities of the present demand it.

3. Although each chapter takes a key component or object of materialist critique — ideology, space, body, fetishism, spirit — these are not meant to exhaust the possibilities for oscillatory practice, the concept in motion so to speak. I have therefore included a conclusion whose theoretical oscillations,

particularly within science, underline some of its further range, if not the details that would be necessary to support it. Two categories alone, culture and class, have sent my research in different directions that themselves demand longer, more thoroughgoing investigations. I hope to remedy this shortfall on another occasion. Until then, oscillation's argument for materialism must remain partial in at least two senses of the word.

4. Who does the concept of oscillation serve beyond the astigmatic gaze of this writer? Obviously, oscillation does not unlock all of the mysteries of materialist theory and practice; it does, however, provide a complex and suggestive means to understand the logic of those aporias. It is not meant as a cure-all for the ills or sins of materialist analysis, but as a heuristic device about the way the world of theory and theory in the world works at this time. This, however, provides a limited political constituency, and to the extent that theory often conspires to render knowledge the ward of intellectual elites, the metatheoretical outlook of oscillation is guilty of that political limit. As my chapter on ghosts affirms, not all philosophers eschew a practical, social consciousness, but if politics has become a more empty gambit in what passes for the public sphere of late (itself a phantasmic projection), then any concept that might further that evacuation must be held with suitable and sustained suspicion. All I do here is offer oscillation as a model of skepticism, one that points to a politics of responsibility — first to materialism, and thus to the world — but it cannot guarantee in advance the constituency in which its consequences might become manifest. Perhaps the political subjects of oscillation remain imagined but unrealized, but then this is no less true of the proletarians to whom much of this century has been dedicated. The paradox of proletarian being is that it becomes self-identical only at the moment of its annihilation — and that is a future that must, as thinkers from Marx to Derrida remind us, continue to haunt the present.

CHAPTER ONE

METAPHORS (OF MATERIALISM)

> Advanced capitalism . . . oscillates between meaning and non-meaning, pitched from moralism to cynicism and plagued by the embarrassing discrepancy between the two.
>
> — TERRY EAGLETON

> To describe the modality of the relation . . . between the class struggle and its representation as "political," we must resort to metaphors. . . . [L]et us say that it is in the (historical) vacillation of ideology that politics appears. — ETIENNE BALIBAR

What constitutes materialism, in particular, a materialism apposite with the complex contours of culture? The question is fraught with difficulty given the long and detailed history of materialism's problematic relationship to cultural material and its conceptual space. Indeed, one only has to mention the word "aesthetics" and the whole project would seem to quiver with doubt (even in Adorno's unequivocal critique of the culture industry).[1] Yet this is not just a key to the contradictions endemic to a materialist aesthetic but also a procedural clue to a materialist analysis of the present. The quivering and doubt, the involuntary movement and vacillation, the oscillations, are constitutive both of materialism's theoretical dilemmas and the logic of culture itself in advanced or late capitalism.[2] While never synonymous, both the dilemmas and the logic must be thought simultaneously (or noncontemporaneously) if one is to offer alternative lines of force in materialist theory and practice. The nature of this force (akin to the architectonic that Alan Sinfield has elaborated, that which produces "faultlines")[3] provides the conceptual ground for a rearticulation of materialism. But what kind of materialism does this imply?

Most of the present chapter will answer this question obliquely through a consideration of the explanatory power of oscillation as a metaphor (metaphor less as an inspirational tool but more as a marker of material change, including the mutability of materialism itself). Certainly materialisms have attended to both the mediatory aspects of culture as various ways of living and the productive capacities of cultural expression (evident, most clearly, in the cultural materialism of Raymond Williams). Many problems constrain the efficacy of this form of cultural analysis: some are produced by the changing socioeconomic dynamic that provides materialism with its transitive form and content; others are systemic aporias that should, I believe, foster both a critical approach to the paradigm and a conspicuous modesty in its practitioners.[4] While scientists have often been arrogant about their cognitive abilities, culturalists have overemphasized their epistemological verve. If one takes seriously the charge of developing a knowledge of culture for science (rather than *as* science), this mutual exclusivity and elitism (an idealism of the vanguard) might yet find the appropriate dustbin — presumably marked "not for recycling."

To think materialism and culture in collision and collusion means to take on the major metatheoretical problems of both. The methodological possibilities that address these emerge from a number of crucial factors: the weakening of historicist and positivist approaches within materialism; the continuing lure of relativism in cultural analysis (intensified to some extent in appeals to multiculturalism); the rediscovery of space as a conceptual coordinate in social theory; the general waning of *les grands récits* in philosophical and social discourse; the emergent formation of postmodern cultural relations; the burgeoning although asymmetrical political force of the new social movements; and the intensification and globalization of capitalist practice. The links between all of these can be fairly easily established, but the question of determination per se is not answered merely by reversing the order of factors. I would, however, state it as axiomatic that materialism begins from an understanding of socioeconomic determination in the production and reproduction of human existence.[5] My interest is in encouraging materialism's oscillation rather than its obliteration by suspicious appeals to the generative capacity of pure thought (in this respect, some strains of poststructuralism have a specifiable prestructuralist characteristic). What value has cultural materialism been in this regard?

Cultural materialism has often read much more like the traditions of philosophical materialism rather than the productivist narrative found in historical materialism. There are many reasons for this, not the least of which is its development within Western Marxism after the Second World War — a materialism with its own peculiar half-life, and one whose specific twists and turns have been well discussed by Sebastiano Timpanaro and Perry Anderson, among others.[6] While not focusing on the corpus of that development (and its historical links to the claims of "actually existing socialism" in the Soviet Union and China — claims that continue to be revised, rethought, or rejected), cultural materialism itself is not simply a symptom of that broader theoretical emergence. Indeed, it is more useful to see its conceptualization in terms of both the *longue durée* of Marxist thought and a culturalist tradition in Western philosophy in general. Williams, for instance, is obviously as much at home in the main currents of British culturalism that lead through Arnold and Leavis to the earlier incarnation of cultural studies as he is, for instance, in the debates on the repudiation of materialism in Western Marxism outlined by Timpanaro. Yet one cannot understand Williams purely in the former vein either, since his thinking is also informed by that linchpin of Marxist thought, the question of human praxis in the production and reproduction of social life that implies a different "sweetness and light" from his forebears. But another part of the usefulness of the Williams project in cultural materialism is that, ironically, it highlights many of the dead-ends in the rapprochement between culturalism and materialism in the first place and suggests some avenues of theoretical articulation that require critical elaboration.[7] The general eclipse of Williams's thinking in cultural studies has much to recommend it (notions like "structures of feeling" and a dependence on an organic conception of community do not adequately address, in their original forms at least, the fragmentation of the social within the apparent integration of the global),[8] but one does not have to be an avatar of British culturalism to appreciate that learning from Williams remains a high priority in any discourse that takes seriously the claims of cultural analysis within materialism. Theory being what it is, academia's own "magic system," conjuring Williams out of the equation, is all too easy.

While Williams will not be the focus of this chapter, he was obviously a materialist concerned with the metaphors of materialism. *Keywords*, for instance, is a touchstone for the critique of terminological waywardness and wonderful testimony to the signifier's slippery career before its current celebration. We should note, therefore, that "materialism," the word, has always lived under the sign of a contradictory "historical residue." Thus, "a materialist" refers both to someone who is primarily interested in making money and accumulating things (materials) and to someone who investigates the very causes and reproduction of that sensibility. Interestingly, it is only within late capitalism that these two characteristics now may occupy the same body. The success, as it were, of Marxist materialism depends upon the attenuation of the other materialism. Even if one accepts the general premises of post-Marxism, the prospects of postmaterialism must remain before us unless or until one detects the universal acceptance of the acquisition of money and things as *the* condition of human existence. The materialism at issue here is simply the name for what doubts that way of life.

The question of theory's metaphors is vast and intractable, so here let me give it a particular resonance: the metaphoricity in materialism is often considered its bad faith with regard to science and the not inconsiderable claims for social transformation, but it is not; it is, rather, the constitutive logic of articulation in materialism's passage from the real to the conceptual. Of course, one cannot rest easy with such a formulation: the point is to eschew the endgame of this ineluctable will to abstraction in materialism for the necessarily different political implications the conceptual holds for the broader aims of radical discourse. Commenting on Engels's rewriting of the central tenets of *The German Ideology* in the *Dialectics of Nature,* Etienne Balibar notes: "If materialism is a specific relation between theory and practice, it ought to be legible in theory itself."[9] My contention is that such "legibility" is instantiated by metaphor — a problematic propensity but a move and/or vacillation that can be historically specified.

Two initial points should be made about the specter of metaphor haunting materialist discourse (the invocation and incarnation of Marx *as specter* will be the explicit subject of a later chapter). First, that the acknowledgment of metaphoricity extends to the metaphor of materialism itself goes beyond the contradiction noted above; that is to say, materialism has a recent history as a metaphor for Marxism that is tied not just to the crises of Marxism but to a more general distancing of Marxist paradigms of analysis. Doubtless an involuntary fear was bound to develop in light of the stunning failure and subsequent collapse of almost every state that dared to invoke Marxism as an operating, or dysfunctional, principle. Yet the metaphor of materialism is also a measure of the marginal political constituency of the intellectual and academic in predominantly Western orders of discourse. There the measure of metaphoricity is a calculus of activist exhaustion with the insufficiencies of the term and its deployment. It is not just the god that has failed, but almost every institutional valence in the construction of a counterpublic sphere of intellectual opposition (by contrast, the successes of the new social movements have further accentuated the metaphorical aura of materialism). To this view one could add a commentary on the emergence of the commodification of theory (as cultural capital) and the general aura of optionality that drives professional if not professorial careers.[10] The important point, however, is materialism's symptomatic metaphoricity for the intractability of certain Marxist dicta.

This leads to a second note on materialism as metaphor, for the notion itself is crucial to a specific critique of Marxism — namely, the discursive polemic of Laclau and Mouffe's *Hegemony and Socialist Strategy.*[11] While I remain skeptical of the attempt to solve the aporias of determinism and causality by the signifier as last resort (the signifying relation as simultaneously the expression and eclipse of the social relation), I would urge an understanding of metaphor not as an evasion of the Marxism in materialism (which extends to the "post" in post-Marxism) but as a structural compulsion in materialism's theoretical edge; that is, its (class) struggle as theory. To borrow from Marx and Engels, metaphors of materialism are not just a case of phrases opposing phrases but signs of materialism's autocritical dynamism.

The Althusserian impulse in the concept of theoretical struggle is more than a gesture, for whatever one may say of Althusser's theoretical war of position within and against the French Communist Party (and the many limitations of his thought would have to be read through that relationship), the basic claims he makes for theory's importance to materialism clarify rather than obfuscate the question of materialist metaphors (since they urge theoretical practice in relation to the "real object" — again, the charges of theoreticism would have to be justified by periodizing Althusser's thought).[12] I will explore the value of an Althusserian detour of theory in my discussion of Balibar's use of "vacillation" below, but here I wish to clarify the deployment of metaphoricity before elaborating its most prescient instances in terms of Marx, theory, and ideology.

As the introduction indicated, oscillation provides a complex and suggestive metaphor for the relationship of cultural theory to the system it is caught within. On the one hand, oscillation describes the pendulous movement between extremes that marks the "being" of capitalism, in all its contradictions; on the other, oscillation is a form of hesitation, a vacillation about what to do, a movement that is actually about a pause. In terms of social domination, oscillation is not just about hegemony's violence or repression, but also about its doubt, its perplexity, its inkling of its own inability.[13] Oscillation occurs under determinate, concrete conditions: it is its own philosophy of limit. From physics one learns that oscillation is about force within limits, energy within confines; as such, the movement can only occur in a determinate space. A swinging pendulum is typical of this motion, but add two magnets along its path and a different sense of oscillation emerges. Indeed, in a resonant condition, that is, where the mechanism is "forced" at a resonant frequency, the pendulum moves with completely random motion — it oscillates wildly.[14] The opposite of oscillation is inertia: by which a matter would "continue in its existing state of rest or uniform motion in a straight line unless that state is changed by an external force."[15] One could say that any mode of social domination is imbued with a sense of oscillation rather than inertia, which, by contrast, offers abject stability under the constant threat of instant redirection.

Although the oscillation of particles in particular and material in general is highly suggestive, I am not interested in simply reproducing the physical properties of oscillation described in physics as a form of crude scientism for cultural theory or materialist theory in general (this, for instance, would only take us back to the materialism of Hobbes and mechanical causality). I do intend to use oscillation as a metaphor for the predicaments of materialist theory. Of course, oscillation is often applied to the realm of ideas and in this regard signifies a fluctuation between opinions, purposes, or principles interestingly characterized as "wavering."[16] Ideally, one would hope that this means the hesitation of ruling hegemony rather than the strategic positioning of its opposition, but there is no neat division of oscillatory practice. But does oscillation imply a binary opposition that even an unskilled deconstructor could mercilessly implode? A single oscillation might provide this opportunity, but here we are referring to complex processes of oscillation that cannot guarantee the poles between which they occur. We know, however, that there must be some limit because, as noted, without it we would be describing a uniform movement with absolutely no change — inertia (and even a modicum of historical consciousness teaches us otherwise). Clearly, the focus is on oscillation as a more agitated condition that emerges in economic, philosophical, and cultural analysis as a way to spatialize the force and relations of contemporary production. As the introduction noted, the types of oscillation may be schematized as those within a theory, those between theories, and those between spaces and places. As isolated examples, these would be just a measure of metaphoricity, but taken together they advance an understanding of oscillation as a concept, as an active component of materialist thinking.

The history of materialism, at least in its Marxist declensions, has been concerned to critique the "agitated" machinations of capitalism (as some of my examples will emphasize); yet it has often been assumed that materialism itself remained outside this movement, grounded by the nature of its metacritique. Most forms of essentializing materialism have proved inadequate to the task of understanding the dynamism of social relations, but that is far from saying that autocritique is a stranger to materialist projects. It is the apparatus of materialist thought that ensures, to a great degree, its oscillation rather than ossification, although there is no metaphysical guarantee to this efficacy. Idealism has no monopoly on the elision of social specificity.

Marx's writing, for instance, provides a trenchant lesson in the power of reflexive thinking as he continually works on his theories in light of the appropriate evidence of the real relations of human activity.[17] Yet in general Marx does not always gauge the impact that the social symptoms he analyzes might have on the conceptual integrity of his own approach. This is particularly true of the phenomenon of oscillation as Marx reads it. Marx's use of oscillation as a descriptive device occurs most often in his analysis of prices and wages. It is one of the ways that Marx understood fluctuations within capital, but it also functioned as a springboard for his critique of classical political economy. In *Capital* (volume 1) he considers how market prices oscillate above or below what Smith calls the "natural price." Marx notes, as Smith does, that supply and demand tend toward an equilibrium, an equilibrium that is often interpreted as a measure for the quantity of labor required for a commodity's production. But Marx emphasizes that the oscillations of market prices over the long term reflect without finding such an equilibrium (except as a mean of their divergence). And, whereas classical political economy defined this equilibrium as a regulating law of the value of a commodity — as an expression of the labor expended to produce it — Marx will argue that average prices do not coincide with the values of commodities because, according to the labor theory of value, the source of value in a commodity depends upon a surplus value extracted from another commodity: labor itself. Oscillation, then, is not just the search for a "natural price": it is a symptom that "value" lies elsewhere in the process of capital. Marx takes the oscillation of prices not as a confirmation of the general law of "natural" or "mean" price but as a sign that the law itself wavers under the pressures of marginalized or misunderstood components of pricing, "congealed labor time" for one.[18]

For Marx, then, oscillation is almost always a foil, a condition that he uses to foreground his own alternative law of value. In *The Poverty of Philosophy* he attacks Proudhon for his principle of "constituted value" as a typical misreading of the function of the wage. This, in turn, will form a subtext to Marx's section on wages in *Capital*. Interestingly, Marx faults Proudhon for his reduction of the problem of labor as a commodity to a "poetic licence," "a figurative expression," and a "grammatical ellipsis." What Marx means to emphasize is that the imaginary "nature" of labor value is actually a material force and not simply a function of lapidary linguistic zeal. I use oscillation not only as a foil but also as vehicle. For his part, Marx's invocation of oscillation could form a separate argument in its own right, but the contours of that reading can at least be indicated here.

If we accept that Marx focuses on oscillation as a foil, we see that in fact it informs a good deal of the structural logic of *Capital* (particularly volume 1), which presents the general form of value then argues its case by debunking the mythologies of classical political economy. Thus, Marx will cite the "continual oscillation in prices" as an example of the contradictions in the general formula of capital. When Marx considers the transformation of labor power into wages in chapter 19, "the oscillations in the market price" are again used to find Smith's theoretical model wanting, since these legitimate a false understanding of the complex formation of labor value (Marx has just noted that "[l]abour is the substance, and the immanent measure of value, but it has no value itself" [*C*1, 677]). But it also appears that the more Marx attacks Ricardo and Smith (and Hodgskin, Say, Proudhon, etc.) for their misinterpretation of the oscillation of prices above and below a certain mean, the more that oscillation recommends itself as an explanatory component of Marx's argument. The foil is also a fulcrum.

For instance, in chapter 23, "Simple Reproduction," the references to "oscillations in market-price" are in keeping with Marx's prior criticisms of the weakness in the conventional economic paradigm. But Marx does not want to argue away from the significance of this dynamism to an understanding of capital *tout court:*

> Capitalist production...reproduces in the course of its own process the separation between labour-power and the conditions of labour. It thereby reproduces and perpetuates the conditions under which the worker is exploited. It incessantly forces him to sell his labour-power in order to live, and enables the capitalist to purchase labour-power in order to enrich himself. It is no longer a mere accident that capitalist and worker confront each other in the market as buyer and seller. It is the alternating rhythm of the process itself which throws the worker back onto the market again and again as a seller of his labour-power and continually transforms his own product into a means by which another can purchase him. In reality, the worker belongs to capital before he has sold himself to the capitalist. His economic bondage is at once mediated through, and concealed by, the periodic renewal of the act by which he sells himself, his change of masters, and the oscillations in the market-price of his labour. (*C*1, 723–24)

Here we see that Marx is not just elaborating an interpretive error in accounts of capitalist oscillation but advancing his own critique about the dynamic of capitalism for the worker. The "alternating rhythm" of this relation is constitutive both of capitalism's exploitation and of worker anxiety: it is a compulsion of capital per se. A similar understanding recommends itself when Marx is advancing a general law of capitalist accumulation in chapter 25 (and it is highly appropriate that this linchpin in his analysis contains the highest concentration of oscillation as an interpretive metaphor). Again, he disputes not the dynamic of capital that classical political economy identifies but the conclusions that are drawn from it. In this example Marx wants to show that variations in wages are produced not by the absolute number of the working population but actually by shifts in the proportion of "active" to "reserve" workers. The source of these shifts is not the product of a working population itself but the "self-perpetuating cycles" of capital as it expands and contracts at uneven rates (cycles that are themselves modified by what Marx calls "smaller oscillations" or periodic fluctuations in capital accumulation) in relation to the pool of labor for capital. Marx comments, "Just as the heavenly bodies always repeat a certain movement, once they have been flung into it, so also does social production, once it has been flung into this movement of alternate expansion and contraction" (*C*1 786).[19] The laws of motion are not identical in Marx's example, but the principle of movement is instructive for it has material causes and effects, and it repeatedly informs his explanatory model. Thus:

> The appropriate law for modern industry, with its decennial cycles and periodic phases which, as accumulation advances, are complicated by irregular oscillations following each other more and more quickly, is the law of the regulation of the demand and supply of labor by the alternate expansion and contraction of capital, i.e. by the level of capital's valorization requirements at the relevant moment, the labor-market sometimes appearing relatively under-supplied because capital is expanding, and sometimes relatively over-supplied because it is contracting. (*C*1 790)

Whether drawing the imagery from existing descriptions of political economy or borrowing from the scientific discourse of the time, Marx reaccentuates oscillation as a ground for materialist critique, in the sense that the latter then works on its substantiation. These are brief examples but serve to underline the specific function of oscillation for Marx's mode of argumentation. If oscillation is part of capital's logic of accumulation, Marx contends, then, first, how has this been misconstrued, and, second, what truth might it reveal about the complex interactions of labor and capital? Oscillation, therefore, is not being used as a concept; nor is it the theoretical material that Althusser might have ascribed to *Generalities I;* rather, it is a means to prize political economy away from the delusions of empiricism, the mere fact of oscillation. But there is a question in Marx's otherwise recondite theorization of the inadequacies of the political economy he surveyed: If oscillation so insistently affects the relationship of the capitalist and the worker, what marks might it make in the material conditions of theory itself? This is where oscillation moves from the position of descriptor to its problematic status as symptom and as concept.

There are several steps to this process, and to accentuate it I will move from the present back to the materialism that, in a sense, makes this possible. The line of thought itself traces an oscillation that does not escape the moment of reflection as pause, as homeostasis. If the primary importance of oscillation as a spatial metaphor is that it embodies the predicament of materialist theory at this time, then it is because it simultaneously arises from a more general cultural logic that has catalyzed the spatial potential in theory. The critique of oscillation, then, draws sustenance from debates about postmodernity, the most overdefined and underdeveloped concept of contemporary cultural theory (although postcoloniality is normally read as postmodernity's natural ally, it also poses a different order of cultural "exchange"). The underdevelopment is a function of postmodern logic, not just because of the waning of affect in the contemporary imagination (as Jameson would have it), but because postmodernity is insistently self-nominating. Impatient with the idea that history will judge its significance, postmodernity compresses time and space to produce a vertiginous simultaneity, "here and now," that defies the linear plod of diachrony. Some critics have taken this to mean that history does not matter for the postmodern, but this misses the point: postmodernity asserts that history is problematic and does so by attending to the spatiality that some histories have been content to overlook. If history plays a role in this study it is because it remains a problem for the analysis of social space and struggles over space. A millennial materialism, for instance, must be historical (rather than historicist in the negative sense) to the degree that the spatialization of contemporary cultural relations is a problem for history. The question of oscillation, again, is a political one.

The allies of oscillation in theoretical analysis are primarily critics of spatiality (for instance, Henri Lefebvre, Michel de Certeau, David Harvey, Edward Soja, Neil Smith, Mike Davis, Derek Gregory), materialists who attend to the dynamic regimes that attempt to master the production of space. Soja, for example, sees the reassertion of space in theory as a specific oscillation of materialism, one that rigorously critiques a historicism that "actively submerges and peripheralizes the geographical or spatial imagination."[20] Since the logic of capital requires spatial organization and subordination (typified in the rationale of ownership) the suppression of space is methodologically disastrous. The spatial imagination is more than just a heuristic tool — it is a crucial component of "dialectical" thinking in Lefebvre's terms, the key to understanding what "takes place." It is materialist geography that now forcefully produces "perspective" on what "takes place" in theory.

But to these social theorists could be added a host of contemporary thinkers sensitive to the logic of dispersal as it is played out within and across cultures. Homi Bhabha, for one, introduces his collection *The Location of Culture* with the following observation on the location of culture in the "beyond":

> The "beyond" is neither a new horizon, nor a leaving behind of the past.... Beginnings and endings may be the sustaining myths of the middle years; but in the *fin de siècle*, we find ourselves in the moment of transit where space and time cross to produce complex figures of difference and identity, past and present, inside and outside, inclusion and exclusion. For there is a sense of disorientation, a disturbance of direction, in the "beyond": an exploratory, restless movement caught so well in the French rendition of the words *au-delà* — here and there, on all sides, *fort/da*, hither and thither, back and forth.[21]

This sense that the next world is also in the shifting forms of the present world has a Marxian ring to it (which may come as a shock to a certain politics of postcoloniality), like Marx's point about the content going "beyond" the phrase in his analysis of the Eighteenth Brumaire.[22] Similarly, Bhabha is aware of the insecurity in such a situation, but he is also generally sanguine about the political possibilities of thinking/experiencing the "other" side of history. One can counter this affirmative oscillation, however, with those who tend to celebrate "disorientation" as its own reward. Yet even Gianni Vattimo, who is not best described as an optimist in his use of the metaphor of oscillation, conjures both the promise and the precipice in liberatory discourse: "To live in this pluralistic world means to experience freedom as a continual oscillation between belonging and disorientation."[23]

Like Lyotard and Derrida, Vattimo begins with history's problem (the problem of history), and much of his postfoundationalist polemics is devoted to destabilizing History's Truth. Not surprisingly, he employs the principle of oscillation to deconstruct stable philosophies of being, and this is worth considering in more detail even if I remain unconvinced by Vattimo's "apologies" for nihilism, "active" or otherwise. Vattimo introduces oscillation into an argument about the central motifs of two essays of 1936, Benjamin's "The Work of Art in the Age of Mechanical Reproduction" and Heidegger's "The Origin of the Work of Art."[24] Heidegger describes the effect of a work of art on its observer as one of *Stöss* (a blow); Benjamin, by contrast, examines the effect of cinema in terms of "shock." While Vattimo is careful not to conflate the sense of both terms, he is clearly interested in the principle of anxiety that both provoke. Noting the existential experience of anxiety discussed by Heidegger in *Being and Time,* Vattimo continues that the work of art is experienced in a similar way since it "suspends the familiarity of the world" as it simultaneously stimulates "a preoccupied wonder . . . that the world is there" (51). The ideas of Benjamin and Heidegger unite at least on this point: an insistence that the experience of art is one of estrangement, alienation, and disorientation — to which Vattimo adds that aesthetic experience can therefore be seen to keep "disorientation alive." As Vattimo points out, this experience of art is the exact opposite of the aesthetics proposed in Western philosophy by a tradition that led from Aristotle to Kant in which stability or security was the key characteristic. Although Vattimo sidesteps Heidegger's romantic conception of poetry and poets a little too quickly (perhaps because that vision of *Dasein* leads to an unfortunate organicism), the thesis is clear enough:

[Aesthetic] experience can no longer be characterized as a king of *Geborgenheit,* a security and harmony. Rather, it is essentially precarious, linked not only to the risk of accident run by the pedestrian, but to the precarious structure of existence in general. The *shock* characteristic of new forms of reproducible art is simply the expression in our own world of Heidegger's *Stöss*, the essential oscillation and disorientation constitutive of the experience of art. (54)

To some degree, the cultural critique signified in the (mis)alignment of Benjamin and Heidegger replays materialism's concern with the daunting difference of Marx and Nietzsche (a primal scene of positivism and its discontents). Yet Vattimo has an ulterior motive — namely, to pry the radical skeptics of Marxian aesthetics from the tradition of Marxism itself (which, predictably, is rendered solely as some Hegelian hangover — one wonders how Vattimo would read Jameson, Žižek, or Bhaskar). True, the disorientation polemic can indeed be registered in these essays of 1936, but the numerous limitations of the Hegelian dialectic do not necessarily render Marxism the purveyor of bad faith, utopian or otherwise, in terms of the experience of art. While intent on recuperating the shock effect of art for the hermeneutic tradition, Vattimo has curiously overlooked Marxism's major theorist of aesthetic disorientation or oscillation within modernism, Bertolt Brecht. Benjamin, an avid reader of Brecht's epic theater, saw in his friend's modernist moves of montage and the alienation effect new ways for art to shock its audiences toward a greater understanding of art as production, as a productive process within broader social relations of production.[25] One need not recount Brecht's long exchange with Lukács over the claims of modernist experimentation or the influence of Russian futurists and constructivists like Tretyakov to realize that "shock" was a constituent feature of modernist Marxism, or what Brecht called "production aesthetics." The point is that the reliance on the Real as an epistemological and aesthetic ground refers to only one strand of early twentieth-century Marxism. Thus, the Benjaminian alternative is characteristic not just of Benjamin's own messianic idiosyncrasies but of an emerging tradition of materialists concerned with what might still remain of notions of artistic creativity in and after explosions of the modern. While this does not make of Brecht or Benjamin a "weak thinker" in Vattimo's terminology, it does suggest that the anxious oscillations of aesthetic experience are not simply anathema to materialist critique.[26] It also, however, places a greater attention on Vattimo, whose characterizations of critical sociology and Marxism elaborate their restrictive practices but, ironically, may also facilitate their renewal (in true "postnihilist" fashion).

There are two other reasons for invoking Vattimo's postmodern polemic. First, his use of oscillation appears to elide our earlier reference to the physical condition of oscillation as a determined principle of movement and materiality. That is, the alternating motion of oscillation Vattimo interprets as indicative of "the precarious structure of existence in general" is a peculiarity of the physical properties of material (the physics corollary), which is also the basis for theories of material existence and/or indeed materialism. However "softer and more fluid" reality may become in Vattimo's theory, the material conditions governing oscillation scratch themselves on his polemic. Indeed, the principle of alternating motion remains (even if the intensity must change); without it there can be no such thing as matter (or electricity, ocean currents, etc.). Interestingly, to suppress all forms of oscillation would leave the world with a "perpetual motion machine" curiously at one with Jean Baudrillard's simulacra, signified by "an immense script and a perpetual motion picture."[27] Conversely, even virtual reality, an infamous electronic infinity of cyberspace, is inconceivable without the structured motion of oscillation, there measured as the difference built into digitized information computed as "bits" of 0s or 1s. In pushing philosophy beyond foundationalism, Vattimo yet invokes a conspicuous foundation of material practice (the working of material and theories of materiality). And, of course, what might be considered an achievement of postmodern thought is also characteristic of its contradictory politics.

A final provocation in the example of Vattimo is partly justified by explaining the Eagleton epigraph with which I began this chapter. Since Fredric Jameson's influential essay of 1984 we have become used to identifying postmodernism as a cultural logic of late capitalism, however controversial or idiosyncratic his particular interpretation might be.[28] Jameson's view suggests that postmodernity is not so much a *coupure*, but a reorganization of cultural relations closely enmeshed with a radical reformulation of the capitalist system as a multinational, global, and "spectacular" dynamic. One of the major contradictions of this epochal conjunction is that while both postmodern culture and late capitalism vaunt dispersal, fragmentation, "flows over unities," decentered subjectivities, and diversification, the effect has been to solidify, codify, and regiment a certain relationship of art to the economic sphere. As Douglas Crimp has noted, if traditional art had an ambiguous commodity status in the past, its current "incorporation" is "a thoroughly unambiguous one."[29] Culture is not just an aspect of the commodity process: it is its defining characteristic. To borrow an example from Jameson, one can no more separate culture from the commodification of life than one can peel the boots from those feet in René Magritte's *Le modèle rouge*.

How does Vattimo respond to this condition of commodification? He remarks, somewhat laconically, that "economic power is still held by capital" (5–6). He continues, nevertheless, to advocate an "ideal of emancipation based on oscillation, plurality, and, ultimately, on the erosion of the very 'principle of reality'" (7). Even if one agrees with this (disposing of the reality principle might offer rhetorical joy, but it is a luxury where a specific reality might provide material needs — Vattimo would have to particularize, in a much more rigorous way, what reality is at stake in his formulation), there is still the problematic complicity of such desire with the working hypothesis of a form of contemporary capitalism that is busily emancipating the world from any alternatives to its globalization. Is it possible for emancipation to proceed through the same operative logic of that which continues to enslave? Like Vattimo, I would say yes, but not for the same reasons he provides. Vattimo's thesis rests on the idea that mass media are not producing a "transparent society," the oversimplifications of the global village, but a more complex and nuanced multiplicity (one that de-natures, in advance, Habermas's theory of communication).[30] It is in the chaos of this plurality that emancipatory hopes must lie. Yet clearly the chaotic dissemination of subversive (sub)cultures does not automatically push (dis)organized capitalism toward its darkest hour. Vattimo knows that the experience of freedom as oscillation he describes is also the logic of late capitalism (resplendent in the epigraph from Eagleton), but he is unable to theorize how one might disarticulate this unfortunate synergy. This, then, describes another need for, and a notion of, an agonistic materialism.

A millennial materialism must continue to develop a counterlogic to capitalism's commodification of culture in the world system. It would be both a means to measure oscillation and an *agent oscillatoire*, a flexible strategy of agitation at any point where capitalist cultural inclusivity is confounded by its own disabling will-to-hegemony.[31] This does not make postmodernism the enemy, but it does question certain facets of its emancipatory strategies whenever and however they reinforce social and economic domination. Thus, while postmodernism is a rather obvious source of radical cultural practice, it is not unequivocally so, and theorists have been prepared to look beyond its expansive and expanding cultural purview with the supposition that one can analyze cultural logics that fall outside its rule of thumb. Simply put: postmodernism may describe a certain globalization of culture, but culture does not have to be postmodern in order to be global. The multiplicity this signifies is not the simplistic and ultimately imperial notion of cultural accretion (an expansion of cultural inclusion as the social management of diversity, as corporatist claims to multiculturalism would have it), but plurality as disjunction, both as a means of demystifying what constitutes culture in the (phantom) international public sphere and as a way of complicating one's sense of the politics of cultural exchange. James Clifford has noted that the future is not only monoculture: in order to understand the contradictory logics of that future, materialism should rethink not just the data of its investigations but the concepts of culture that inform them.

Oscillation provides a useful metaphor in the sense that it accentuates the dynamic intensities of theory. It reflects on the politics of theory and culture but not within the rubric of conventional, coherent political strategies (those that seek to limit the centrifugal and situational logic of social praxis). Part of the problem of cultural materialism, for instance, has been its reliance on a conceptual coherence in apparent opposition to a transcendent idea. Ironically, this has often produced an advocacy of historical forms that are themselves paeans to metaphysical thinking. The theoretical impasse is obviously complex, but one that is significantly engaged in the work of Raymond Williams, whose cultural materialism attempted to ground the productive capacity of culture in terms of social development and change in general. Yet one must also take Williams at his word about the potential of a materialism "to find itself stuck with its own recent generalizations"[32] and necessarily move cultural materialism "beyond" (in Bhabha's interpretation) the limitations of the Williams model.

If materialism itself has been marked by a significant practical oscillation, then this only begins to characterize the theoretical pause that is altogether immanent to such thought. This means distinguishing the structural necessity or truism of oscillation from its particular theoretical value. Thus, materialism's move from social being to abstraction does not guarantee theoretical change simply as a "reflection" of reality: the conditions of theory are always already a symptom of materialism's inscription in reality. As I contend, oscillation also refers to the elisions of theory, or theoretical limits that precipitate various forms of displacement. The metaphors of materialism are, then, both the signs of its conceptual limits *and* the changed circumstances of its object. Materialism's relationship to culture should therefore be read within the framework of these dilemmas and contingent reformulations, not just as a persistent intransigence but as the tissue of a specific moment in movement.

We have noted the instance of vacillation that is systemic to capitalism and to a certain regime of culture, postmodernity — but I would like to examine in some detail the case for this condition in terms of materialist theory, for this in itself would tend to support the argument for mobile or tactical thinking (somewhat along the lines of nomad thought with, perhaps, less inclination to lines of flight as fancy).[33] A pertinent and pivotal example in this regard emerges from Etienne Balibar's exposition of the vacillation of ideology in Marx and Engels's writing, which I will use both to reconsider the question of ideology in materialism and to embed this reflex in the otherwise "weak" or equivocal thinking of our time.[34]

Balibar reads the changing articulations of ideology in the thinking of Marx and Engels as part of a general critique of the antimonies of Marxian politics. In terms of ideology, he detects a series of "theoretical vacillations, …eclipses, antithetical deviations, or displacements of problematics" (88). From its initial articulation in what we now have as *The German Ideology*, ideology disappears from the theoretical agenda of Marx and Engels only to be reformulated some twenty years later in Engels's systematic attempt to present the case for historical materialism. As Balibar notes, there is nothing about ideology in *Grundrisse,* in *Theories of Surplus Value,* or in *Capital* itself, but after these texts ideology appears once more as a substitute, or perhaps as a metaphor, for fetishism, the imaginary power of commodity value (the subject of chapter 4). While commodity fetishism is like ideology in the sense that both offer a division between an appearance and a concealed reality, clearly ideology has more theoretical sway than that. Balibar quickly outlines the task for theory: "This extraordinary shuffling of identities suggests that if the question of ideology is constitutive for historical materialism, then several relatively incompatible approaches are involved, each of which has to be pursued in its turn. The study of these differences then becomes a privileged means of access to the internal contradictions of the Marxist problematic" (90). To some extent, this is but another chapter in *Reading Capital* and is valuable enough for that pedigree. The general aim is to read from the problems of Marxian principles, then apply this knowledge to the dilemmas and directions of a more contemporary reality. But the interpretation of this critique in the wake of Althusserianism provides a necessarily different perspective, as if the progressive tense of "reading" reads into the current predicament of culture, of theory, in a significantly discrepant form (for we are not only "after" Althusser but after a particular representation of communist desire).

Much of the success of Balibar's contention rests on the centrality he accords ideological critique within historical materialism, defined as a "program of analysis of the process and of the formation and real production of idealist representations of history and politics — in short, of the process of idealization" (91). Since Balibar has just suggested "illusions" as an alternative for "representations," an intriguing problem offers itself: How is a scientific approach that is primarily empirical (though not in the "vulgar" sense) in its analysis of the mode of production and of the forces and relations of production going to fathom their "inverted" forms in consciousness or even the unconscious? The short answer would be that historical materialism is concerned to show how social contradictions are misrepresented at the level of consciousness (that materialism begins from the fact of *méconnaissance*) and is not primarily inclined to unravel the form and content of representations themselves. Balibar, however, wants to force the issue by arguing that full-blown ideological critique is the conceptual essence of the materialist project.

One clear reason for Balibar's emphasis here is the need for an understanding of abstraction, an understanding that is built into Marx's materialist concept of history. The real is a relation, not a being identical with itself; indeed, social beings themselves are the product of abstract relations, not something they, as individuals, can produce by themselves.[35] But the more we consider this abstraction, the more difficult it becomes to sustain the argument that separates the being of the proletariat from the imaginary relations of ideology. Here a stripped down version of ideology as false consciousness might provide solace, but Balibar's point is that if revolutionary practice occurs when ideology is separated off as idealism, and if this view is only possible through and from the social relations of the proletariat, then how can historical materialism itself provide this knowledge? Furthermore, can one be satisfied with the impasse that Balibar points out as the lot or endgame of this logic: that the working class has an ideological consciousness only when it is not revolutionary? Surely it is such absurdities that hastened the demise of many a regime fed by the Second International.

Balibar invokes this model of Marxist theorizing to argue for a more nuanced conception of the abstract in ideology. Marx was quite clearly struggling with an interpretation of ideology that would not negate the revolutionary thought of the present (his, and others) but yet retain a critical perspective on the real relations of bourgeois consciousness, the more or less precise constraints on revolutionary praxis. The need for abstraction opens up a dialogue between the political and philosophical aspects of practice that do not necessarily resolve themselves in a sublation called "science" but remain the tissue of its possibility. The indecision, or vacillation, is intrinsic not just to a theoretical dilemma (Balibar mentions *The German Ideology*'s outline of a dominant ideology without a dominated ideology) but to the practical forms of irresolution in revolution, an incompleteness wrought both by the effect of ideology (its functionality) and by the nature of ideology (its epistemology). The abstraction of ideology lies in the need to think these categorical differences simultaneously without collapsing them — which is part, at least, of Marx and Engels's project in debunking the Young Hegelians.

Balibar reads a similar disjunction in the function and epistemology of ideology in Engels's introduction of the term "worldview" (*Weltanschauungen*) in the *Anti-Dühring*, which is Engels's way of separating-off bourgeois ideology from communist and materialist ideas. In wanting to purify the scientific claims of Marxism, Engels reverses the polarity of materialist thought, and Marxism swings back to an ideational base that is its specific aim to refute. If, as Engels avers, ideology is "the deduction of reality not from itself but from a concept,"[36] then the professed centrality of "Marxist ideology" in the Second International would seem to have invoked once more the aporia that is both the subtext and substance of *The German Ideology* — except on this occasion the problem becomes Marxism's virtue and is ultimately formalized in Lenin's position that ideology is (also) a scientific theory of socialism. The worldview, then, is taken as ideology's metaphor (particularly in Kautsky and Bernstein's reading of the *Anti-Dühring*), and the scene is set for what often reads as a pseudoscientific standardizing of a term that, as we have seen already, is intrinsically contestatory.

Engels is guilty not of papering over the problem of a certain incommensurability between thought and practice in a developing workers' movement but of underestimating the political need for clarification (at, perhaps, any cost) within the Second International, which desired a rigorously communist outlook more than oscillating aporia. Clearly, for Balibar, the vacillation of ideology authorizes, as he says, "another reading," one that looks to the complex relations in the twin histories of, on the one hand, the dialectic and, on the other, warring materialism and idealism as representing the very instance of the class struggle (where "represent" underlines that this is the class struggle within theory). If the time was not right at the end of the nineteenth century when the class struggle engaged a practical political consciousness, how is such a historically concrete analysis possible today? It is more possible now because the history that Balibar calls for would also include what happened to the forms of State when they assumed the ideology of the mass; that is, when the state became a noncontradictory expression of mass ideology — its revolutionary party. And, of course, such a history is not an autonomous narrative of inchoate materialist dogma but a concrete reflection on the changing dynamic of capitalism as a world system in the twentieth century.

Interestingly, Balibar shows that Engels was well aware of the difficulties of his theoretical position, right up to one of his last texts, "On the History of Early Christianity," where he comments that "mass movements are bound to be confused at the beginning; confused because the thinking of the masses at first moves among contradictions, uncertainties and incoherences and also because of the role that prophets still play in them at the beginning."[37] But Engels constructs from this a teleology that culminates once more in a proletarian worldview, the thought of the masses at his historical moment. The proletarians' relationship to history is ideological in the same way as worshipers' relationship to Christianity, according to the dictates of mass consciousness as a mode of production. Thus, Engels gets back to the work of history that Balibar suggests is crucial for an understanding of ideology (even if a history of ideology is not history's object) only to couch that narrative in terms of evolutionary ideas on mass consciousness. The circle is squared, not broken.

Rather than pass judgment on the particular argument against Engels here, my point is to stress the value of Balibar's conceptual critique for the contingencies of materialism. It is not, after all, the truism that theories oscillate that interests me here, but how these vacillations impede or enhance the political integrity of materialism itself at particular moments in history. Without doubt the pause in materialism's exegesis of ideology has proved to be crucial to an understanding of the history of Marxism, both in its shortcomings and in its vibrancy.[38] The intensity of oscillation has determinate conditions at two levels: within the conceptual grid that constitutes a theory's differential identity; and in the real relations that constitute historical change. These levels do not exist in a binary opposition; nor do they fit snugly in the useful categories of base and superstructure; they do, however, provide a process of articulation that can be specified. The indecisions of theory do not necessarily augur the paradigmatic eclipse of a particular way of thinking but can be symptoms of its dynamism and reflexivity. The "end of ideology" thesis, for instance, was meant to close off an argument sustaining materialist thought (handily at one with the triumphalism of the New World Order), but on the contrary it has only spurred its urgent rethinking. Indeed, the renewed attention to the substance of ideology underlines why the genuflections of theory assume a political importance among and in relation to other mediatory practices now possible (an importance that has grown since Balibar first wrote his essay and one that will cause me to reflect on its moment below).

Balibar extends his thesis about the role of vacillation in ideology within Marxist thought to the profoundly ambivalent forms of the "party" in working-class movements (needless to say, like the thought of many members of the French intelligentsia, this is not unconnected to an experience of the material conditions of French politics in 1968 and the activities of the French Communist Party [PCF] in that regard, which is both a primal scene of Left structuralism and a catalyst of poststructuralism in French thought). Balibar goes on to affirm that the constitutive force of the concept of ideology has its correspondence in the practical identity of working-class movements, which therefore bear, in their substance, if not their effects, all the aporetic propensity of their correlative. Since Balibar is clearly interested in the knowledge production of dialectical thinking, one should add his point that ideology itself "expresses in a privileged way the historical contradictions of the party form" (which is no less pertinent more than a decade after his essay when the party, we are told, is over [152]). From this he postulates that "the impossibility of talking about a proletarian ideology (as will readily be done later within the Socialist and Communist parties) and the oscillation between the concepts of ideology and worldview can here be considered to be a decisive symptom." Why?

Clearly, if the distinction between worldview and ideology collapses the political difference of a party by and for the proletariat, then the theoretical autonomy advocated by Marx and Engels is compromised; indeed, the process foregrounds the intractable tension between party centralism and antistatism. There is a specific history to that tension that seems destined to illuminate the events in Eastern Europe in 1989–91 once the dust of shock therapy, market reform, and punditry has settled. The symptom itself explains a practical impossibility: the unity of "theoretical thought" with the thought of the masses. While the proletarian worldview might seem to provide the conceptual bridge across this divide, it in fact only accentuates the original aporia in the formulation of ideology. The autonomy of theory is not an elitist sleight of hand (although it can obviously be read that way) but a conceptual necessity whose practical negation leads first to various cults of leadership within nominally worker movements, then to a fetishization of the mass itself as a governing mythology. The movement from this, or oscillation in another direction, now threatens to extinguish the accessibility of the political problem that the concept was initially intended to address — namely, the dominance of capitalist social and economic relations.

Since we speak here of metaphors in relation to Eastern Europe, it is worth noting the rather literal deconstruction of the mythology that was communist Romania invoked by Slavoj Žižek in his discussion of the hole in the national flag made by rebels opposing the Ceausescu regime. What, of course, the masses have removed is the red star that vacuously symbolized their centrality. Typically, Žižek reads this in Lacanian fashion as that sublime moment when the "hole in the big Other, the symbolic order, became visible."[39] There is a certain truth to this, in that the psychological investment in the "hole" marks the hegemony that has been overturned. What is more contentious is the notion, which directly links to the question of theory's autonomy, that the critical intellectual should "occupy all the time" the "place of this hole" in the way that it signifies, however briefly, an overlap of the masses' enthusiasm and the attitude of the intellectual.[40] Here the value of Balibar's approach becomes clear because while there is certainly a strategic advantage to "tarrying with the negative" (as Žižek calls this positioning, borrowed from Hegel) — making visible the invisible workings of the "Master-Signifier" — for the intellectual to "occupy" this "hole" replays the disjunction between ideology and worldview. Simply put, the spontaneous worldview of the Romanian masses is not synonymous with the desired, that is, willed, position of the intellectual (which, surely, would be an ideology in this case). One could add to this Judith Butler's pertinent criticism that Žižek grounds the contingency of the symbolic through the assertion of phallic law (and thus, his "real" is phallocentric rather than phallocentrifugal), which would seem to replay the Master-Signifier even as it is denied.[41]

To the extent that there is no identity adequate to the formula used to describe it, the metaphors of materialism are the signs of "discursive limits," as Butler describes them. What is often misunderstood, however, is that the theoretical aporias under discussion are not explicable solely within a discursive approach. The reasons for this should be emphasized. For instance, the description of an ideological discourse does not mean that ideology functions only as discourse even if it can be a discourse with a significant role in social life.[42] As more than one critic has noted, by inflating the term "discourse" we risk trivializing the dominance of specific ideologies, those, for example, that gird the extraction of surplus value within capitalism or the subjugation of women within patriarchy. Ideology, then, may be internally contradictory as a concept within Marxism, but it is precisely because the latter attempts to think the discursive and nondiscursive elements of social formation within the dynamics of their negotiation. Similarly, although there are strong arguments for the description of discursive practices, to conflate this with practice per se erases the distinction between the idea and the material. Once more, to understand oscillation is to examine the determinate conditions that structure even the febrile life of materialism.

On this point, Balibar provides a materialist critique of the theoretical limits within specific materialist concepts. Perhaps his most devastating commentary is on the consummate lack of history in Marx and Engels's appeals to historicity; that is to say, they fail to provide an adequate history for the present capitalist relations they describe and thus *project* the conditions of capitalism they see in the nineteenth-century as the instance *and* the history of capitalism itself. This tendency (a form of presentism) is not uncommon in contemporary critique. Class struggle as such preserves the form of nineteenth century capitalism to the extent that it does not destroy it (as Balibar points out, trade unionism often provides a normative approach to contestation rather than a mechanism for a transformation of the structural relations in which such norms are manifest). With proletarian ideology impossible to formulate, capitalism's history appears as its privileged form rather than as a dynamic instance. In response, the blockage in particular conceptual tools of Marxism has periodically fostered a kind of teleological catastrophism ("Don't worry, the revolution is coming"), a compensatory reflex that does not address the structural mutations of capitalist exploitation. While Western Marxism can be read as a logical correction to this tradition, the oscillations within its theoretical apparatus have not been adequately explored as symptomatic of the paradigmatic crises within its initial formulations. The main force of Balibar's argument comes not from a dismissal of the materialist paradigm but from his insistence that it be treated as a program whose last instance can never arrive before the demise of the conjunctural object of its analyses. The point, however, must be pushed further so that one understands the vacillation not just as a symptom of initial conditions (from which the "chaos" of its twentieth-century cognate ineluctably proceeds) but as a continuing sensitive dependence on the concrete manifestations of change within capitalism itself.[43] It is within this particular dialectic, for instance, that the problem of culture for materialism can be reformulated.

For his part, Balibar reads the conceptual difficulty of ideology for Marxism not just as a blind spot but as Marxism's own recognition of the unrest in class struggle. Yet this is not the same point: ideology may well "connote the imaginary correspondence between the practice of organization and theoretical knowledge in a 'program' that could be formulated once and for all" (173), but this falls short of its implicit value for materialist critique. Indeed, Balibar is quick to provide another definition that is both much broader and more vexing for those theorists untangling a different knot in the orders of representation. Thus, "the concept of ideology denotes no other object than that of the nontotalizable (or nonrepresentable within a unique given order) complexity of the historical process" (174). This explains both why proletarian ideology corresponds to the unrepresentable *as* proletarian identity and why ideology is so powerfully linked to representation and totality (indeed, representations of totality), the bugbear of cultural materialists among many others. The vacillation of ideology therefore provides a salutary and crucial lesson for a materialist analysis of culture because culture constitutes a horizon of historical processes that structure the unconscious of capitalist logic without ever seeming, at least in noncontradictory ways, to "represent" it. It is for this reason that the concept of culture is another site of materialist hesitation, wavering, and oscillation (and, by the way, why "proletarian culture" has been much easier to formalize at the level of state ideology rather than to formulate theoretically).

Just as a critical complexity emerges in the concept of ideology as materialism moves from material to its abstraction, culture is also implicated in this dynamic. Similarly, if we accept the Bakhtinian credo that "without signs there is no ideology,"[44] then culture, as social processes of the production of meaning, ineluctably embodies material and its metaphors. Again, the aim here is not to provide a summary of materialism's extensive treatment of the topic, but instead to urge a reevaluation of materialism's symptomatic inscription in the dynamism of social relations. The impurities of the concept of ideology tell us not only of the limits to pure ideology but also of the constraints on ideology as culture. This is some distance from the notion of culture as a relatively unproblematic or transparent "expression" of content and much closer to the contradictory arena of metamorphosis and metaphoricity in the actual social reproduction of everyday life.

Like Balibar, Williams sees the impasse in the Marx/Engels formulation of "ideology" as basically unresolved. True to the metaphor at issue he notes that " '[i]deology' then hovers between a 'system of beliefs characteristic of a certain class' and 'a system of illusory beliefs — false ideas or false consciousness — which can be contrasted with true or scientific knowledge.' "[45] As we have noted, this equivocation can be rejected according to certain categorical and historical imperatives (e.g., in Lenin's *What Is to Be Done?*), but sooner or later the problem returns as if borne by Minerva. Williams, of course, does not dismiss the ambivalence of the term (in this light, his theoretical production is a preeminent form of materialist metaphor critique) but explores it as evidence of the fundamental role of signification in all social processes; that is to say, the theory of ideology opens out into a theory of culture. As Terry Eagleton has argued, this expansive notion of ideology and culture not only opens out but empties out a good deal of the political edge of both categories despite the fact that it pushes culture in particular beyond its more elitist confines ("the best that has been thought and said," etc.).[46] Ideology and culture can both serve legitimating functions and arise from specifiable social relations (commodity fetishism, for instance, can be read across these concepts in fruitful ways), but they diverge considerably with respect to their inscription within hierarchies of power. Wearing one's hair a certain way can be subversive within a given context but does not share the same political register as, for instance, the U.S. government's definition of national interest in the bombing of Iraq during the Gulf War. If oscillation means conflation, then the radical senses of conceptual vacillation may be lost. The latter is the idea that oscillation reveals the theoretical limits available at any one moment in history and that oscillatory intensities are themselves indices of crisis (not just in a paradigm but in the sociopolitical confines in which that paradigm is manifest).

There is no doubt that theory has produced a much keener understanding of the political valences of, by, and through culture, but part of the political crisis in materialism is that a very Williamsesque recognition of culture as a productive material process can slide into an argument about culture as the primary arena of political critique. In "vulgar" interpretations of cultural studies, the thin line between culture *as* politics and culture *is* politics is often erased with ideology devolving into a question of cultural expression and the critic emerging as the doyen(ne) of political savvy. This situation is symptomatic of an oscillation about forms of political engagement or displacement within the university as an institutional site of hegemony and resistance (which is why cultural studies looks very different according to its location).

In *The German Ideology* a materialist notion of ideology as socially determined is crucial (particularly in the attacks on Feuerbach and Stirner), but this is coupled with the idea that ideologies tend to deny that very determination. As we have seen in Balibar's analysis, the conceptual space for oppositional thought, which must be internally persuasive to generate a mass movement, is highly problematic (can it be persuasive without being ideological, and if it is ideological how can it avoid the ultimate charge of idealism?). To some extent the later writings of Marx rethink this impasse: in *A Contribution to the Critique of Political Economy* he notes that we cannot depend upon the ideological forms in which people become conscious of conflicts in economic conditions as an explanation for a particular moment of social transformation. That is to say, the ideological struggle between oppressor and oppressed is not coextensive with the knowledge of that struggle that can be explained from "the existing conflict between the social productive forces and the relations of production."[47] The moment of proletarian ideology, for instance, arrives in the revolutionary confrontation with capitalism but is its consciousness in that moment and not a judgment of the conflict itself (just as, Marx comments, we would not think of judging an individual based upon what they say of themselves). Of course, the subjectivist critique is no cure-all either, for Marx does not suggest a practical way to distinguish proletarian ideology in a revolutionary period from the knowledge of social contradictions that might facilitate the development of such ideology (or "dominated ideology," as Balibar calls it). The question of critical explanation of social contradictions and ideological struggle cannot be the reserve of postfactum debates for it is part of the revolutionary narrative itself. Again, however, this has implications for the problem of culture in materialism.

Culture as a concept undergoes as many mutations as ideology and crosses paths with it because forms of living and forms of domination share the same human narrative. If, however, culture were simply an instance of ideology, the difficulty for materialism might seem less daunting, especially if one subscribed to a version of the dominant ideology thesis. It is far more provocative to look at culture's own ideological shadow rather than the subject of culture as ideology within materialist methodology because it is this that draws attention to the pressure points in the latter's inconstancy. To do this I would suggest that the tremor in the relationship of materialism to culture is not just an expression of the vacillation in materialism's concept of ideology but is in part a product of culture's asymmetrical (and therefore conflictual) relationship to the aesthetic.

Here I am primarily interested in culture's ideological purview, particularly in its legitimation of particular forms of symbolic practice, and not the full range of its conceptual sway. The reason the aesthetic emerges as the *mise en abyme* for materialist conceptions of culture is precisely because it continually rekindles the problem of ideology and of whether materialism is just another form of ideological discourse. Perhaps Terry Eagleton offers a solution even in the title of *The Ideology of the Aesthetic* (that is, that the aesthetic contains an ideology but is not coextensive with the concept), but the equivocation remains, not just in the history he traces but also, symptomatically, in the fact that he writes a second book on ideology more or less simultaneously, in order to clarify the nature of the other book's irresolution. Let us start, then, with *Ideology* and move to the specific dilemma of Eagleton's theory of ideology for his work on the aesthetic.

Eagleton certainly does not want to embrace a notion of ideology that is rigidly negative because that would preclude the advocacy of its most prominent processes ("unifying, actio-oriented, rationalizing, legitimating, universalizing, and naturalizing")[48] within oppositional ideologies. Tactically, to dispense with these attributes within radical social movements would more or less suppress the radical, the social, and the movement (a move that is not uncommon in "endist" philosophy). Thus, when Eagleton supplies definitions of ideology, they are open-ended enough to be applicable to a sociopolitical hegemony and various oppositional groups to it. Ideologies are "usually internally complex, differentiated formations, with conflicts between their various elements which need to be continually renegotiated and resolved" (45). Of course, this open-endedness does not extinguish oppositional practice (although it can make it very difficult) but provides it with its agonistic potential. From our reading of Balibar, however, a fundamental weakness remains: if the only difference in the unifying and legitimating discourses of a dominant group and various forces of opposition is their relative positions along an axis of power, then should one of those groups displace the dominant power, how will its hegemony not replay the deficiencies of its antecedent? As we have noted, the assumption of such unifying thought as an ideology is precisely what allowed putatively proletarian parties to ossify. Certain pundits might here intervene to suggest that it is the moment of revolution that transforms the concept of ideology into a more positive correlative (i.e., an ideology that secures the mandate of liberation), but this is the kind of promissory note that itself defines ideology. My point is not to reject Eagleton's expansive notion of ideology (it certainly recommends itself over false consciousness arguments or illusionist discourses), but to note that it does not exculpate Marxism for the cycle of vacillation integral to its conceptual field (it remains its symptom). What it does do, of course, is to prepare the ground for Eagleton's systematic and detailed engagement with the aesthetic, the ego of culture, if not bourgeois consciousness sui generis.

Because ideology is not simply the superstructural tool of the dominant, the aesthetic need not be the ruler's ruse about taste, discernment, and what human expression counts. Rather than pit materialism against a dogmatic and unbending aesthetic edifice, Eagleton shows how the aesthetic is a form of materialism. Thus, *The Ideology of the Aesthetic* begins, "Aesthetics is born as a discourse of the body."[49] The maternal metaphor would be reason enough for detailed elaboration and argument, but here it is the explicit link to Marxian materialism that is at issue. If sense perception was a linchpin of Alexander Baumgarten's *Aesthetica,* then it is also the rational kernel of Marx's developing materialism ("Sense perception must be the basis of all science").[50] Marxism seeks to return the realm of sense perception to the ravaged body of capitalist social relations (there are many reasons for the divisions of Marxism and feminism, but one source of solidarity has often been this form of body politics, as the next chapter will underline). The sense perception of objects is transformed in exchange value so that a particular form of the body, the laboring body, has its sensuous relationship to the world displaced first by value extraction and then by the money-form. Aesthetics attends precisely to this deracinated self, seeking constantly to suture the space between subject and object, a realm of sensuousness sundered by the harsh existence of commodity life. With the parallelism in a discourse of the body established, Eagleton then delivers Marx, the aesthetician:

> Marx is most profoundly "aesthetic" in his belief that the exercise of human senses, powers and capacities is an absolute end in itself, without need of utilitarian justification; but the unfolding of this sensuous richness for its own sake can be achieved, paradoxically, only through the rigorously instrumental practice of overthrowing bourgeois social relations. Only when the bodily drives have been released from the despotism of abstract need, and the object has been similarly restored from functional abstraction to sensuously particular use-value, will it be possible to live aesthetically. (202)

The neatness of this formulation does not mean that Marxism and aesthetics signify the same political space but that Marxism is a positive form of aesthetics (materialism, in this declension, might usefully be interpreted as a form of what Michael Taussig calls "mimetic excess"),[51] just as a proletarian worldview is a positive form of ideology. Negative aesthetics, then, functions like commodity fetishism by reifying a world of objects into an ideal form. If "aesthetics seeks to resolve in an imaginary way the problem of why, under certain historical conditions, human bodily activity generates a set of 'rational' forms by which the body itself is then confiscated," then materialism is not aesthetic. But, to the extent that "there can be no liberation of use-value as long as the commodity reigns supreme" (which is why "the resolution of the *theoretical* antitheses themselves is possible *only* in a *practical* way" [207]), materialism provides a way out of the idealism in aesthetics. Why is it necessary, however, to call this materialism "aesthetic" or, as Eagleton suggests, "the Marxist sublime"?

Eagleton's political intervention is to intertwine what seem like disparate notions in order to demystify *both*. Marxists cede too much ground to bourgeois humanism by stereotyping the aesthetic as an epistemology of immense idealist proportions while suppressing the "sensuous" agenda of the Marxian project (in a later chapter I will link this agenda to the problem of imagination in the world system). For my purposes, the ambivalent nature of materialism's relationship to culture is caught up in the basic multivalence of aesthetics. The relationship is oscillatory because in aesthetics materialism confronts both its enemy and ally — significant features of its own critique *and* some founding principles of capitalist domination. In Eagleton's polemic the oscillation is pronounced:

> The aesthetic is at once...the very secret prototype of human subjectivity in early capitalist society, and a vision of human energies as radical ends in themselves which is the implacable enemy of all dominative or instrumentalist thought. It signifies a creative turn to the sensuous body, as well as an inscribing of that body with a subtly oppressive law; it represents on the one hand a liberatory concern with concrete particularity, and on the other a specious form of universalism. If it offers a generous utopian image of reconciliation between men and women at present divided from one another, it also blocks and mystifies the real political movement toward such historical community. (9)

Eagleton does not describe the movement between these wildly different notions, but it is my contention that because materialism cannot adjudicate the separate politics implied in the deployment of the same term *in advance,* hesitation and vacillation often follow (unless, of course, materialism decides to settle accounts by voluntarism and/or relativism). A Marxist aesthetic is only a contradiction because materialism cannot purge the contradictory elements from aesthetics itself: just like the conceptual limits that form Marxism's own political purview, aesthetics embodies a porous history that, if it were homogenized, would elide the reasons for its shifting formulations.

Michael Sprinker's solution to this dilemma is to divide up the theoretical practice requisite of materialist critique. Thus, he recommends two modes of inquiry (or "sciences"): one that elicits a specific "aesthetic modality" (a critique of art in general); and another that explains its possible function within a structure of particular historical ideologies.[52] The distinctions are valid enough, although it is unclear how one could specify an aesthetic modality in a materialist way without simultaneously invoking the realm of ideologies in general (which is at least one of the meanings of dialectical thinking). In addition, if we accept any part of the narrative on terminological contamination in Marxism (including Balibar's exposition, Althusserian or otherwise), then the practical claims for scientificity would have to include the ideological underpinnings of scientific discourse, a place where metatheory wants to bang its head against a receding rainbow, the constitutive outside.

But the lesson of oscillation is not the impossibility of any theoretical ground or the infinite regression that such textualism apparently confers; it draws significant attention, instead, to the political folly of assuming a pure form of theoretical engagement or a stable set of methodological principles (caught in the inertia of their own convictions). The problem remains, however, that once one has deconstructed the monolithic edifice of materialism, the fragmentation of the discourse makes it very difficult to specify at all — as if it can only "exist" in the logic of movement and vacillation itself. Like Sprinker, this leads Eagleton to separate aspects of the aesthetic as procedural imperatives, as a way, therefore, to spot the contaminating residue of that which must be opposed. The "ground" here sounds like the "predetermined yardstick" that Eagleton strenuously resists, but the nature of his question reminds us that the conditions of materialism are themselves conditional: "What will inform this constantly shifting process of freely evolved powers?" (212).

The negative aesthetic in this schema is a "bad" sublime *informed* by capitalism itself, the one epitomized by Marshall Berman in the title of his work *All That Is Solid Melts into Air,* the one characterized by Eagleton in terms of "its relentless dissolution of forms and commingling of identities, its confounding of all specific qualities into one indeterminate, purely quantitative process" (212). The "good" sublime is the one conjured by Marx in *The Eighteenth Brumaire* and the historical sense invoked by Benjamin, a sense that dreaming the past or repeating it is not just fanciful or farcical parody but a recognition of its radical content.[53] The negative aesthetic describes this content with disinterested aplomb: the materialist aesthetic seizes hold of memory "in a moment of danger" (Benjamin) as that which exceeds the phrase of the present. The trick, as it were, to the "good" sublime is that the content of its desire cannot be blueprinted because it is caught in a philosophy of the present where, for one, the reconciliation of form and content is denied by exchange value itself. The materialist aesthetic says one can imagine the world differently, but only within what Eagleton terms the "limits of representational resources." Again, this harks back not just to the conceptual limits of ideology but to what determines its concrete manifestations. The danger in both ideology and the aesthetic is that critique has often assumed the good and bad elements as transparent rather than as characteristics that are knowable only to the degree that the critical tools allow as much. This describes a realm of responsibility (or answerability in the Bakhtinian sense) but one where, as Wallerstein suggests, "[w]e can only be responsible for that which it is in our power to affect."[54] To this extent ideology and the aesthetic constitute the liminal worlds of materialism and culture respectively.

In Balibar's analysis the vacillation of ideology is a metaphor for the concept of ideology itself, so that, as we have noted, "the concept of ideology denotes no other object than that of the nontotalizable (or nonrepresentable within a unique given order) complexity of the historical process." In traditional theories of art the aesthetic has functioned in a similar way, tied as it is to a certain will to universalism in the imaginary of ruling orders. That these are contradictory concepts is certain, but it is only relatively recently that the oscillation in meaning common to metaphoricity has been seen to either texture from within or overdetermine what is definable through a range of social relations and economic conditions. As Balibar points out, this is what Althusser explored, albeit indirectly, in the notion of the "absent cause": what was less clear in his theory, however, was how people might act except as its embodiment. That ideology is now as nontotalizable or nonrepresentable as ever might seem to support the idea that "causes" are even more absent in our present, but this is due as much to the intensities of oscillation as it is to the intrinsic mischief of the ideological signifier itself. For both, the characteristic clues lie in what grounds the theory at any moment of history, and it is to that reality (the grounds, like hegemony in Gramsci's thought, of "shifting equilibrium") that we now turn.

The attempt here is not to provide a conceptual history of the major terms in materialist analysis but to indicate the mutability at base in their formulations. The point is that the degree of oscillation is historically specifiable — the wavering is indicative of various crises. The wild oscillations of the present do not necessarily weaken the rational kernel in the mystical shell, although the proliferation of mysticism might signify as much. What I will explore as materialist feminism in chapter 2 is symptomatic of materialism's internal oscillation and the movement of sociohistorical context. While it does not solve materialism's internally constitutive struggle with the concept of culture, nor culture's own struggle with the aesthetic, it does address the forms of such movement within the realm of social change itself. The grounds of the latter are, after all, the real relations to which materialism has provided methodical attention.

Just as capital is a relation, so materialism must continually attend to process, to the dynamics of the social and social change. It is ironic, given Marx's warning, that so much materialism seems intent to let the dead weigh on its brains (and I will work more with the irony and urgency of this spirit later) because this has made it that much easier for primarily bourgeois thought to celebrate that the social has moved beyond its comprehension. The speed of capital has obliterated a specific sense of space in which it operates. True, much of this intensification in capital transfer and accumulation can be read in terms of class formation and status symbolization (the place where forms of cultural materialism most often cut their teeth — a place where Williams and Bourdieu might be read contiguously), but it is primarily an economic process that depends ultimately on an increasing percentage of proletarianization.[55] As we know, the state regularly attempts to intervene in the process of unequal exchange to maximize the flow of surplus to particular states (including itself) over others. North/south and periphery/core arguments often focus on state intervention of this kind. The free-trade-zone movements of recent years do not necessarily minimize state regulation, but actually attempt to make state interventions in capital flows more efficient (an efficiency that does not necessarily accrue well-being to the wage laborer whose value is intrinsic to accumulation). The state may appear to recede into the background (the will, in the 1980s, of Thatcherism and Reaganism) but only to the extent that its interventionist strategies do not significantly impede the globalization and intensification of capital relations at this juncture. One reason materialism must oscillate wildly now more than ever is that the economic relations that form the core of its critique are mutating at a much faster rate. Punditry about apocalypse aside, the adequacy of materialist tools is in question if the world economy or world system is merely seen to be playing out nineteenth-century models of capitalist "development." The complexity of those models is not at issue; it is the forms of complexity that necessitate vigilance in materialist thought.

The metaphors of materialism are at once historical and symptomatic: they are the tissue of its transitive objects of inquiry. If we take seriously the conceptual power of oscillation, it necessitates an attention to the historical conditions of its articulation. For his part, Balibar analyzes this movement as a series of conceptual vacillations within the initial conditions and subsequent articulations of Marxist thought. But metatheory is not outside this process, as if theoretical oscillation can occur only within the object of critique. By way of conclusion, therefore, I want to provide an example of how the reaccentuations of metatheory are themselves subject to an oscillatory potential. Thus, from Balibar as an *agent oscillatoire* I will proceed to Balibar as a *sujet d'oscillation*. This means taking account of the event of articulation (what Bakhtin would call an "utterance context") and then seeing under what terms and conditions that theoretical position may be revised.

"The Vacillation of Ideology in Marxism" was first written by Balibar for a special issue of *Raison présente* that appeared in 1983, an issue that both commemorated the centenary of Marx's death and reviewed Marxism's troubled relationship to Darwin and Darwinism. For Balibar the question of Darwinism was less interesting (although it does make the odd appearance in his article); the more pressing agenda was to present a materialist critique that did not depend on apologia for "actually existing socialism" or adherence to the line of the French Communist Party (PCF) (from which he had recently been expunged because of his criticism of its arcane and racist position on immigration). With the theoretical opposition to Althusserian structuralism intensifying (something clear in the Anglo-French debates of the late 1970s and compounded by Althusser's departure from the intellectual scene in 1980) and with a corresponding lack of political apparatus for its articulation, Balibar sets about a reassessment of "the class struggle in theory" by historicizing materialism's most controversial concept, ideology.

Against the ossification of the truth of Marxism he sees in the "party line," Balibar argues for a conceptual hesitation in Marxism's project, one that allows for various (and sometimes debilitating) interpretations of its founding principles. This is not just a sign that Balibar is moving to what could broadly be described as a New Left position; it is also a symptom of the changed circumstances of Marxist theory in French intellectual life (which Balibar seeks to wrest from the "ideologues" — an obvious reference to the PCF). Interestingly, this specific moment of marginalization gets reconfigured in the English translation of Balibar's essay published five years later. The essay, with the shorter title of "The Vacillation of Ideology," appears in the volume *Marxism and the Interpretation of Culture,* a book pieced together from a conference of the same name that took place in 1983 in Champaign-Urbana.[56] Obviously, much of Balibar's essay is in the spirit of the conference and the volume. For instance, the introductory essay by Lawrence Grossberg and Cary Nelson notes that "Marxism is no longer a single coherent discursive and political practice"; "an ability to problematize Marx's writings has been central to the whole renaissance in Marxist theory"; and "by refusing to take its own categories for granted, contemporary Marxism has reappropriated the critical power of Marx's interpretive practice" (11). But the introduction ends on an ominous note, one that, again, could be read into Balibar's discrepant critique but that this time speaks more to the situation of Marxism in the United States: "Marxism is a territory that is, it would seem, paradoxically at once undergoing a renaissance of activity and a crisis of definition" (12). My point here is to underline that the political aims of Balibar's intervention are not identical with those to which they are attached in translation. More important, however, is the third moment of Balibar's essay: its inclusion in a collection of his essays in translation published as *Masses, Classes, Ideas.*[57] This reaccentuation is decisive both for the notion of the metaphoricity of materialism and for the concept of oscillation within it.

Balibar "jumps over twenty years of history" in order to consider the mutation of ideology in the work of Engels: we will jump eleven to understand the conditions of Balibar's revisions of his initial statement. The vacillation of Balibar in this example can be summarized as follows: (1) if, in the earlier version, the attempt was to differentiate Marxism from its party cognate and to refuse an interpretation that would simply root the errors of Marxism in the banalities of "actually existing socialism," then the latest rearticulation does not have the luxury of that foil — Balibar is forced to legitimate conceptual sway on its own terms; (2) the consequence of the changed historical conditions of Balibar's argument, now reinscribed after the collapse of Eastern Europe and the end of the Soviet State, tends to accentuate the weakest aspect in his critique, namely, the failure of Engels's epistemological project, whereas clearly the intention is to avoid precisely that emphasis;

and (3) the implications of Marxist vacillation, now unhinged from both the verities of the Cold War and the illusionist history of the communist state, become its defining characteristic so that the more Balibar revises his text the more it becomes the very instance of the logic he describes. If, for Vattimo, the opposition of Heidegger and Benjamin is a modernist prologue to a postmodernist predicament and, for Eagleton, the reevaluation of the early philosophical manuscripts provides a conduit to the aesthetics as a materialist sublime, then for Balibar, the event of oscillation now marks a decisive philosophical and political break so that he can proceed according to the logic outlined in his book of 1993, *La philosophie de Marx:* namely, that the *doctrine* of Marx does not exist.

This is not to say that there is no evidence of such an argument in Balibar's original articulation of what he would call the "problematic." But Marxism now enjoys the luxury and liability of a perspicuous nondoctrinal apparatus, one signaled in the first revision to Balibar's text, the addition of an epigraph from Gaston Bachelard that notes that "all rational organization 'trembles' when fundamental concepts are dialectized" (87). The trick for Balibar does not rest in reading the postmodern condition back into Marx but in understanding how the present liberates the potential of dialectical thinking, something that is implicit in his mode of argumentation. The "new" version of "The Vacillation of Ideology in Marxism" is split into two sections (the original essay was too long for *Raison présente* and was continued in a subsequent issue, not, however, according to the divisions we have here). By my count there are over 150 revisions to the text (including not only corrected translations, repunctuation, and stylistic polishing, but the deletion and addition of words, phrases, sentences, and indeed, whole passages). Since I do not intend to make oscillation equivalent to the basic exigency of textual revision, I will focus on two additions that substantially respond to the essay's new utterance context (although I would maintain that most of the revisions can be explained on that basis). We recall that Balibar has argued Marx and Engels failed to historicize capitalism sufficiently (a point punctuated in the new version by its description of their articulation as "pseudo-historical"). By formulating an "essence" of capitalism, the proletariat is equally essentialized and locked into a consciousness of identity (or not — it is an either-or dichotomy) that explains away class exceptions and precisely inhibits alternative modes of identification. Thus, to the point that "the working class becomes the blind spot of its own politics" Balibar will later add: "leaving the field free for messianic ideologization" (161). Lest the reader mistake the object of this criticism Balibar revises the accompanying footnote to conclude: "To a large extent, this would explain how, in 'really existing socialism,' workers could be dominated (and condemned to silence) *in their own name*" (239). This is not just hindsight but a shift in the structural logic of the argument afforded by changed historical circumstances. Balibar then adds a long passage that ends with a devastating conundrum: "And now it is our turn to be ironic: thus there is no more history, but there will be.... A small detail — the fact that the concept of a 'proletarian ideology' remains decidedly impossible to formulate — leads to a large result: 'history' becomes the other name for eternity (and 'materialism' the other name for idealism?)" (162). The purification of class and class antagonism impedes the very dialectic meant to critically engage such concepts. Is this summary now a break from the "historicity" made concrete in the period 1917–91?

Balibar pushes the point still further to consider the "concept of politics at work in Marxism" itself. Here, as in the initial articulation, the metaphors begin to multiply. Thus, "it is in the (historical) vacillation of ideology that politics appears" ("historical" was added, since history now proves it); then, another metaphor of oscillation, "the twisting of the relation between state and ideology, which must be undone for the relation to be twisted again in the other direction, as a many stranded-rope twists one way and then the other under the effect of two forces" (164); and finally, "politics itself can become the 'mask' of politics" (165). Again, however, the implication of the initial observations has been intensified so that Balibar will readily concede that "we do not believe any longer in the univocity of words, apart from their use." Does the force of structuralism now lie buried in the debris of the Berlin Wall? Not quite. Balibar's position comes through in the added words of his revision (here emphasized): "It is not a question of substituting, by means of a hyperbolic transcendence of 'grand narratives' and 'worldviews' *(or, if you will, in a highly problematic 'withdrawal from the political')*, the metaphoricity of language for the identification of ideological differences, but of inscribing ideological effects within the *historical* element of language" (167). Rather than poststructuralist reverie we are in fact presented with what is, in essence, Bakhtin/Volosinov's materialist conception of sign.

From this Balibar proceeds to his conclusion, which again is marked by the difference that history, not mere volition, offers his critique (one of his revisions states: "we *now know* that history tells the story of the change of form or even of the change of the function of crises" [169; emphasis added]). If the historically determined condition of oscillation is supportable, perhaps it explains why what was originally a question becomes a statement in the revision: "This evolutionist representation also underlies the epistemological notion of an absolute truth as 'process of integration' of relative truths (or relative errors) as it was put forward by the *Anti-Dühring*" (170). The question of politics and truth within Engels's evolutionist paradigm is (still) rejected, but the "constant vacillation of the concept of ideology" in Marx and Engels now inflects the terms of its rearticulation so that oscillation itself provides the promise of new possibilities in the field of politics. Nothing, it seems to me, could be clearer from the new sentence that ends what was already a major intervention in Marxist theory: "For if proletarians or, more generally, the people from below are no longer portrayed either as completely lacking ideology (*Illusionslos*) or as the potential bearers, by nature, of a 'communist worldview' — providing revolutionary theories with an ideal guarantee — they will themselves have more, not fewer, opportunities to introduce and test their ideas (the 'thought of the masses') in the battlefield of politics, from which they had been excluded in their own name" (174). The metaphor of oscillation is just this, the opening of possibilities within history and within the very logic of concepts available to it. For materialism has learned, almost at the cost of its own exclusion and erasure, that "the people from below" must begin with history, and not its abstraction, in exploring the possibilities that now present themselves. This does not "end" the crisis of Marxism that Balibar outlines, but it goes some way to explaining its constitutive logic — the ground of its materialism and the necessary contradictions that attend it.

CHAPTER TWO

BODIES (OF MATERIALISM)

The body of materialism trembles. This is a function of its dynamism, which in turn is symptomatic of its dialectical flair (as Balibar and Bachelard have just reminded us). Certainly, its oscillation is predicated upon an impossibility, that it might arrive at a point of absolute knowledge, as if change might be rendered transparent to itself. Forms of materialism shiver in specific ways: Marxism, for instance, in various declensions, anxiously purports to report its own annihilation, for capitalism's demise is Marxism's death knell as much as it heralds the coming and departure of proletarian being. It is somewhat ironic that materialisms are so often characterized as metanarratives when their very being is so inextricably linked to agencies that are necessarily beyond their control. Of course, this does not nullify a justifiable incredulity toward materialism's grander manifestations (of which dialectical materialism is perhaps its most obvious and egregious example), but it does draw attention to the materiality that conditions materialism rather than reproduce the myopia that simply reads such a scenario as a conspiracy in reverse.

The corpus of materialism is subject to material consequences, including death for those materialisms that seek not just to critique specific social formations but somehow facilitate their attenuation. The grounds for these materialisms shift most palpably, for their theoretical objects will mutate almost beyond recognition in order to preserve the essence of their material domain. Importantly, the same logic of self-preservation cannot be true for materialisms themselves unless they assume the mantle of social relations as a system to which their logic gives the name. For historically specific materialisms of this kind such an overreaching of immediate aims has produced cataclysmic fantasies that contradiction, and the odd counterrevolution, painfully deconstruct.

The corporeality of materialism is something of which Marx was well aware, which is why perhaps he so obviously drew materialist philosophy from the sensuousness of the human body. Unfortunately, the material, sensuous being of that body lacked a key spatial, and not simply biological, coordinate. And this is another reason why, for instance, materialist feminism has not only engendered Marx but critically reconstrued the corpus of

materialisms in general. The thesis of this chapter is not that materialist feminism introduces an appreciable multiplicity into the ossified practices of its
often more celebrated forebears, but that it accentuates in a transformative
way the constitutive impossibility of materialism's situatedness — that the
body of material exceeds or superadequates bodies of knowledge. This is a
second lesson about how oscillation as a concept works for materialism. The
transformative methodologies of feminism are those that critique not just
how bodies are made but how they are made otherwise, other to themselves.
The forms of this noncoincidence are of paramount importance to any materialism that seeks to understand the modes of its disjunctive conjuncturalism,
the shifting equilibrium of its wild oscillation and homeostasis in relation to
feminism. The noncoincidence itself is a function of the body's double register. Like oscillation, the body is simultaneously a physical and metaphorical
space: for theory it trembles between *corps* and *corpus*.[1] Marx, in the manuscripts of 1844, erred on the side of the body's conscious species-being —
its sense perception — rather than propose an abstraction that precedes its
determinate relationship to nature. The argument, at this level, is against
abstraction as alienation and against abstraction as a "logical, speculative expression for the movement of history" (i.e., the Hegelian dialectic).[2] It does
not, however, rule out the cognitive abilities of mental sense that, if they
cannot ultimately suture the body to its sensate being (a social being that
is never simply "being flesh"), can, in the transcendence of private property as an abstract relation of humanity, make the senses, "in their practice,
theoreticians" (87).

Different forms of feminism have fought a similar mode of alienation,
that which separates off the woman's body from the lived relations of a
woman's practical existence. But again, this critique of metaphoricity (the abstraction of assigned roles over practical existence) does not preclude mental
cognition so much as argue for its realization or actualization in social being.
When Luce Irigaray contests the "feigned" reason of masculinism, it is to disturb a particular form of rationality — a specific economy of metaphoricity
(woman as Nature, for one) — by proposing an alternative "specularization"
that destabilizes a dominant mode of specularity, the "denigratory metaphors" that make up the subject of subjection.[3] Thus, Irigaray counters the
logic of visual objectification, of fetishization, of the gaze, by exploding that
realm of metaphoricity itself: the eye that looks is a different eye; the mirror that shows reflects the sun and thus sets fire to a "female" "cathected by
tropes." This is oscillation as ocularization. It is the way that the eye can become a *human* eye; a way, indeed, that the eye can be, directly in its practice,
a theoretician. The point is not to restore the body (which is why many have
dismissed Marx's conceptualization), but reconfigure it. And this remains a
problem of matter, material, and materialism.

Clearly, the reconfiguration of the body is not the only message of feminism for materialism because its politics are always already more than the fact of the body as material. Yet I want to suggest that specific feminist approaches to the body go beyond the ability to make masculinist materialism tremble (although that political effect is significant in itself): what they can do is ground the body in a materiality that does not depend on a humanist essence in order to constitute a political force (to realize the body as human is not synonymous with the Idea of Human — which itself is an ideology of humanism). The vacillation of the concept of the body in materialism has in part been produced by an inability to theorize the material of the body with its abstraction (the story of the labor theory of value is symptomatic of this impasse), but it is also testimony to the logic of body politics itself that cannot, for its integrity, rest easy with a unifying abstraction for a mutating form of materiality.

Rather than summarize the transformative potential and effects of feminism for and as materialism, I want to examine particular strands of philosophical and political materiality in feminism, efforts that problematize in fairly precise ways the body of materialism. The fact that materialism and feminism have often been consonant because they both think the body is not the vital issue; it is, rather, the centrifugal impulse in their mostly less-than-mutual interruptions that interests me here — including the catechresis effects that Spivak has often invoked. To unpack this problematic interrelation leads outward not just into an appreciation of feminism's interrogative power but into the troubled correlative of global critique. How might feminism explode the discourse of multiculturalism, for instance, so that materialism is less than a massive reductionism of material difference on a world scale?

Feminism's demystification of the classical body of Marxism operates in multiple registers,[4] but I will begin with the grotesque body whose formulation rewrites the material body under the sign of oppressed excess. In a brilliant reading of Bakhtin's thoughts on the grotesque and also a rather literal projection of the material body for Marx, Laura Kipnis's *Marx: The Video* engenders the material body of materialism.[5] The video takes a simple fact of Marx's biography, his lifelong struggle with agonizing outbreaks of carbuncles, and reads this into a series of crucial issues for materialist feminism. How better to understand the material of the body than to narrate the body of a materialist? As Marx writes about the fate of the laboring body his own body repeatedly breaks out in carbuncles (described as a "proletarian disease"). The proletarian body is excessive to capitalist desire (capitalism must produce it nevertheless), but Marx seems to repress the connection between that and his own body's tortuous excrescences (just as capitalism must suppress the noxious symptoms of capital accumulation). By turns witty and polemical, Kipnis's video explores the consequences of Marx's misreading of his body and the masculinist implications this holds for his critique of capitalism. As a worker asks within the narrative, "[F]or Marx, which bodies were absent, unspoken, unacknowledged?" (255).

Just as Jean-Martin Charcot is starting to characterize and treat a new disease, "traumatic hysteria" (in part diagnosable from cases that emerged in light of the failure of the 1848 revolutions), Marx appears to embody its most prescient symptom: he suffers from ideas. And yet, while caught up in a discourse of body politicking, Marx fails to address adequately the gendered division of labor his analysis implies. Throughout the video, Marx's body appears to take revenge on him, as if to write on his body that there can be no theory of labor without a concomitant and complex understanding of gender. *Capital* is written anyway, despite the carbuncles that tell Marx otherwise. Thus, the video quotes Marx writing to Engels: "I had decided not to write you until I could announce the completion of the book, which is now the case. Also, I did not want to bore you with the reasons for the frequent delays, namely carbuncles on my posterior and in the vicinity of my penis, the remains of which are now fading and which permit me to assume a sitting (that is, writing) position only at great pain" (287). There are many lessons that derive from *Marx: The Video,* including one that questions the theory/practice split in media work, and another that tells of the necessity to rewrite the body of materialism within the contingencies of the possible, but I want to take the metaphor of the excessive body itself as a way of exploring a materialism that is both limited and exorbitant in its structural compulsions, and thus a body that oscillates beyond its initial formulations within the metaphorics of masculinity.

The chief danger for cultural materialism has been its tendency to aestheticize politics in the guise of foregrounding culture as a mode of production. Its main advantage has been that it has reintroduced the subject and the subjective as contestatory points of reference in the production of meaning. While formulating the cultural for materialism has necessarily produced intractable problems, the question of subject/object relations is really only an elaboration of Marx's sense of the central concern of practical materialism — namely, that the sensuousness of the body is a practical activity that produces historical subjects. This is achieved not by viewing ideas as separate from the body (an idealism perhaps best answered by carbuncles) but by seeing them as a practical manifestation of the body that, while independent of things — the other matter of materialism — is nevertheless an active engagement with reality. Marx's basic insight, that social life is essentially practical (eighth thesis), remains crucial to any materialism that attempts to understand how humans might come to undermine the sensuousness of their very being by producing forms of social life that are, in essence, impractical or irrational. Materialism lives on in every form of social thought that seeks practical solutions to a logic of living that denies humans' interdependence with each other and with nature. The body must not be made a stranger to itself.[6]

Kipnis's video tells the story of how Marx's body revolted at an idea, an idea that seemed to deny how much the practical activity of the body was organized through gender differentiation. But materialist feminism is not simply a "correction" to Marx the masculinist, nor a moral compensation for male malevolence in the history of ideas, but a profound reconceptualization of the matter of materialism — indeed, how the body matters. Aspects of this narrative are familiar: several recent studies have tracked the effulgence of materialist feminism from the inadequacies of Marxist feminism, the latter caught unabashedly on the centrality of class contradiction.[7] What has been less clear is whether such theoretical sea changes are symptomatic of the eclipse of Marxism or an attempt to integrate key notions of Marxist critique into a different mode of analysis. For some this ambivalence adds up to the same thing, and, however credible "post" has become in various discourses, such criticism is not easily dismissed.[8] In this study, the attempt is to examine how far Marxist criteria can be pushed before they become simply terminological dross in what would otherwise be anti-Marxist thought. Yet if the conceptual metaphor of oscillation is useful, it is in showing how the matter of materialism might come to look very different under alternative circumstances, like those that now radically overdetermine and disperse trajectories of theory on a world scale.

Rosemary Hennessy's term for this oscillation in materialism's wayward reinscription in competing and sometimes incommensurable theoretical modalities is "discourse," in some, but clearly not all, the ways common to Foucauldian critique. For Hennessy, materialist feminism distinguishes itself from socialist feminism by its embrace of "postmodern conceptions of language and subjectivity," and most of these focus on discursive constructedness.[9] To separate her materialism from ludic postmodernism (the language game gambit), Hennessy stresses discourse as ideology and makes use of Michel Pêcheux's notion of the interdiscursive to buttress this contention.[10] While this allows her to critically distance her efforts from simply discursive reverie, it remains unclear whether Hennessy's claims for materialist feminism are undermined by its own status as ideology.[11] Hennessy rightly critiques post-Marxism's consummate inability to distinguish the discursive from the nondiscursive (with the danger that the former becomes the metaphysical guarantee previously coveted by the latter), but as we have seen with Balibar's symptomatic approach to certain Marxian texts, the vacillation of ideology does not resolve itself in discourse if those claims simply cancel through the theory that describes it. This question would seem to fall somewhat obliquely on the problem of the body for materialism, but it has everything to do with it as we shall see.

There is nothing particularly excessive about feminism, except as a trope within dominant articulations of patriarchy. The same is true for woman's body, although this has complicated repercussions for a materialist understanding *of* the body. As a political imperative, feminists have had to continually contest the legislation of women's bodies, for instance, in labor and in reproduction, that issues from patriarchal, normative conceptions of woman and woman's work. Obviously, this aspect of political practice does not need theories from Marxism or poststructuralism in order to actively engage a specific form of social subjection. In a similar way, materialist feminism certainly offers a knowledge of oppressive practices, but it is not itself the primary mode through which those practices are addressed (that form of vanguardism is a modernist conception). How, then, is the body a contested site within theory, and how might this be rearticulated within materialist feminism's broader possibilities as global critique (if not ideology)?

If one views value as the process and name for transcoding, then the labor theory of value depends upon a particular transcoding of the worker's body, one in which use value must find surplus value but also value enough to sustain the body that has provided it (unless or until, of course, that body itself is rendered superfluous). Only labor power provides the kind of super-adequation of the body requisite for capital's use value, which capital duly extracts and negates through exchange. In a world of critical theory that rightly questions essences and essentialisms of all kinds, the notion of labor as the essence of value sounds overwhelmingly recidivist, but much depends upon how labor is defined and how its value is effaced in the commodity form. Obviously, a labor theory of value has been around for quite some time (it predates Marx's reformulation by about five hundred years), and its usefulness has been not as a universal but as a mutable theoretical tool for analyzing specific instances of the human body's social practice. Marx transforms political economy by detailing how a particular mode of production harnesses and thereby defines the labor of humanity. A Marxist interpretation of the body within capitalism begins with this insight: that the body's materiality is constituted as a commodity relation in the production of surplus value. Labor's relation to capital has changed quite dramatically since the Second World War (for one thing, labor power, as variable capital, continues to expand more slowly than constant capital, which includes "labor-saving" machinery), but the question of labor power remains hooked on capitalism's necessity for surplus value. For capital, this is the only way the body matters.

To be sure, this is an abstract body: it matters little to capital what physical form it takes, as long as it provides the basis for surplus value. But the body's abstraction for capital extraction does not mean that the laboring body has not been specified in capitalist history. Here, feminism, as Kipnis underlines, has had to say much more than the contributions that Marx and many Marxists have made. The engendering of the division of labor has meant reformulating all manner of elements that "define" labor in contemporary societies. The old "domestic" labor arguments, for instance, hardly explain the massive proletarianization of women in the global economy in recent years. The international division of labor now defines woman as a primary motor even as sexism and patriarchy still find it propitious for her to do most if not all of the "domestic work" as well (I will explore the question of the globalization of women's labor within a particular regime of capital below, and in chapter 4). But the concept of the laboring woman also finds itself as an abstraction in the body's matter.

There are several issues here that, if they are to continue to be useful for materialism, must be kept separate. The body, as a ground for capitalism, is a source for surplus value produced by the social practice of labor. But surplus does not mean excess in this formulation: as Gayatri Chakravorty Spivak has pointed out, it refers to "value difference."[12] Materialism itself may well be a form of mimetic excess, but surplus value certainly is not. In her critique Spivak warns against textualist extrapolations from Marx's use of "surplus" that may obfuscate precisely the question of value in labor — that is, that it produces more than it uses up in the time/space coordinates of work but not in a way where the exact moment of surplus can be measured (after two hours' work, three hours', etc.). One of the lessons of new historicism as a cultural materialism, for instance, is that to take metaphors of political economy and deploy them in textual readings does not make cultural critique a more materialist form of analysis; on the contrary, it opens the doors to idealism precisely where the brute fact of economic exploitation is at issue. The difficulty, however, is that the process of valorization does indeed foreground questions of representation because a worker herself is a representative, if not an embodiment, of the value form. The fetish of labor, the cult of labor, is certainly deconstructed by attention to the abstract reality of the worker, the representational links, the metabolic aura, that cathects labor in a process of production. It is this aspect of labor's abstraction, which is not secondary but coterminous with the production and circulation of value, where a materialist feminism intercedes most forcefully.

What Spivak calls the "feminization of superexploitation"[13] is a key facet of late capitalism, perhaps even more so than that much-heralded "flexible accumulation" itself. Globalization, in this sense, means the increasing colonization of the woman's body as the abstract form necessary for the expansion of accumulation. Of course, if one limits one's analysis to recent "postindustrial" societies, the question of services becomes a primary arena, but globalization is much more about the process of value extraction in the factory system worldwide where the term "sweatshop" signifies the interpellation and incorporation of women's labor at unprecedented levels. Most cultural critics rightly cringe at the thought of global critique, not from ignorance but from the suspicion that it involves one in a new round of epistemic violence. Yet surely criticism falls short of understanding the new regimes of integration and fragmentation that characterize transnational capitalism through defensive forms of localism. One of the strongest elements of Hennessy's (and Ebert's) articulation of materialist feminism is precisely her appeal to a global social analytic, one that attends to the "workplace and home, suburb and ghetto, colony and metropolis as specific and interrelated sites of exploitation."[14] Obviously, stating this does not remove the dangers of authoritarian knowledge production, tendencies produced as much by the site and subjectivity of the critic as by lapses in commendable desire. But as I have argued elsewhere, the critic must speak to this problematic alterity, the other-being intrinsic to global exploitation even as, from my position, I cannot speak for it.[15]

In a polemical essay on the writing of Mahasweta Devi, Spivak argues for an understanding of the "socially invested cartography of bonded labor," one that might come to terms in a rigorous way with the capitalization of the woman's body in India's political economy.[16] Certainly bonded labor predates India's development of capitalist social relations, but Spivak via Devi underlines the immense generalization and overinvestment in the good, clean images of low-paid service industries by accentuating the persistence of bonded labor in the present. Mindful of the difference this represents in forms of capitalism, Spivak yet presses the implication of the bonded-slavery trade Devi narrates:

> Woman's body is thus the last instance in a system whose general regulator is still the loan: usurer's capital, imbricated, level by level, in national industrial and transnational global capital. This, if you like, is the connection. But it is also the last instance on the chain of affective responsibility, and no third world–Gramscian rewriting of class as subaltern-in-culture has taken this into account in any but the most sentimental way. (82)

The representations of capital are not synonymous with Devi's representations of capital, but this is far from saying that her inscription of the separateness, or difference, of the woman's body is unthinkable within a mode-of-production narrative. Rather, such fiction "spaces" or specifies a logic that capital itself cannot represent. Materialist feminism need not detain itself with the bad conscience of capitalism, but it should elaborate (as Spivak has done in her work on and with Devi) the systemic limits to capitalist representation — the very heart of its contradictory social relations. The other being of capital is that which exists to produce value but cannot be represented without negating the grounds of capitalization. And that being is gendered.

There are moments in Spivak's argument where Devi's story appears to operate within a mimetic economy (for instance, where "Douloti the Bountiful" might be read alongside Gyan Prakash's work on labor servitude in colonial India),[17] but the larger issue concerns what the socioeconomic relations are compelled to deny, and there Devi's story, like Spivak's critique, serves the aims of materialist feminism extraordinarily well. At the end of the story, Douloti, dying from venereal disease and exhausted from her journey toward home, lies down in the dark on a bed of fresh clay. This clay has been shaped into a large map of India by a schoolmaster intent on teaching his students a nationalism apposite with the celebration of India's independence the next day. Douloti's body literally interrupts and brings to crisis the schoolmaster's (and other masters') nationalist negotiation. The schoolmaster and his students are presented with the following disarticulation: "Filling the entire Indian peninsula from the oceans to the Himalayas, here lies bonded labor spreadeagled, kamiya-whore Douloti Nagesia's tormented corpse, putrefied with venereal disease, having vomited up all the blood in her desiccated lungs" (93). The story ends, "What will Mohan [the schoolmaster] do now? Douloti is all over India." The question might as well be asked to literary critics in general and cultural studies advocates in particular. From these different positionalities and modalities what can be done to enable and not just record the knowledge of a socially invested cartography of bonded labor? Spivak, who remains one of the most committed to such tasks, immediately contextualizes the tale within, and not as excess to, the international division of labor: "[S]uch a globalizing of douloti, dissolving even the proper name, is not an overcoming of the gendered body. The persistent agendas of nationalisms and sexuality are encrypted there in the indifference of superexploitation, of the financialization of the globe" (95).[18]

One of the answers, and a forceful one, to the immense complexities that inhere in oppressive social practices remains the discursive turn. Hennessy, in her conceptualization of the term, and Donna Landry and Gerald MacLean, in their book on materialist feminisms, invoke discourse as an operative technique and critical object. Hennessy in particular makes discourse analysis an integral part of materialist feminism, and since she explicitly proposes a global analytic, I want to consider this in terms of the material body. As a Marxist, Hennessy knows the thin line she treads by taking on (both opposing and incorporating) a discursive paradigm since, although some form of discourse analysis is fundamental to an understanding of the materiality of oppressions (it demystifies the social), it is also the mainstay of theoretical projects that signal the eclipse of Marxian approaches. Steering away from what she reads as liberal eclecticism, Hennessy is also compelled to distance her critique from Foucault, Laclau and Mouffe, and Kristeva as examples of discourse analysis that, consciously or not, fail to adequately distinguish between discourse and the nondiscursive, or woman as subject and women's lives. The usual retort is that since language is a prime mediator of discourse, the nondiscursive can only be rendered discursively anyway: wherever you admit the signifier, there lurks discourse too. This makes discourse analysis something like a totalizing critique, but it does not totalize in the same way as, say, economistic Marxism, and there lies much of its allure for Hennessy. Discourse is certainly material, but whether discursive practices are more material or materialist than others has specific political implications, particularly for critics who wish to link micro- and macrological materialities. Interestingly, the vacillation or hesitation in Foucault's conception of materiality clarifies Hennessy's sense of discourse as relational and causal (if not ultimately so), but in a way this only exacerbates the theoretical lacuna explored in chapter 1, one that cannot be resolved by the appeal to ideology as the mediating category, as a sign that Marxism has been materially discursive all along.

Nevertheless, the body emerges as a key site in the articulation of the discursive with the nondiscursive: it is the very litmus test for how "material" is predicated. Without detailing his many permutations of discipline and punishment, power and knowledge, Foucault makes the case for the subject as subjected, for a body that is disciplined by the discursive practices in which it is made knowable.[19] As Hennessy points out, body consciousness is very close to class consciousness in Foucault's work, something that leads directly to the suppression of working-class sexuality by an emerging bourgeoisie fearful of the unconstrained energies such a body might represent. This is, of course, a key element in Bakhtin's articulation of the grotesque body where the "lower" orders, by their very association with the lower bodily stratum, are held to be subversive, uncontrollable, and a threat to the dictates of rational order. In this sense, Foucauldian and Bakhtinian critique make possible a deeper understanding of the body's political implications, even when Marx's self-disgust (with his own body) is at issue. For Hennessy, the body is the linchpin of Foucault's materialist claims: "As the taproot of genealogy, the ultimate micro-instance, the body for Foucault is the fundamental materiality on which history has been inscribed" (44). But the body's materiality is fundamentally unstable and therefore cannot "serve as the basis for self-recognition or for understanding other men [sic]" (44). It is because of pronouncements like this in Foucault's Language, Counter-memory, Practice that Hennessy ultimately warns against the Foucauldian body as a "discursive object." She asks, "What does it mean for the body to be a force of production? In what sense are the body's subjection and production reciprocal relations? What is the materiality of the productive, subjected body?" (45).

Hennessy concludes that such questions are only volatile with respect to Foucault because he fudges the relationships between specific instances of disciplinary discourse and other elements of the social. But it seems to me these questions are just as appropriate when directed to materialist feminism as they are to Foucault and his legacy. For instance, it is undeniable that Landry and MacLean, like Hennessy, maintain a critical interest in the in-equalities of the world system as they directly affect women. At one point they note the expansion of export-processing zones (EPZs) and the inter-pellation of women as primary workers for transnational capital. As we have noted earlier, douloti is not only all over India; she is all over the globe: "Preferred to male workers for their so-called innate dexterity and ability to perform repetitive activities, not to mention the expectation that they will be less likely than men to organize into trade unions, these young women workers trade their eyesight for cash, often as the sole income-earners for entire families."[20] One may quibble with the idea that these practices are the monopoly of EPZs (information processing in postindustrial societies exacts similar tolls on women workers); the problem, however, is whether this con-cern is congruent with the theoretical model Landry and MacLean propose. Thus, they may invoke the bodies of women workers currently being dis-abled around the globe, but what is to be done about these material bodies? At other places in their work, the answer is not very reassuring: "The world to which we refer must be inscribed, must itself become a text, in order to be thought about or lived in" (139).[21] Deferring to Laclau and Mouffe (the object of Hennessy's criticism in her notion of materialist feminism), they continue, "[E]vents are never not discursively constructed" (140). Are the ail-ments the women workers suffer textual, discursive, inscribed? The familiar tautology that they are discursive to the extent that they can only be rendered discursively does not exactly provide a material understanding of the social production in question. As I will argue later, the global proletarianization of women does present a crisis in imagination when it comes to the cognitive abilities of critical theory, but this is not the same knowledge as that which is lived by the superexploited (a knowledge that itself may teach the difference between the discursive and the nondiscursive). The deployment of oscillation as a concept means challenging every excess of economic determinism in materialist analysis (this is the starting point, for instance, of Williams's in-tervention on behalf of a cultural materialism), but the answer to economism is not textualism, formalism, or what Michele Barrett used to call "discursive imperialism." You cannot articulate the "discontinuous movements of mate-rialism and feminism" by simply making all material discourse (where is the discontinuity of the social there?). Blindness can be a discursive effect, but it is not enough to describe it in such terms.

The short answers to Hennessy's questions are: first, the body as a force of production means that sociality cannot exclude or separate the body (discursively or otherwise) from the political — the nexus of production and value marks a site where a good deal of oppression and liberation is not just inscribed but socialized; second, Foucault's point about the body as both productive and subjected indeed signals its centrality in relations of power and domination, but, as Hennessy avers, it is reductive and politically inhibiting to maintain a privilege for discourse inside and outside social relations (44); third, the disarticulation of such privilege makes the body's agency a social if not sociological problematic, the tissue of the body's materiality.

This reading does not deny the discursive constitution of the body, as if meanings do not powerfully construct the socius; it does, however, question whether realist science is simply the immovable Satan before the angelic oscillations of discourse (not least for the dualism and moralism this implies!). If the debate is really about what counts as a body (although for much materialism and feminism it is also about what bodies count), this is a symptom of a proliferation of materialisms at the present time rather than the laudable if premature eclipse of one or two of them. As I have contended, the oscillations of theory are signatures of determinate inabilities and possibilities within and without a prescribed teleology of interests. In this regard, I want to consider the body politics of Kristeva because her formulations have a strong purchase on how the body signs and is signified within gendered critique. The trembling of this body is symptomatic of its limits for materialism and the fact that, in terms of the body, more than one economy of materiality is at stake.

The chora is an *agent oscillatoire,* a presymbolic figuration and specularization that erupts in language as the sign that has indeed been otherwise repressed. Toril Moi has argued convincingly that although the chora is most strongly associated with the pre-Oedipal mother, it is not, in itself, a basis for femininity.[22] But if that particular charge of essentialism is misplaced, Kristeva's materialism seems to falter on a naturalizing functionalism that reifies the maternal body in terms of drives that are only specifiable as a pulsional pressure on language. The body's path to subjecthood is registered through a thetic phase in which the semiotic chora is split and differentiated (i.e., specified) in the symbolic: language (particularly poetic language) therefore bears the trace of a semiotic, disruptive heterogeneity that cannot itself be otherwise represented. The body bows to signification and paternal law, but not without gestures of defiance: "The body, as if to prevent its own destruction, reinscribes rejection and, through a leap, represents it in absentia as a sign."[23] Hennessy comments:

> Here the multiplication of matter in the form of energy charges is offered as the ground for a *materialist* theory of the subject. As a result,

the terms of the "ferment of the dialectic" — material *contradiction* and *struggle* — which supposedly constitute the dynamics of this process, no longer refer the historical construction of difference to disparities in social production. Instead, the dynamics of difference are yoked to universal life and death drives. (50)

For the body, Kristeva's theory seems more a leap of faith than of figuration. An original libidinal multiplicity is posited to confirm the disruptions in the symbolic in a metaleptic move that is also proleptic and positivist. It is as if all the complex overdeterminations of the social have always already been worked out in the relationship of the semiotic to the symbolic. And because Kristeva reads the semiotic as ultimately beholden to the symbolic as patriarchal law, many feminists question whether the semiotic is especially subversive, particularly where the maternal drives of the body are concerned. The terms of the semiotic process also sanction homophobia, or what Judith Butler calls a "heterosexist matrix" in identity formation.[24]

The charge is significant for many reasons, not least of which is the gender trouble that emerges when the body's materialization is based upon a psychologism riven with masculinist and heterosexist precepts. The maternal body itself is defined in terms of a libidinal drive for birth that Butler suggests is the effect of the paternal law it (occasionally) disrupts. Thus, "maternal instincts," for instance, are a code for and are supportive of a matrix that operates by way of excluding any and all desire that might challenge the logic of its reproduction. Indeed, as Butler points out, Kristeva limits homosexuality to the presymbolic (in the birth relationship of the mother and girl-child), and then only to an "absence of meaning and seeing" that borders on psychosis (83). Poetry might well signify a manifestation of homosexuality as linguistic excess, but again only as a form of psychotic reverie, or as Butler terms it, a "libidinal, displaced homosexuality" (86). If drives constitute the material/maternal body, it seems they do so only by channeling rather than by liberating desire.

The masculinism and heterosexism that Butler finds permeating Kristeva's work is not simply a product of the Freud/Lacan nexus in French feminism but connects both to a cultural elitism and to specific modes of Eurocentric thinking. The aesthetic is not intrinsically individualist but has readily been interpreted to substantiate as much, a tendency redolent in Kristeva's penchant for the European modernist avant-garde. Here, the point would not be to enumerate the exceptions to the elitist rule of thumb (even Joyce, say, or Brecht) but to press the issue that Kristeva generalizes the semiotic from "revolutionary" poetry far too narrowly defined to encompass something as important and as heterogeneous as the body. As Hennessy notes, this particular aestheticism is not out of step with a conservative backlash in Europe and North America that now places the individual before forms of political collectivity and multiculturalism that support as much. In her essay "Psycho-analysis and the Polis," Kristeva goes so far as to say that psychoanalysis will provide an antidote for the discourse of Marxism,[25] but if feminist criticism of her work counts for anything it shows how psychoanalysis can repeat some of Marxism's own muddled materialism.

Is there a way to rethink the materiality of the body without cathecting its constitution to limiting ontological prerogatives or ahistorical instincts or drives? Spivak knows that even when she specifies a body (like Douloti in fiction, or Shabhano in recent Indian history), it is not as a philosophical ground or as a political certainty. It is as if signification itself names the discontinuity in the material body. Spivak, who admits her "Europeanist" training precisely to undo it by recoding, thus learns and unlearns the body from European feminism not to take pride in a kind of voguish internationalist vacillation (which has, nevertheless, determinate formations, as other parts of this book suggest) but to question the logics (if not always logos) of "situational imperatives."[26] The recognition and questioning of situation are hallmarks of Spivak's materialism: "In *our* time-space of feminism, we have kept uncertainties at bay by binding mother to daughter in our theories and strategies. But we cannot make the whole world fit forever into that devoutly-wished embrace" (146). This is a conditional and contradictory limit on the global analytic of a millennial materialism — it eschews the embrace that globality might imply for the agonistic specificity that cultural difference compels. Spivak's particular example concerns "The Mother" chapter in Beauvoir's *The Second Sex* (within a series of situated readings of French feminism):

> It is possible to read Beauvoir's description of the female body in gestation as exactly not biologism. The pregnant body here is species-life rather than species-being, to follow Marx's famous distinction in the *Economic and Philosophical Manuscripts*. It is the site of the wholly other, rather than the man-consolidating other that woman is supposed to be. This is where "the whole of nature . . . is woman's *body without organs*." There are no proper names here. To read this as bio-*logy* is abreactive, for that assumes that someone reads where being is nature. A bio-*logized* reading makes this mode — if mode it can be called — merely intuitively accessible. It then becomes a space before access to the properness of the species-being of each female subject, where she is proper to herself; thus prepropriation. (148)

Spivak reads the Mother in Beauvoir's text as a "situation," one that cannot situate itself but yet marks the difference between "proximity and accessibility to knowing" of Heideggerian *Dasein*. A consideration of the complexity compressed in Spivak's sentences is a way of addressing what is useful and dangerous in the Marxism/Mother imbrication. Marx describes the species-life of humans as that which lives on inorganic nature. Nature is both the direct means of life and the material object of life activity: "[N]ature is man's [*sic*] inorganic body" (to the extent that it is not in itself the human body).[27] Species-life is the life activity of the species. Active species-life requires "working-up of the objective world": this is a human's species-being. Marx continues, "The object of labor is, therefore, the objectification of man's [*sic*] species-life" (76). Spivak quite rightly views this sense of labor and production as reductive. In an earlier essay, "Feminism and Critical Theory," Spivak suggests: "The possession of a tangible place of production in the womb situates the woman as an agent in a theory of production. Marx's dialectics of externalization-alienation followed by fetish formation is inadequate because one fundamental human relationship to a product and labor is not taken into account."[28] It is important to keep in mind that Spivak is not seeking to analogize from Marx: the labor of gestation *is* productive of more than itself, thus the child is thrown open to species-being from the species-life of woman. The properness of the female subject is actually the space of her subjection — that is, when that labor is appropriated as alienating, when it becomes a means to satisfy a need external to it. Engendering labor means in part elaborating the estrangement or alienation that renders even "life-engendering life" (76) external, "unproductive," and appropriated.

There are a couple of difficulties here that require further comment. The first concerns Spivak's reaccentuation or retranslation of "the whole of ... nature is man's *inorganic body*" to read "the whole of nature is woman's *body without organs*." This usefully invokes Deleuze and Guattari's de-essentializing of gendered ontology, the structuring or hierarchization of bodies, in the body without organs (the BwO),[29] but why attribute this concept to Marx? True, like Deleuze and Guattari, Marx is interested in defamiliarizing a thoroughly propertied and propriated body of capitalist rationality, but all three seem to recuperate woman's body within an economy of masculinism — Marx, in the being of man's dominion over nature; Deleuze and Guattari, in the highly questionable stagist philosophy of "becoming-woman." While the BwO is "never yours or mine. It is always *a* body,"[30] and once that body is specified (although even in its "molecular" form it is still not a body), the dubious image of the little girl, decorporealized and "universal" (277), stands in as a masterful, fluid abstraction. One could argue, and quite convincingly, that Spivak's bold catachresis here unhinges the masculinism of Marx, Deleuze, Guattari, and Sartre (along the way) merely by juxtaposing them with Beauvoir's complex articulation of the figure, if not the body, of the Mother. These masculinisms, however, are of a different kind and require qualification case by case. Perhaps woman, like the BwO, has become a sign of what Spivak calls a "miraculating agency," but even with the idealism that trips through the *Economic and Philosophical Manuscripts* the praxis that woman is denied is not its equivalent, at least not in the equivocation that Spivak carefully unpacks.

A second difficulty in Spivak's formulation derives in part from the first, and that is in accepting the idea that Beauvoir's woman in gestation is an inclusive "situation" of mothering and not one marked by a heterosexual matrix. The question of gay mothering that Spivak mentions is crucial, since this too would depend precisely upon not framing gestation through biologism and therefore presenting the intuitively inaccessible as a little less so. Certainly lesbian parents in particular would emerge as a significant interruption of capitalist and patriarchal laws of appropriation; propriation is not smothered by property rights, or at least not in the same way as normative heterosexual subjecthood. But even if one did read this thesis into (1) Beauvoir's Mother as "figuring forth the fundamental difference — between proximity and accessibility to knowing — that marks *Dasein*" (a difference that is unrealized in Sartre's translation of Heidegger),[31] it is unclear whether this also (again, in the mode of Spivakian catechresis) (2) undoes a philosophical/empirical binary *and* (3) exemplifies the Marxian distinction of species-life to species-being (which itself may be read to restage such a binary). In deconstructing the mother/daughter "embrace," the body in gestation is here also made to bear the weight of three rather different forms of the political: an inclusive mothering that "denatures" normative heterosexuality; a philosophical demythification of being and reality; and an engendering of labor in "the act of production."[32] These are all objects of materialist feminist inquiry, but the body is not made, or made up, in the same way in each mode of elaboration so it remains difficult to articulate their disparate but overlapping materiality *in the same concept.*

One could reply that the task in any reading of Spivak is to conjoin as best one can each statement to another one that it invokes, contradicts, or extends (certainly this is the case in Robert Young's critique in *White Mythologies*),[33] but here the issue is of a different order. Could it not be the case that, rather than brush the deferral or *différance* in materialism from within and through feminism, Spivak is in fact tracing the conceptual limits of their less-than-mutual articulation? The deconstructive mode would then be a symptom of contemporary vacillation in general but also a conceptual tool in the oscillation of materialist practice, one that stands or falls in the name and desire of feminism. With this in mind I will extrapolate further from Spivak's provocation to argue for the materiality of the body as a primary but not primordial space of political contestation.

Marx sets the Hegelian dialectic on its feet; Bakhtin carnivalizes the body politic by turning it upside down. For materialist feminism these theoretical acts are not unconnected for they both, in varying ways, predicate the body on forms of sociality. Significantly, women are often the objects of oppression within these forms of sociality because their labor is integrated and marginalized in the same process. Within capitalism the similarities of this oppression with that of the working class are pronounced in that, as we have noted, neither patriarchy nor capitalism wants to admit the body that produces its being. In expanding the implications of her reading of "Mother," Spivak quotes herself as a warning about the danger of collapsing two categories of labor and production: "Incanting to ourselves all the perils of transforming a 'name' to a referent — making catechism, in other words, of catechresis — let us none the less name (as) 'woman' that disenfranchised woman whom we strictly, historically, geopolitically, *cannot imagine* as literal referent" (156). This, I believe, is the woman of labor as well as the woman in labor sometimes named, marked, as "subaltern" but in any case the direct object of a historically specific mode of economic socialization. What is for Beauvoir's philosophy an existentialist dilemma is also an "undecidable" in a human's socialization of nature. The capitalist labor market is actively proletarianizing women's labor as never before. For Marx and Engels this is consonant with a weakening of the patriarchal monogamous family: as Engels puts it, "The first condition for the liberation of the wife is to bring the whole female sex back into public identity."[34] Yet this "liberation" is still proletarianization for working-class women, and especially subaltern women. The woman without organs may well be prepropriative and the unimaginable as literal referent, but by far the strongest form of her emancipation as material body is being done in the name of *ap*propriation. To quote from Spivak once more, this is "the undecidable in view of which decisions *must* be risked" (156).

Previously we have looked in some detail at Balibar's symptomatic reading of Marx and Engels, as he traces the constitutive oscillation, vacillation, and ambivalence in what have been held to be principles of a Marxist-materialist approach, particularly with regard to ideology. Without endorsing the Althusserian claims for an epistemological break, it seems clear that the 1844 manuscripts also partake of certain formative ambiguities, of which the relationship of human species-being to nature is but one. The bodily metaphors that spin out of Marx's argument on the subtended sensuousness of the body in capitalism have often led to a confused or contradictory equivalence between economic exploitation and forms of patriarchy (the question of the uses of "reproduction" alone is the subject of significant debate among materialist feminists, as the work of Mary O'Brien for one underlines). There is no sense in rescuing Marx from the masculinism of his particular interpretative mode (he must be left to suffer from carbuncles); there is much value, however, in a materialist understanding of the body. If labor as alienation depends upon a particular appropriation of a prepropriated woman's body without organs, a political (mis)reading of the practical activity of species-being, then one must do more than, for instance, bemoan the Hegelian hangover in the 1844 manuscripts; one must come to terms with the infinitely political prospect that feminism *is* the refiguring of the materialist body — it is the "being" of the body that is materialist *avant la lettre*.

This does, of course, make some bodies of materialism tremble — and from fear, as Spivak well knows, but the political implications of this are diverse. Some will argue that everything depends upon how the body is predicated. But this itself misses what "grounds" materialist critique, which in Marx's case at least is the attention to process. It is not the object of capital that Marx elucidates in innovative ways (after all, Ricardo and Smith can do that); it is his insights into the processes of capitalism that are remarkable. If materialism is to continue to provide an understanding of culture, it is only through its abilities to explain the relations of cultural production; that continuation is not dependent on whether materialism's language is adequate as a description of cultural objects. Similarly, materialism is considerably constrained if it is merely to provide descriptions of the deracinated self of capitalism: it is the processes of the production of a body within and for various formations of capitalist exploitation that provide an epistemological and ontological horizon for materialist politics. But the laboring body is an equivocable body, despite the attempt to harness and rationalize its abilities, its processes, its dispositions. Thus, on the one hand, materialism must attend to the structural compulsions of various orders of socialization; on the other, it must never forget that the body is not reducible to its functions within a regime of socialization. The equivocation between the body and its labor is crucial in understanding forms of materiality and the resistance to particular modes of materialization. This, of course, has a philosophical provenance. Deleuze, for instance, summarizes Spinoza's discourse on the body through the latter's critique of two vital questions: "What is the structure (fabrica) of a body? And: What can a body do? A body's structure is the composition of its relation. What a body can do corresponds to the nature and limits of its capacity to be affected."[35] This doesn't necessarily have materialist consequences for Spinoza (or Deleuze), but it does point to the difference between a potential of the body and a capacity calculated for it. The philosophical difference is a political difference where the body of labor is concerned. Again, however, the mode of materiality is itself brought into question when a body is specified. The problems and possibilities of such an approach are precipitate in Judith Butler's *Bodies That Matter*, in which the matter of material dissembles not just from the Marxian concept, but from within itself in a process of citationality.

Butler's argument would seem to be a highly unlikely choice as a source of oscillation in millennial materialism, since her approach is primarily discursive, and where discursive practices are not coextensive with material.[36] Rather than rehearse Bhaskar's extended critique about the difference between transitive and intransitive objects of reality to bolster the incommensurableness between materialist and poststructuralist (and post-Marxist) positions, I want to use a reading of matter like Butler's in much the same way as Spivak's intervention, as a rearticulation of the "moment of materialism," one bound by the oscillatory urges of the present, but present too in the vacillating procedures of otherwise stable bodies of thought. In *Bodies That Matter* Butler is primarily interested in the regulatory norms that constitute the materiality of the body, particularly those associated with "sex" differentiation (although along the way she produces a provocative reading of race as well). Materiality, then, is read as "an effect of power, as power's most productive effect."[37] The normal, and normative, materialist immediately balks at such statements seeing not only the panoptic power of Foucauldian critique but the cart before the horse.[38] Yet clearly what Butler sets out to do is make already ambivalent categorizations oscillate more wildly. In part this means complicating somewhat knee-jerk versions of constructionism, but it also means attempting to undo "matter" as a posited limit. Butler therefore argues for "a return to the notion of matter, not as site or surface, but as *a process of materialization that stabilizes over time to produce the effect of boundary, fixity, and surface we call matter*" (9; emphasis in original). Obviously this is a *very* specific notion of matter: the "we" here would not include a scientist out to test the theory of matter's indestructibility. There is a materialism dedicated to the changing content of scientific belief, but the materialism here is of a different kind, one with its feet in political philosophy, and one more creative when considering the centrifugal forces of "culture."

I would agree that there is a process of materialization that congeals as an effect of fixity, but this defines ideology or power, not matter per se. True, ideology wants to produce matter and thus has material effects, but that is a very different proposition than claiming that the process of materialization *is* matter. Certainly that is not a move made in historical materialism, but it is logically consistent with Butler's stress on performativity as an agency without a subject (in both cases process supplants the traditional node of its possibility). To the extent that a process cannot also be the content of the process Ebert is correct to label Butler's concept of the materiality of materialism a "mystification."[39] The elements of this mystery depend upon a "misreading," which is not always the same tactic that deconstruction has legitimized.

Significantly, Butler deploys Marx's first thesis on Feuerbach to support her contention that it is the process of materialization that constitutes the "very matter" of objects. But Marx does not say this. One of his criticisms of Feuerbach redolent in the first thesis is that not just idealist but materialist philosophies elide the importance of "'revolutionary,' of practical-critical, activity"[40] — in other words, that much philosophy denies the relationship of the "thing, reality" to "human, sensuous activity, practice." It is not that human activity makes matter but that activity *transforms* matter. Socialization entails this process of transformation (this defines social change), which indeed can be called "materialization," but to call it matter itself is to lose the sense of the activity involved and the determining role of social being and agency this implies. Thus, when Marx and Engels extrapolate from the "Theses" in *The German Ideology* they are careful to distinguish the forms of activity humans engage in from "the actual means of subsistence they find in existence and have to reproduce."[41] This difference, to borrow from Marx's second thesis, is a *practical* question, not a "purely *scholastic*" question of the reality or non-reality of thinking (144).

Why, then, argue for Butler's contribution as profoundly materialist feminist? The conflation of matter as the site of activity with matter as activity notwithstanding, Butler nevertheless elaborates a "modality of materialization" that is crucial to theories of social change. Starting with a concept of materialization as a form of citationality (somewhat apposite with Althusser's use of interpellation), Butler goes on to map the exclusionary practices that render materiality itself a sign of irreducibility, one that grounds an otherwise masculinist fantasy of autogenesis and reason. In doing so, Butler points to the political promise of oscillation:

> To problematize the matter of bodies may entail an initial loss of epistemological certainty, but a loss of certainty is not the same as political nihilism. On the contrary, such a loss may well indicate a significant and promising shift in political thinking. This unsettling of "matter" can be understood as initiating new possibilities, new ways for bodies to matter. (30)

For my purposes this means reading Butler herself against the grain, the grain of a certain obsessive discursivity, but the point is not to correct somehow her philosophy (like Aijaz Ahmad wanting Said to be a Marxist),[42] but to read her strategically for the limitations she perceives in conventional or traditional materialist practices. As Butler notes, part of the problem resides in the etymological associations of classical Western philosophy where matter is linked to *mater* and *matrix* (womb). If, in the 1844 manuscripts, nature is "the material, the object, and the instrument of his [*sic*] life activity" (75), then there is some justification to Spivak's earlier point that nature is feminized, but without organs (i.e., that nature is "not itself the human body"). The "nature" of femininity in "woman" emerges in the projection of nature as man's body but without his organs. When the body is defined in terms of man, nature has no organs as woman. Needless to say, this version of *mater*ialism is *anti-mater*ialism in that it affirms and denies a sexist differentiation in the production and reproduction of social life or species-life. Unlike Spivak's approach, Butler mixes in Marx with Aristotle and Plato without exploring how Marx might partake of a phallogocentric division of labor. The implication, however, is that a given version of matter will determine, and determine to a great degree, "what will and will not appear as an intelligible body" (54). Thus, "to invoke matter is to invoke a sedimented history of sexual hierarchy" (49).

To invoke matter otherwise requires explanation about not only how the exclusionary mode of categorization defines itself but also how it can delimit responses that explicitly set out to deconstruct the violence of such logic. This is demonstrated in Butler's innovative approach to Irigaray's reading of Plato, to which I will add a couple of brief points.[43] The form/matter binary is a Platonic rationalization of masculine and feminine. The feminine exceeds this figuration, as Irigaray argues, not by reversing the mode of appropriation (what is proper to this or that as negotiating the nature or their relation) but by "miming" or "citing" it as Butler suggests in the manner of a displacement (the manner, indeed, in which Spivak writes nature as a woman without organs). Yet even miming, as Butler points out, risks the "inadvertent uses of . . . containment" (46) that the Platonic erotic economy itself proposes. On one level, the task would be to provide an account of the metonymic signification in the less-than-stable borders of the maternal (thus the mime would be, as it is in Bhabha's work, an ambivalent de-essentializing of the Same). On another level, one would have to come to terms with an inevitable conceptual contamination, something that cannot be expunged or expelled but is transformed with the categories of signification themselves.

Butler wants to fight this, but she seems to know that the struggle involves more than the terms of discursivity; that is to say, there is a long history of materialist critique that might be brought to bear upon this very question, the "modalities" of which distrust forms of philocentrism *and* varieties of exceptionalism that simply nominate the attenuation of prior theoretical formulations. Dialectical materialism has not simply purged itself of the problematic forms of the dialectic in classical antiquity (including Plato), but clearly it is not identical with those either. Similarly, it would be nice to believe that all versions of dialectical thinking were simply dualistic or binary in their procedural moves, but this is not the case as, for instance, the value form in Marx extensively indicates. Thus, Butler's argument begins to waver, and necessarily so, because to argue otherwise would be to master the exclusions that is reason's outside. The "task," as she describes it, is actually the argument that she has performed, "to refigure this necessary 'outside' as a future horizon, one in which the violence of exclusion is perpetually in the process of being overcome" (53). This is why Butler would never argue that all heterosexuality is compulsory or that all reason is masculinist, for this would cancel through the terms of her own intervention and make it the absolute that it is not.

Perhaps such comments do not explain why Butler hesitates in her adjudication of Forms in classical Western philosophy so that "the regulation of sexuality at work in the articulation of the Forms *suggests* that sexual difference operates in the very formulation of matter" (emphasis added), but it certainly indicates why such terms as materiality and materialization become progressively more obtuse in her argument. Thus, Butler notes:

> This is not to make "materiality" into the effect of a "discourse" which is its cause; rather, it is to displace the causal relation through a re-working of the notion of "effect." . . . Discourse designates the site at which power is installed as the historically contingent formative power of things within a given epistemic field. The production of material effects is the formative or constitutive workings of power, a production that cannot be construed as a unilateral movement from cause to effect. "Materiality" appears only when its status as contingently constituted through discourse is erased, concealed, covered over. Materiality is the dissimulated effect of power. (251)

And then:

> Materialization can be described as the sedimenting effect of a regulated iterability. (252)

The paragraph begins by admitting that materiality "causes" discourse but then redefines "effect" so that it means "cause" in a dissimulated kind of way. Materiality then "appears" only when the fact that discourse has constituted it has been denied. Thus, materiality has actually been "caused" by discourse, something that power tries to hide. It is true that certain forms of materiality are the dissimulated effects of power (there could be no Althusserian theory of ideology without such a notion), but the materiality in the first sentence cannot be identical with the materiality that follows it. Similarly, not all forms of materialization are "effects," sedimented or otherwise, of regulated iterability, or else there can be no revolution in social practice and never has been one, just layer after layer of effects that may, or may not, turn insects into oil. Again, materialization *can be* described in this way, just as the regulation of sexuality *suggests* a sexual differentiation in matter, but more than that Butler will not say because this would give up the shifting grounds that provide these possibilities in the first place. Far from dismissing such an approach, I would argue that it is precisely what must be risked to clarify if not clear the detritus "sedimented" within the very terms of materialist analysis. To say that I disagree with the sliding of certain signifiers in Butler's argument is obvious, but that is not the same as saying that the argument itself is politically unnecessary or unrewarding.

The destabilizing of specific tropes in philosophy and psychoanalysis is a political imperative because it weakens repressive notions of materiality (if not matter). This is most evident in Butler's critique of Freud and Lacan through the paradigm of the lesbian phallus. Here Butler undoes Freud's stolid and masculinist desire to define the borders of erotogenic body parts. She notes that in *The Ego and the Id* Freud links erotogenicity (sexual stimulus) to the consciousness of bodily pain. This is not a point about sadomasochism but one about what is real and what is conjured in bodily definitions. Characteristically, perhaps, Butler finds a distinct oscillation in Freud's argument: "This ambiguity between a real and conjured pain, however, is sustained in the analogy with erotogenicity, which seems defined as the very vacillation between real and imagined body parts" (59). The politics of this reading are then connected to Freud's elaboration of the "symbolically encoded phallus" as distinct from the penis, where the originating idealization of the one decenters the erotogenicity of the other: "Insofar as the male genitals become the site of a textual vacillation, they enact the impossibility of collapsing the distinction between penis and phallus" (61). This failure to approximate is a constitutive ambivalence, one that phallogocentrism cannot hope to overcome but vigorously attempts to stabilize (this is at least one of the meanings of patriarchal ideology).

Having established the imaginary procedures of Freud's notion of erotogenicity (including an important note on his pathologization of body parts that allows a link between sexuality and disease — a characteristic reproduced in homophobic discourses on AIDS), Butler draws on its implication for the body's matter: "[I]t is no longer possible to take anatomy as a stable referent that is somehow valorized or signified through being subjected to an imaginary schema. On the contrary, the very accessibility of anatomy is in some sense dependent on this schema and coincident with it" (65). Clearly, Butler is not denying the materiality of the body; she is, however, arguing that specific conceptions of the body attempt to stabilize it within economies of Truth. As Elizabeth Grosz has noted, the body is continually reminding us of its materiality in different ways. For instance: "Body fluids flow, they seep, they infiltrate; their control is a matter of vigilance, never guaranteed. In this sense, they betray a certain irreducible materiality."[44] Yet as Butler points out, "it must be possible to concede and affirm an array of 'materialities' that pertain to the body" (66) — not just its fluid reminders, but age, weight, and so on, leading to the ultimate "betrayal" of irreducible materiality, death itself.

But conceding such materialities does not provide a knowledge of the ways in which they are explained at various moments in history, and within different regimes of intelligibility. One of the many values of Butler's approach is that it offers a critique of such modalities as they collude with and/or constitute repressive forms of power. In that sense, her use of the question "Are bodies purely discursive?" is purely rhetorical since the key component of Butler's reading of Freud, and indeed Lacan, is a negotiation of the material and the discursive, however inconsistently this principle is applied. Materialist feminism is a staging of this continual dilemma, that the power of discursive critique must be acknowledged but not in a way that negates, rather than sublates, the political project of identifying and collapsing the material basis of masculinist formations. To a certain extent this perplexity is evident in the schisms between the Hennessy and the Landry/MacLean arguments — in the difference, for instance, between their respective versions of postmodernity and deconstruction for materialist feminism. When Butler calls for a "displacement of the hegemonic symbolic of (heterosexist) sexual difference and the critical release of alternative imaginary schemas for constituting sites of erotogenic pleasure," this must include the hegemonic symbolic within materialism itself. Materialist feminism signifies an ongoing attempt if not the name for that displacement.

In her discussion of the lesbian phallus Butler uses a symptomatic approach toward the textual ambiguities of Freud and Lacan (the broader question of the master's tools and the master's house are not at issue here). The founding ambivalence in the concept of the phallus supports Butler's claims for alternative sites of identification and desire. While always a political question, the argument is not read primarily into the actual social hierarchization that currently obtains (for instance, the phallus is ambivalent historically, geographically, etc., and not just bodily). I have already noted how thinkers like Spivak are compelled by that step, although it is also evident to some extent in Butler's reading of *Paris Is Burning* and her approach to the works of Willa Cather and Nella Larsen. Here, however, I wish to materialize the body in two "(dis)appropriate" ways to the analysis of social hierarchization: spatiality and the carnivalesque. This is not by way of returning matter to material, but it will press the issue of materialization in a less circumspect manner than that of the citational body.

There are several cogent critiques that have developed and taken issue with the carnivalesque body politics of Bakhtin (Stallybrass and White, Russo, and Jefferson, among others). Within the rubric of materialist feminism discussed so far, only Kipnis makes use of Bakhtin on the body, and then only in her reading of *Hustler* magazine. What she finds is that the classical body and the popular festive lower bodily stratum are still lurking in the social imaginary (albeit in different forms) and that publications like *Hustler* feed on gendered disgust and class resentment in projecting body parts. Of course, the fact that *Hustler* challenges hegemonic, bourgeois conceptions of the body complicates what constitutes a political intervention in popular culture, but Kipnis is well aware of the particular limitations this example represents (its liberation of the lower bodily stratum is not at woman's behest even when such a woman is specified as working-class).[45] Since it is Kipnis, however, who has focused on a carnivalized Marx, a Marx whose body symptomatically revolts at the idea of *Capital*, the carnivalesque body may offer a paradigm for material determination that citationality wants to suppress (at least where an actual body is concerned).

The objectification of the body in nature as woman represents an intractable political problem. On the one hand, fixing this definition masculinizes the object, often in contrast to passivity or the inactive (precisely Bakhtin's characterization of the other in his early philosophical essays), or feminizes the subject as an array of essential physical or mental features (an essentialism that has its own history within feminism); on the other hand, to posit "woman" as itself a masculinist signifier, the symbolic *geist* of the Law of the Father, can lead to a more fluid or conflictual sense of being for woman in response (citational, performative, situated, etc.). Yet even the notion of a foundational ambivalence in woman is also recuperable within patriarchal discourse (woman as untrustworthy, wayward, irrational), so this hardly presents itself as an unproblematic strategy in the politics of difference. As I have suggested, however, while oscillation cannot presume social change (change that, for instance, materially deconstructs oppressive gender hierarchies or phobic sexual matrices), it does provide an understanding of the dynamics of this or that social formation, including the body logics that support them. And since theory is not outside the articulation of these logics, it too is a measure of oscillatory practice.

Just as Dostoyevsky cannot possibly bear the weight of all Bakhtin's claims for the dialogic, so Rabelais is scarcely able to represent the thousand-year history of popular, folk forms through which he is interpellated in *Rabelais and His World*.[46] Rabelais, one could say, is grotesquely out of proportion to the stunning critique that Bakhtin offers (a grotesqueness entirely necessary, even if not consciously so, in terms of the obscenity of Stalinism in which it was produced). Within this representation, however, the body emerges as an intense site of social contestation; indeed, its surfaces mark the quintessence of cultural struggle. Thus, although the chthonian desire in carnival as a specific, historical form may be dead in France, the carnivalesque body retains a certain explanatory power. As such, it is promiscuous, malleable, subversive, basic, humorous, exaggerated, and exaggerating. The carnivalesque mocks propriety (and appropriation), civility, pomp, officialdom, regulation(s), and the perfectibility of the human body in those who lord over us. And it understands well the carbuncles that threaten Marx's penis.

But since the sign is materially situated, body imagery too is subject to struggle, and the "lower" orders and the marginalized have no monopoly over the "lower bodily stratum" (a point to which I will return). How is woman figured into this popular discourse? In the Gallic tradition that Bakhtin outlines, the "popular comic" and the "ascetic" war for hegemony in the popular imaginary, a conflict in which Bakhtin favors the former:

> The popular tradition is in no way hostile to woman and does not approach her negatively. In this tradition woman is essentially related to the material bodily lower stratum; she is the incarnation of this stratum that degrades and regenerates simultaneously. She is ambivalent. She debases, brings down to earth, lends a bodily substance to things, and destroys; but, first of all, she is the principle that gives birth. She is the womb. Such is woman's image in the popular comic tradition. (240)

The danger of the lower bodily stratum and woman's incarnation within it is precisely its ambivalence. It is neither the corporeal space of pure negativity nor positivity but in this way can only guarantee struggle rather than outcomes in its articulation. Woman as the "principle that gives birth" can confine real women to the sphere of species reproduction, as feminism well knows, or destabilize summary notions of production and value per se (which is much in the spirit of Spivak's intervention). Woman is undecidable in Bakhtin's formulation because the grotesque body is "a body in the act of becoming. It is never finished, never completed; it is continually built, created, and builds and creates another body" (317). The woman's body is only grotesque to the extent that it shares this greater logic with the grotesque body in general: it embodies process.

For Bakhtin, as for Marx in this case, there is a more desirable form of becoming — through erasing the subject/object split of history, that which has demarcated the borders between the body and the world ("man and nature" in Marx's parlance), that which has sundered the sensuousness in human activity. In the grotesque figuration of the body, such separation (or alienation, *entfremdung* in Marx's schema) is constantly if not consistently ridiculed. This self is counter to what the body knows. Rabelais's fascination with bodily orifices is, in Bakhtin's argument, nothing less than an affirmation that the body is in the world; its orifices are the points of "interchange and interorientation" (317). Here "excess" of the body does not mean just wasteful (the waste of defecation, etc.) but creative, socially productive processes. That the image of the womb can be both has meant that it has been a powerful image in a variety of cultures for what the body can mean, or what the body can be. To extract from this a prescriptive body (literally, one to be always already inscribed) is not the point (by this token, neither Rabelais nor Bakhtin would have much to offer feminism), but there is some political sustenance in bodily transgression itself, the principle of challenging normative notions of the body and bodily activity.

It is a truism that the body is a signifier par excellence, but perhaps it is only now, when signification has become an eminently ambivalent enterprise, that the body's material transgressions can take on a revolutionary agency. The grotesque in its literal forms is easily dismissed in what constitutes a consequential symbolic act (people do not change the world just by eating, bleeding, sneezing, farting, or birthing), but what regime of truth it undoes now gains greater purchase within broader theories of changing relations in the worlds that bodies make. One need not share Bakhtin's exuberance for protuberance and the artifice of the orifice to understand why this might be so. Certainly there are moments in Bakhtin's study where it is unclear if he is merely describing Rabelais's own celebration of bodily functions or partaking in that imagery in yet another version of, in particular, the objectification of woman. All that Mother Earth discourse and the thematics of death-renewal-fertility that focus on the womb as, in one paragraph, a well, cow's belly, cellar, gaping mouth, hole, and an ur-text of masculinism, the mouth of Satan as *vagina dentata*, the jaws of hell, are not necessarily the stuff of dehierarchization in gender relations, however much they decenter the "official discourse" Bakhtin identifies. Much depends, therefore, on the contextual instance of bodily topography that he proposes since this will determine to a significant degree whether the exaggeration of the inappropriate will disappropriate specific examples of masculinist grotesquerie.

Bakhtin makes his case in several interesting ways, including a provocative critique of G. Schneegans's *Geschicte der Grotesken Satyre* (The history of grotesque satire [1894]). Specifically, Bakhtin takes issue with Schneegans's reading of the "clownish" in a scene from the Italian *commedia dell'arte*. A stutterer is talking to Harlequin but cannot pronounce a difficult word. He becomes short of breath and sweats and trembles "as if he were in the throes and spasms of childbirth" (304). Harlequin's solution is to run at the stutterer and hit him, head first, in the stomach. Thus, the word is "born." Bakhtin resists Schneegans's psychological interpretation of this scene in favor of its "objective content" (308). Perhaps, however, the ambivalence of one can be read into the other. The stutterer as pregnant with the word is not just a feminization of man, as the psychoanalytic literature on stuttering purports to show. But even if we did assume for a moment that masculinity is destabilized by the birthing motif, the product is language — and there the symbolic might seem to reassert its hegemony (women have babies, but men have words, and which has been the more powerful birth*right*?). In Bakhtin's materialist reading it is the attack on official religious iconography that is emphasized. Thus: "We specify that it is the word that is born, and we stress this fact: a highly spiritual act is degraded and uncrowned by the transfer to the material bodily level of childbirth, realistically represented" (309). Because the lower bodily stratum displaces the upper bodily stratum (the word is born in the belly even if it is "conceived" in the head), the materiality of language itself is problematized, as if the rational head wants to deny the materiality of words themselves, just as it marginalizes the materiality of birth (better to hypostatize it in the immaculate discourse of Christianity, which is itself one of Rabelais's grotesque objects). Through his analysis of Rabelais, Bakhtin continually presents us with the risk of ambivalence: turning the classical body upside down may also feed a more general degradation in the body parts of woman, but it can also call into question the discrete categorizations of a rational, ordered self that belong to a specific history of phallogocentric thought (interestingly, in the "Hippocratic anthology" Bakhtin reviews, the soul is born "through the apertures in the head," but this topography occurs within a rather different category from birthing, "Death" [358]).

That the bodily subversions Bakhtin identifies may work best within a historical Rabelaisian economy of difference has been increasingly affirmed within contemporary cultural critique. Achille Mbembe's essay "The Banality of Power and the Aesthetics of Vulgarity in the Postcolony" argues that the binary opposition of nonofficial and official discourse in Bakhtin's account of popular festive forms fails to account for the *recherche hegemonique* of the *commandement* in the postcolony.[47] Within this discourse, the juxtaposition of official and nonofficial imagery suggests a "promiscuous relationship" between the two and problematizes the easy equation of resistance and domination in terms of the people and the state. Not that Mbembe's analysis is un-Bakhtinian in spirit: his understanding of the grotesque provides a springboard to a novel reading of the postcolonial state's imaginary. The "poaching" of meanings Mbembe describes, however, is not just the populace ridiculing the ruling orders (the example of the Togolese party acronym R.P.T. rendered as *redépécer*) but a condition of the *commandement*'s penchant for lecherous living. Two points derive from this: the ruling orders can join in the mockery and laughter ostensibly leveled at themselves; and popular hilarity itself may be a measure of the people's agreement with the "face value" officialdom puts on it. Contrary to the model of European decorum that Bakhtin examines, the leaders of the postcolony delight or indulge in their ridicule: "[I]n fact, the *commandement* derives its 'aesthetics' from its immoderate appetite and the immense pleasure it encounters in plunging in ordure" (10).

The inversion that Bakhtin describes is itself inverted as power appears to rejoice in its own redundancy. The postcolony's place in history is marked by its "chaotic plurality," a wild oscillation not too far removed from two other contemporary symptoms, postmodernism and poststructuralism. But then Mbembe's argument itself begins to sway: first, through truism ("I would argue that defecation, copulation, pomp, and sumptuousness are all classical ingredients in the production of power, and that there is nothing specifically African about it" [11]), as one remembers that European carnival was always already an "all-licensed" affair; and second, by the continuing implication that resistance does indeed reside with the people. The first point takes us right back to Bakhtin's difficulty in generalizing from the particularities of the Rabelais example (the heady claims for folk and popular cultural forms open his periodization to intense criticism). In Mbembe's case, the articulation of the postcolony in this way immediately invites contradiction from critics in other places and discourses (as a follow-up issue of *Public Culture* adequately emphasizes). If the postcolony is this, then what of Indonesia, asks one commentator? (My answer appears in chapter 4.) In addition, as Judith Butler points out, once Mbembe decides to generalize, gender and race seem to drop out of the politics of power.[48] The question of resistance is not displaced simply by arguing against its binary manifestations and for its chaotic contingencies, as Mbembe's argument makes patently clear:

> What gives rise to conflict is not the frequent references to the genital organs of the men of power; but rather the way in which the people who laugh kidnap power and force it, as if by accident, to contemplate its own vulgarity. (12)

> The applauding crowds of yesterday have become today a cursing, abusive mob. (15)

> [W]e have to conclude that what we have in the postcolony is a case of theophagy where the god himself is devoured by his worshippers. (16)

True, "the practices of the ordinary people cannot always be read in terms of 'opposition to the state,' 'deconstructing power,' and 'disengagement'" (22), but this hardly represents Bakhtin's analysis of the banquet, the body, or the marketplace. The grotesque may find itself inscribed within an economy of resistance at particular moments of crisis (indeed, even a book about the grotesque can function in that way, as Bakhtin's intervention suggests), but resistance is not immanent to its representation. If there is a resistance ritual in grotesquerie it emerges in the way that historically specific hegemonies have compartmentalized and disciplined (in the Foucauldian sense) what counts as the body, which parts matter. The grotesque appears to carnivalize best in the weak spaces of the body's ideologization, the body as a trace of the dominion it cannot name. Thus, the materialization of the body in history speaks to ideology that has none.

Mbembe's essay has already intensified discussions of what constitutes the "postcolonized subject" (23), and his analysis of real and imagined bodies also underscores that the body is always already about material metaphors, the body as space, location. The specific feminization of space has a long history of investigation, but I want to draw together the examples above by relinking the material body to the body of materialism. The trope of femininity caught between corporeality and image is as much an insignia of modernism and modernity as it is a symptom of the paroxysm of the postmodern. Perhaps this means only that patriarchy continues to fester in the cultural logic of the hour. Yet it seems to me that the specific mode of spatialization in postmodernity maps woman's body in a particularly contradictory way, and there the otherwise pietistic accusations of dualism in conventional models of materialism are on the mark.

Even if one looks at literal motifs, for instance the Statue of Liberty, its reaccentuation *after* modernism seems to parody the spatial logic of the late nineteenth and early twentieth centuries. There was much that was grotesque about spring 1989 in Beijing, and not in the particular sense that Bakhtin uses the term, but who could have been prepared for the students' stunning act of defiance when they installed a facsimile of Liberty in Tiananmen Square? The claims for democracy were epitomized in a white woman dubbed "The Goddess of Democracy." I have written elsewhere about the mediazation of that moment, both about the marginalization of Chai Ling, the woman leader of the movement, and the savvy maneuvers of the protesters in the face of impossible odds (although there would be few tactics that could have avoided the crushing intervention of the military in June).[49] One could argue, with true postmodern aplomb, that the students' statue was a wonderful pastiche primarily directed at the fundamental inequalities of postrevolutionary China, but this would also have to take into account the image of democracy invoked. The pastiche in the latter continues to mock the evacuation of meaning in the Western correlative, an unintended consequence no doubt but one dramatically punctuated by, for instance, the beating of Rodney King and the L.A. riots that followed the mock trial of his assailants. My point is this: the spatialization of the woman's body on a world scale means both the imbrication of sedimented patriarchal imaging and a concomitant and no less complex denaturalization of that body's situated aura. Again, appeals to the spatial logic in, say, a Lefebvrian materialism are not out of order, but feminism continues to offer and/or articulate a revolutionary knowledge of these dispersed and sometimes integrated bodily abstractions.

The body is always in space even if this condition of its materiality has actually been suppressed in materialism at different moments in history. The provocation of what Elizabeth Grosz calls "corporeal feminism" is that the materiality of the body in space is coordinated along several cognitive axes — those that link a body image to sensual data. As Grosz indicates, the body image has a long history and exists in different forms within and across cultures (think of the meridians in acupuncture, for instance, as tracing a sense of the body that one can only image). This neurophysiological mapping of the body is fascinating in its own right but serves here to underline that the material body depends to a certain extent on the imagination of its surfaces, on its schema. The most conclusive evidence for this is the phenomenon of the phantom limb in which body parts continue to be experienced despite having been amputated or "lost." As Grosz points out, the phantom is not the same as the flesh that preceded it, although its approximation is closest immediately after the excision of the original. The phantom extremity is usually lighter, less mobile, and less amenable to voluntary movement. For the amputee, the phantom limb is a sign of perpetual sensory oscillation because she or he simultaneously experiences a missing arm, for instance, in two necessarily incommensurate ways: as a "reality" with sensate reactions and as a real stump with an imaginary extension. As such, "these two 'limbs' occupy the same space and time, one the ghostly double of the other's absence."[50] Two bodies cannot occupy the same space simultaneously, but this is possible in terms of a single being's sensorium.

From here Grosz quickly moves her argument to the gendered differentiation of this absence. According to her reading of the neurophysiological evidence, there is precious little analysis of the phantasmic imaging of the woman's body, after hysterectomies and clitoridectomies for instance; indeed, the question of the woman's body image is closely linked to masculinist formations of scientific power. If woman's sexual organs are already a sign of "lack," then she is always already an amputee, forever destined to conjure the ghostly "limb" she never had. Why worry about an actual amputation, this logic goes, unless one is prepared to rationalize the lack of a lack? The phantom limb is, of course, a compensation, an active nostalgia for the body as a complete entity, but this has its uncanny correlative, as Grosz well knows, in psychoanalytic theory where the phallus and "phantoms" like the castration complex dance around one another in woman's "truncated" being. Perhaps we are still too far removed from the time when penis envy will refer only to the phantom-limb condition of a man whose penis has been amputated, but Grosz's argument is clear that positive feminist knowledge cannot be developed without a greater understanding of the links between the body's sensory and imagistic selves.

The analysis of amputees provides a key example of the body image as a psychosocial construction, the phantom as a necessary adjunct of self-identity in worlds that place a high premium on complete, fully functional bodies. But this fantastic investment is not the monopoly of amputees: the body image is more generally required to orient the body in space and in relations to other objects in space. The zone of the body image alters under different conditions and cultures as it continually coordinates sensory data with experiential conventions. For instance, I am aware of a body image when I walk past a mannequin. I perceive the mannequin as an inanimate object, but the form of that object suggests that I should keep an agreed upon distance (even though no such agreement could exist for the mannequin). That the body image is mutable extends to the otherwise mundane experience of driving a car. It is as if the body must drape its image over the car in order to coordinate the requisite body movements for driving. A crash need not injure one's actual body, but it will always fracture one's body image, whose liminality is at that moment bound to the contours of the machine. Needless to say, the body image is different again when one is a passenger in any moving vehicle. In general, the body image is an index of the subject's relationship to the object, which opens out materiality to questions of prosthesis and cyborganics — two more forms through which materialism must be reinscribed.

Marx, as I have argued, did not go far enough in analyzing the implications of narratives of human sensuousness (perhaps because he did not always begin with the evidence of his own "volatile body"), but there is no doubt that he would not have been able to theorize alienation or commodity fetishism without linking a history of the senses to a particular mode of production. His materialism is, in this interpretation, an economic critique of the culture of the body. The dualism of material and culture dissolves in Marx, if not in Marxism, as early as the 1844 manuscripts precisely because of this concern for the fate of the human body in socialization. As Marx notes, a dualism is a theoretical antithesis that can only be solved in a practical way.[51] In this regard, feminist materialism is not a polite addition or correction to more malleable notions of Marxism but a necessary sublation of theoretical antitheses that block an understanding of the social. It augurs, if not formalizes or guarantees, a practical solution.

The body in space and the image of the body are not adequately understood outside their gendered differentiation. Capitalism may well have entered the realm of flexible accumulation wrapped in a cultural mantle of dispersal and fragmentation, but this does not subtend the gendered hierarchies of social space. As critics have pointed out, the weakness of many contemporary geographical materialists' accounts (Harvey and Soja in particular) is that they continue to intervene on postmodern terrain using modernist masculinism (one that trivializes feminist body-mapping by reducing it to questions of, say, the mirrored phallus of the urban skyline). Lefebvre is to some extent, as Derek Gregory points out,[52] the notable exception, for he understood fairly early on that the hyperreal abstractions of capitalism in the twentieth century are but another form of phallic rationalization, one that not only denatures the human being but specifically departicularizes all concepts of woman's subjectivity that might stand outside the commodity form. If, as Lefebvre insists, "the body, at the very heart of space and of the discourse of power, is irreducible and subversive,"[53] it is only because its contours and surfaces are materialized or corporealized through multiple determinations that construct the very texture of change.

These determinations can, of course, be trucked out as an obligatory mantra in theoretical work, but the force of materialism lies in the explanatory power of their specific articulations, not in the mere fact of their irreducibility. Although there is no single theory that can untangle, as a matter of course, all the complexities of articulation (this is usually marked as an error of totalization; in reality it is because totalities are in continual flux), there are some that are more sensitized to such multiplicity and to the limits of the same. Their advantage lies in more than their descriptive power of social problems: it rests in their attention to the process of practical solutions, sometimes called "praxis." And the body is not the instrument but the embodiment of praxis.

In the above, I have considered several conceptual difficulties in the meaning of the body for materialism. In the case of Marx, a primary suppression led to a major structural problem in understanding the body's relationship to nature. This has been transformed by subsequent materialist critique, but the engendering of the space of the body has occurred at the borders of materialism itself — in the liminal spaces where its theoretical integrity wavers. The oscillation of theory here pivots on the body's own ambivalent borders in the recognition that its phantasmic identifications and quotidian functions render it excessive to the rationality of the Same. One does not solve the question of the body's abstraction (say, in abstract labor) by simply returning us to a material, concrete body — the body that bleeds or defecates or scars or fractures. Feminism's interruption of the masculinism within the history of materialism is based upon a negotiation of the abstract (in its most radical senses), rather than fixating only on a fleshly correlative. This has been true for some time, but if what we have suggested about the intensity of oscillation is brought to bear, body politicking has an entirely prescient valence. As Spivak's argument makes clear (and it is implicit in a good deal of contemporary materialist feminism), the intensity of a particular regime of capital is not just proletarianizing but feminizing the body of the worker in nature. Because this space continues to be relatively unimagined in materialist theory (a normative logic of abstract/concrete totalization resists this move or movement), its corpus trembles. The vacillation is constitutive of its crisis but also of the possibility of its further transformation. The metaphor need not be a substitute for praxis: it can also be its symptom.

All of this still requires concrete bodies and not just a body for theory. These are bodies that live and breathe and struggle with a material reality when theory often considers them a means to materialize itself. There is no sense, however, in trivializing theory as rhetorical play or as mythic space even when specific theories indeed indulge in such gaming. Neither can we be satisfied with the Marxian implication that, because human senses are not yet theoreticians, theory itself is a measure of that inadequacy or self-alienating body. Yet curiously, perhaps, the latter still defines a task for theory, and one that materialist feminism has more critically addressed wherever materialism hides its investment in patriarchal norms for the body. This critical function also drives a creative function, an ability to connect various theoretical aporias in materialism to an emphasis on completion, wholeness, and totality in understanding. In this respect, the body's function for materialist theory is as an *agent oscillatoire:* it not only places bodies, theoretically and cognitively, on the map, but also presses the issue that body-mapping itself is central to processes of social change.

To some extent, Marx realizes the body's materiality for materialism from the start (as many materialists before him). He also understood, I believe, the problem and promise of artificiality in the construction of the body. For some, this is only a desire to return the body to a primordial state, to heal it, to render it authentic. It is feminism that has most often revealed the ideological underpinnings of that desire (even if it has not been exempt from reproducing it), and materialist feminism in particular that has engendered the process of socialization this entails. But how intense can this oscillation become, the naysayers say, before the artifice of the body dominates its real instantiation so that gender is style and sex is produced and never a breath is heard? Of course, some theory and practice are already there (Donna Haraway stated the case for socialist feminism over a decade ago). To fear this intensity is to deny the forces that "make up" the body in and outside theory. Millennial materialism will learn the lesson of the artificial body as a clue to its own artifice as a body of theory. But it cannot forget the socialization of that body, the actual difference that corporealization entails on a world scale. And if it does, then Marx's carbuncles are never far from view.

CHAPTER THREE

SPACES (OF THEORY)

> History is sea.
> —Derek Walcott

> North Atlanticism [is] in decline.
> —Immanuel Wallerstein

Notes on the Atlantic Zone of Flow:

The space of theory *and* a theory of space? One dilemma of materialist theory has been a persistent inability to think the difference between these two categories simultaneously. The space of theory is its positional mode — the way it is taken up, deployed, inscribed. The theory of space has been viewed in a number of ways that have been kept entirely separate from this inscription, and this has had far-reaching effects in ontology and epistemology. For instance, the theorization of abstract space in scientific discourse suggests science believed itself to be beyond the ideological fray in the construction of spatial knowledge, yet who would now doubt that this knowledge was not only a product of but also the mechanism of a colonial machine from the fifteenth century on? Spatial abstractions found their way into the technology of discovery (the instruments of navigation) as well the guides that marked and/or facilitated possession — maps.[1] Similarly, the theory of space was seen as a separate branch of knowledge (social geography) that has only relatively recently been understood as a conduit between the humanities and the social sciences and, more particularly, as a contestable site in reimagining the world. Maps and mapping are no longer monologic: the cognitive abilities they require mark arenas of social struggle. Interestingly, just like oscillation, "map" has a physical and mental range that depends upon a theory of representation. Analyzing that metaphoricity not only produces a narrative on spatial oscillation but leads back to the structure of theory itself. In this manner, abstract space can be concretized or specified. This is the only way, perhaps, that mapping can mean something other than its history as colonization and dispossession. Certainly, this is a utopian mode of mapping and follows not only the logic of "utopistics" alluded to ear-

lier in the work of Wallerstein, but also the trenchant admonition of Oscar
Wilde ("a map of the world that does not include Utopia is not worth even
glancing at").[2]

The space of theory locates it. Against the suppression of real space in
ideologies of the dominant (call this normative "worldliness"), articulating
the space of theory coordinates it in a specific time/space continuum: the
space of theory is the conscience of a space. From this point of view, the
"culture wars" about the place of the Western tradition in Western institutions of learning are literally about locating and location. It is no longer
tenable to separate the content of knowledge from the time and space of
its formation. Note, however, that the conscience of a space does not mean
disregarding its knowledge. It means focusing on the conditions of the production of knowledge and its subsequent deployment. The answer to a theory
of space that suppresses the active modes of concretization (an ideology of
the modern — and the modernist, if Lefebvre's critique is anything to go by)
is to spatialize the theory, to map its possibility. To the oscillations within a
theory we should add and maintain a contextual possibility. For materialism
this is not just a struggle over theory but about the forms of politics most
appropriate to it. By engaging the space of theory, millennial materialism
not only maintains a practical autocritique but contests a concretized political
space. No theory can ensure its position on the map (to believe this would
misunderstand both theory and the history of maps); it can, however, provide
better evidence why it should not be written off that map.

But even a cursory look at the space of theory invites suspicion and hostility to the politics it implies and has implied. Why? Think of theory's location
in the metropole — its specific and long association with dominant centers of
knowledge production. This is not serendipitous or a surprising coincidence
(as the odd new historicist would have it) but a symptom of insistent synergy.
Obviously, it is difficult to talk of the territorial provenance of theory without
reference to the production of relative space — an index of power, certainly,
but more accurately a function of capital accumulation.[3] Thus, the metropole
locates theory, but in what sense can theory dis-locate the metropole?

The space of theory, the conscience of a space, immediately reveals a sordid history. Rather than detail the full range of synergy invoked I want to
concentrate on a particular architectonic. Just as, in the previous chapter, we
saw materialism oscillate through and by feminist intervention, here we will
consider the ways in which space gets created or redrawn. That documents of
civilization are simultaneously documents of barbarism is no less true when
those documents are cultural theory.[4] But if barbarism is inscribed within the
very moment of cultural criticism's genesis, it scarcely describes the tortuous
jetzteit[5] of "traveling theory." When theory flaps its wings, epistemic violence
has been seen to follow. No one should underestimate the aggressivity of

cultural theory's epistemes, which, like Derrida's exegesis of the Pharmakon, can poison and cure in equal measure. There are many ways to elaborate this double-instant (perhaps even double-session) of critical crossing, but I will demonstrate the problem of the space of theory in "the Atlantic zone of flow" (in which "flow" connotes not just movement but change, not just current but deformation, not just gliding over but quicksand, not just moving between but melting, not just circulation but fluctuation — for the etymologist the meanings of "flow" flood every connecting stream).[6] The Atlantic zone of flow has a specific history and political purview and is not synonymous with other contact zones (the Indian, the Pacific, the Mediterranean, etc.). But it does serve to highlight some intriguing and vexing questions about the formation and circulation of theory at the end of the twentieth century, questions about nation, institution, identity, and power. Following Arjun Appadurai's "scaping" of the global cultural economy, it would be tempting to add the Atlantic zone of flow as a "theoryscape," for it too plays a role in what he calls "imagination as a social practice."[7] Yet it is difficult to imagine a historical grid in which "scapism" might fit, at least in the elaboration provided so far, even if we agree that it shares the fundamental disjunctures of disorganized capitalism.

These notes are offered not to configure some kind of league table in cultural theory but to explore an expansive notion of what James Clifford describes as "the global world of intercultural import/export"[8] in terms of theory. This now assumes a greater concern not just because of the seemingly exponential increase in the movement of intellectuals across the globe (exilic, diasporic, professional, escapist, etc.) but because the commodification of theory has not altogether extinguished the radical import of theory on the move. And how and why theory moves tells us not only about the shape of its own politics but about what politics produces theory in exchange. I foster no illusions that the trade in theory can be simply traded in for broader transformation, but there is a political necessity to examine this logic for the insurgent contingencies that obtain. Such an approach is a materialist inquiry of theory's space more than a materialist theory of space, and yet, I would argue, these knowledges must enable one another if one is to realize any difference against exploitative circuits of global integration.

There is, in the tenor of this term, the Atlantic zone of flow, an obvious reference to the major articulation of the black Atlantic by Paul Gilroy.[9] The "flow" diagram in this discussion traces a complex net of race, class, and gender relationships, trajectories of power and exchange that crisscross the Atlantic among several continents. The production of theory along these flows is not meant to complement Gilroy's black Atlantic, however, nor indeed incorporate it, but does draw sustenance from the political and historical efficacy of his project, which productively specifies the "in-between" and "intercultural" as an informing condition of the black diaspora in all its transnational creativity.[10]

The logic of movement in this reading depends very much on the kind of theory transacted, which leads me to an important qualification — namely, that the theoretical flows at issue are primarily cultural and philosophical and cannot stand in for the production and circulation of theory in general even when (as in economic and scientific theory) some trajectories appear consonant. Certainly the overall production of theory shares the same determinants, particularly as an index of hierarchies of power. As I have suggested, even the most abject idealist is no longer so naive as to believe that her or his theory does not come courtesy of the location in which it is framed, an utterance context that cancels through the current investigation. Yet the specific logic of movement in cultural theory is paramount not as a metonym for theory per se but because many of its strands have attempted to account for its own possibility without necessarily addressing the spatiality that is fundamental to such an understanding. This has the tendency of suppressing or underdetermining key social components in the production of theory, particularly since narratives of theoretical movement are always already about matters of race differentiation and the engendering of space. And spatializing theory also inexorably leads one to reconsider another coordinate recently banished to the margins of theory's travels precisely at the moment when its globalization might be informed by it — namely, the international division of labor.[11]

Pace Edward Said's work on traveling theory, one can say that purely content-oriented approaches to theory fail to adequately account for their situation or how they are situated, and thus how they might come to cross, traverse, or travel — that is, how they oscillate across a specific geographical space.[12] Without recalling the entire debate about "traveling theory," I want to build on its lessons. The immediate context of address, as Bakhtin reminds us, is at once constitutive of receptive understanding. This is a question not just of the point of origin but also about the successive or disjunctive reaccentuations that occur in the movement of a theory which, of course, that original moment, *in situ,* cannot comprehensively predict. The internationalization of theory is probably of deeper significance than its local instantiation because it is often read as a symptom of geopolitical import, and the noncorrespondence of one with the other is indicative of important dislocations in cultural logic and the politics of exchange.

Said suggests there is a "recurrent pattern" in traveling theory, although I would aver these are possible elements (the elaboration of a pattern is not evident in Said's essay) that include a point of origin (or set of "initial circumstances"), the distance traversed, the conditions of acceptance or resistance, and finally the accommodated or incorporated or transformed idea in its new position. Said's example of theory on the move is an argument about what happens to Lukács's theory of theory in *History and Class Consciousness* when taken up by Goldmann in *The Hidden God* then by Williams in *Problems in Materialism and Culture*. I am not going to rehearse the minutiae of Said's procedure, but he does explain in some detail how Lukács's urgent theorization of coming to consciousness is born of a philosophical concern not just with reification but with the political and economic dynamic that characterized Hungary's crisis after the First World War. The journey from Budapest to the Paris of the post–Second World War is an arduous and ameliorating one, for Said's discussion of Goldmann emphasizes that the consciousness of insurrectionary desire has become the privilege of scholarly homology: theory has become part of the existential tryst, rather than peripatetic praxis. Said then comments on how Lukács via Goldmann comes to Cambridge, and Raymond Williams and theory "doth suffer a sea change into something rich and strange" (that is, cultural materialism). Interestingly, the trajectory that Said sketches seems to end there, with a fault line opening up between that theoretical tradition and the one that ends his essay, concerning the example of Foucault. Except, of course, that because of Said's own relationship to Foucauldian critique he himself becomes the possible bridging term between the materialism of Williams and the genealogical and discursive schema of Foucault. There is a significant anxiety of influence and resistance to theory in the injunction and disjunction of theory's travels in Said's essay, enough to warrant a full-blown psychoanalytic reading perhaps, but here the approach will be restricted to the categories of traveling theory as Said describes them rather than the impasse that marks Said's own theoretical deployment.[13]

First, there is the problem of theory's initial conditions, for the principle is not deducible either from Said's discussion of Lukács or from his distinction between critical consciousness and theory, in which the former provides a metatheoretical *explanadum* of the latter's inconstancy. Critical consciousness is surely of paramount importance to an understanding of the Atlantic zone of flow, but the stress on initial conditions elides the iterability of theory that continually prefigures and disfigures theory's formal integrity (in the previous chapter we read this into body politics). Indeed, iterability governs the matrix of theory's flow and its integration into global zones of engagement. In what sense is the theory produced by Budapest's revolutionary moment separable from Lukács's close reading of Marx, and Marx's reading of Hegel, and Hegel's reading of Kant, and so on? It would seem far more useful to specify the unique conditions of the Budapest moment rather than to attempt an origin for theory amid a complex constellation of overdeterminations.

Second, while Said's notion of traveling theory gives us some sense of theory's dislocation, the function of space and place in its articulation, it does not make much of theory's detours, which, although implicit in Said's use of "resistance to theory," play a forceful role in theory's dissemination. In other words, there are active suppressions and denials in theory's articulation, but there are also more febrile circumlocutions in its utterance that indicate less conscious disavowal and more a constitutive logic of elision and displacement.[14] When theory travels, therefore, we must be sensitive to the shortcuts it makes or offers, and ponder what Pierre Macherey calls the "non-said" of its narrative possibility, for this too is part of epistemological practice.[15]

Third, theory has always been on the move, but in the time/space compression of this epoch, the abstruse simultaneity of the present, the speed of traveling theory is quite pronounced.[16] The twenty-year journey from Budapest to Paris would now seem pedestrian, if not fatal, since the lust for the new precludes or severely inhibits the contemplative zeal of *longue durée*. The high speed of cultural theory is linked, rather obviously, to its function as cultural capital.[17] The question of cultural capital in theory's travels is extremely important for many reasons, including its function as cultural elitism in the guise of openness to new ideas. What might have been elitist in the content of theory has now been eclipsed by the inherent elitism in the speed of retrieval or circulation.[18] Of course, the equation can be undone by how theory is deployed, which is a noteworthy component of Said's methodology and those that have taken issue with it in the past, but the tendency remains. The speed of theory also connects to its "post" possibilities — post-ism is the very integer of theory's rapid acceleration, as if those of the theoretical persuasion might scramble ahead of history's judgment by nominating their exceptionalism. I am not, however, a staunch advocate of gradualism (there is something in theory's oscillation — as I've argued earlier — that remains radically transformative), but sometimes the receptiveness to theory is ahead of the reflexiveness to theory, and that way relativism and voluntarism lie.

The speed of theory along the zone of flow is not just a function of its "newness" or "post" polemic: it is also a stipulation of exchange between specific cultures according to the values systems of each. While Said does remark on the problem of assimilation, the *rate* of assimilation is highly sensitive to the material conditions of theory's actants. A study of the rate of flow between France and the United States in the last twenty years would be instructive for many reasons, not least of which would be its index of the relative marginalization of radical intellectuals within both states. The speed of assimilation increases as theory itself becomes a form of politics otherwise denied in the public sphere.[19] There are other issues of course, some of which derive from the experience of 1968 (of which more in a moment), but in general the question of speed draws attention to the contextual apparatuses at work in theory's circulation and not just the user-friendly aspects of a particular theory's content.

One other point needs to be made in relation to Said's conceptualization of traveling theory. While it is certainly the case that some theories will meet with mighty resistance at different moments and versions of their travels, there is little room for rejection in theory's outlook. This is not just an indication of an appreciable congeniality in intellectual exchange that makes the importation of theory less threatening than force of arms but a symptom of an inherent flexibility in theory's formulations, a propensity to variation vital to longevity. It is only when theory loses its dynamism or oscillation that rejection becomes possible, and it is in that rejection that it becomes feasible to imagine an entire paradigm shift in an explanatory model. Critics tend to think of this only in terms of scientific theory, but I think the case can be made for specific cultural theories as well, even when revolution is not always the relevant term.

The hegemonic flow in the Atlantic model is that between Europe and the United States. Interestingly, whereas Europe consumes great gobs of American popular culture (although at a slower rate, perhaps — *l'effet* Eurodisney), the reverse is true when it comes to the trade in cultural theory, which is just ahead of the nostalgia mode in the American cultural imaginary. The Euramerican nexus clearly has its corollary in the economic and social fields, but in general theory's Atlantic zone of flow is as relatively autonomous as the intellectuals who produce and "trans-act" it. That is not to say, however, that one's analysis can remain oblivious to theory's role in the social, which is the point in spatializing its dynamic, its pulsion in the politics of culture. As Immanuel Wallerstein notes, "North Atlanticism [is] in decline":[20] here I will trace that space in theory in terms of the alternatives that have exploded it.

There are certainly other ways to construct such a narrative, most obviously in Aijaz Ahmad's *In Theory*, which sees "theoretical development" as radically ironic and therefore provides a critical contrast to Said's approach. In the first couple of chapters of Ahmad's book he reads the proliferation of theory, particularly since the late 1950s, as a systematic (and sometimes less than that) displacement of the political in literary studies. "Avant-garde" theory is viewed as "technicist" (and in terms of technical expertise required for some theories Ahmad is on the mark) and increasingly elitist. In general, Ahmad tracks the journey of French critique to the United States in terms of the specific histories of each. For instance, the difference in perspective on that annus mirabilis, 1968, is quite pronounced. As Ahmad points out, what was for the French intelligentsia a year of defeat and betrayal (by the government and the Communist Party respectively) was in the United States a scene of indefatigable opposition — to the war, to Johnson, to racism, to the overall status quo. In Ahmad's argument, the intensities of the latter galvanized new approaches to the teaching of literature with more or less explicit reference to the black civil rights movement, the women's movement, academic Marxism (academic because of the absence of a "real socialist movement"), and the twin demons of imperialism and colonialism. The specific context, therefore, affects the way theoretical issues are taken up. Thus, even if one reads an extensive if unprogrammatic inscription of the colonial question in French poststructuralism (for which, as Robert Young points out, the Algerian war of independence is the stronger formative crisis),[21] in the United States that problem was initially posed from within black nationalism, on the one hand, and the debate on Vietnam, on the other. One of the values of Ahmad's approach is to offer that contextual disjunction as vital.

An important target in Ahmad's elaboration of theory is the production of Third World literature as a subject (which has functioned very much like the divisive ghettoization that separates off feminist critique into women's studies), although its institutional status is not quite as mighty as he would have one believe (the more pernicious ideology is the one that soaks through otherwise neutral terms, like "literature" itself). Where Ahmad's polemic begins to break down is around the relative emphasis that one can attach to the tendencies he notes: first, the "sheer weight of reactionary positions in the Anglo-American literary formations"; second, the greatly expanded discussion of race, gender, and empire; and third, the radical literary intelligentsia's inability "to constitute a properly Marxist political or literary culture." It seems to me that, given the more detailed analyses of the world system that Ahmad offers, these tendencies are reductive and misleading. The first two elements do not cancel each other out, and their combination does not precipitate the third tendency, except through assumptions that Ahmad does not entertain. One is left with the sneaking suspicion that, somehow, the reactionary elements have singled out Marxism for suppression while being unable to contain the other insurgent social movements. As I have already suggested, part of the reason for the relative weakness of Marxist theory is the vacillation within the very terms of its critique (which, paradoxically, also provides it with a regenerative edge). That element, the logic intrinsic to a theory, is apparently unthinkable in Ahmad's approach (vacillation is simply non-Marxist). It is also for this reason that he is unable to schematize the logic of movement in the theory he surveys.

Like Said, Ahmad tends to hypostatize the initial conditions of theory even as he is more sensitive to its determinate instances. Thus, while Ahmad does outline elements in the commodification of theory (just like my comments on its function as cultural capital in circulation), the metaphor of the marketplace needs to be qualified in important ways. As Marjorie Howes points out, the eclecticism in theory that Ahmad bemoans (and with which I generally concur) does not mean, however, that a theory "arrives" on the shelves as a product internally undifferentiated.[22] The diversity within a theory is a symptom not just of its contamination but also of its dynamism both in its deployment and at the origin where overdeterminations, theoretical and otherwise, affect the constitutive "moment" of a theory in space and time. Ahmad is clearly aware that this spatialization of theory affects his own contribution ("it was quite to be expected that the book's crossing the Atlantic would touch many nerves and that tempers would fly" [144]), but *In Theory*'s travels underline that the movement itself reconfigures conceptual space.

To Althusser's proposition on the (class) struggle in theory, one can productively add Lefebvre's point that "the class struggle is inscribed in space."[23] Not all that struggle in space and theory is class struggle, and the spatialization of theory is testimony to as much. Indeed, on the one hand, the more one analyzes the spatial coordinates of the production of materialist thought itself, the more one must acknowledge that its own situatedness cannot be accounted for purely on its own terms, or specifically those that cognitively map on the basis of class alone. On the other hand, expansive notions of materialist theory must not proceed along the lines of an implicitly imperialist gambit that ingests the cognitive abilities of every radical theoretical modality in the name of righteous materialist totalizing. Just as poststructuralism cannot adjudicate its own truth claims (including those that jettison Truth as some hermeneutical fib), so materialism should address the continuing (and necessarily insoluble) ability to reach and overreach through tactical openness. The spatial problematic in materialism is not its globalizing propensity per se, but the arrogance of assuming the story is told by doing it. The distinct advantage of materialism lies in its attention to the material processes of globalization, not in globalism itself, which is never attained nor transformed by theory alone.

Theory's travels, then, are indices of much more than the content of this theory or that and symbolize an intricate collocation of ideologies, economies, values, and social forces in collision as much as collusion. The currency of cultural theory in movement has risen as much through time/space compression as it has through a democratization of cultural exchange (one might call this the differential mobility of theory). Yet although the Atlantic zone of flow is coextensive with Euramerican hegemony, it is not synonymous with it. In a similar vein, the circumstances of theory preclude or at least destabilize summary notions of origin if not originality. Thus, theory proceeds not just by reflection but by inflection, consciously or not, of other minds and other places. A theory is precipitate of a process.

The Atlantic zone of flow provides an architectonic understanding of theory on the move — it is an imaginative grid of the circulation of specific cultural formulae within a history that produces the Atlantic as a conceptual space, as a conduit for theory's situatedness. In this sense, the zone of flow lends itself to Bourdieu's field analysis, to specific laws of functioning, the autonomy of which are prescribed, but not absolutely, from the power flows of the economic and the political.[24] Of course, Bourdieu takes the strong view on autonomy whenever his cultural fields border on Marxism. Yet for all the appropriateness of his accusations of reductionism in the literary critiques of Lukács, Goldmann, and Adorno, his sociology of culture is not simply anathema to the Marxist tradition (for instance, identifying laws in the field of cultural production is precisely Williams's move in his "structures of feeling" argument as well as in his formation analysis). One aspect of the importance of Bourdieu's work is that field critique spatializes the circulation of culture, but whether this is primarily a motive of metaphor remains a vexing question.[25] Bourdieu's approach to the social conditions of the production of utterances (of different forms) is dependent upon not simply the place or instance of the utterance but also the space, or logic of connection, between utterances (in Bakhtinian terms, this is the difference between "event" and the "eventness of being" and a constitutive tenet in understanding the dialogic). One cannot talk of the zone of flow as a field of theoretical production without also implicating its structures of transaction, which, however much they signify, like the writer in Bourdieu's reading, the dominated among the dominant, are the effulgence of a particular mode of circulation — the logic of capital itself.

The process of crossing or transaction can be characterized by placing, replacing, and displacing, or more accurately (but woefully neologistic) spacing, respacing, and despacing. If "place is space to which meaning has been ascribed,"[26] then the Atlantic has been a catalyst in that process rather than a place that the category implies: it is an imaginary zone drawn by theory's motion, a cognitive map of socially produced space. And cultural theory cannot survive, except perhaps as a hollow abstraction (and then, not for long), without being worked upon in movement. That is to say, it has to move at the spatial level in order to survive at the temporal level (and therefore theory cannot guarantee the *Aufhebung* of Hegelian teleology, or spatial ontology). The space of *h*istory detotalizes the time of *H*istory; it preempts it. To a degree, the process I am describing is closer to Deleuze and Guattari's on de- and reterritorialization, although the idea that the cultural theorist is therefore a veritable schizophrenic, an agent of "asubjectivity" who performs "subjectless action," might confirm the worst suspicions of the antitheorist. Their sense of theory's architectonic subscript, however, remains indispensable.[27] What happens when theory crosses the Atlantic is that its spatiality is transcoded. On one level, it speaks differently (with or without translation, the utterance context, as Bakhtin calls it, alters the mode and content of enunciation); on another, theory is potentially answerable (again, in the Bakhtinian sense), which refers to the way in which it takes up a position or space in relation to other theories or discourses. As noted, the traveling at issue is context-specific rather than only an index of theory's righteous content.

I would suggest that spacing denotes an assimilationist agenda, that respacing signifies an elaboration of the formative concepts of a theory, and that despacing renders the integrity of a theory questionable so that it is either transformed or "rejected" (keeping in mind the qualification appended to the latter). These processes of answerability occur simultaneously and give to the epistemologies of cultural theory their agonistic shape. A similar antagonism characterizes the work of metatheory, which mitigates against the brusque adjudication of theoretical flux.

There are many narratives that can illuminate traveling theory. Examples could include the importation, through spacing and respacing, of European Marxist cultural theory in the States in the 1960s and 1970s (rooted further back in the "arrival" of the Frankfurt School, then later in Althusserianism) against the relative quietude of such theory in the opposite direction (explained, for one, by the fact that Jameson's *Political Unconscious* crossed to Europe after the despacing of Althusser, which in England, at least, was achieved by the scandals of Hindess and Hirst and Thompson's somewhat rabid crunching in *The Poverty of Theory*); and dozens of examples from the history of feminisms, including the respacing of French theory in North America within poststructuralism and the despacing of the same by feminists more interested in catheting the question of woman in cultural theory to liberal humanist discourses on rights (the difference this opens up between, say, Carol Gilligan and Judith Butler itself describes a veritable ocean). As we have already noted, the space of theory for feminism is precisely a differential space, one in which the body in space and the body in theory are critically refigured (the coordinates themselves are rendered suspect). In general, however, the major theoretical examples tend to support the hegemonic flow across the Atlantic and are subject to the political qualifications that accompany this "mainstream." But there are other ways to read the Atlantic trade in theory.[28]

One method would be to highlight how the hegemonic flow is internally distanciated by what is smuggled along its path or what departs from its governing logic (this is intrinsic to *In Theory*'s intervention). The case of sociocriticism is instructive in this light, since clearly the work of Claude Duchet was despaced to Canada in crossing the Atlantic, and to Quebec in particular, while sociocritics to the south of that border settled for Edmond Cros, and then minimally.[29] What happens to cultural materialism when it crosses the Atlantic is also informative, especially given its mutation into new historicism.[30] There are, then, at least two levels of epistemic violence in cultural critique: one inscribed within theory's formulations, the other produced in the moment of spacing, the content in which it is taken up, despaced or respaced. As an abstraction, the zone of flow is what distinguishes those levels.

Paul Gilroy's *The Black Atlantic* argues for an exemplary model of radical intercultural relations. He redraws the map of the Atlantic in terms of the literal crossings of blacks and their representative cultures. It is a stunning indictment of traditional narratives of the modern and a cogent disarticulation of white mythology — in particular, that which made the Atlantic the white space of imperial and colonial adventure while suppressing its function as a middle passage, the inglorious conduit of the slave trade. The black Atlantic functions as a heuristic device in the reevaluation of a supranational culturalism. Thus, Gilroy explores and highlights the syncretic and hybrid formations of black cultural production as it crisscrosses the Atlantic seaboard. One icon for this countercultural logic is the figure of Martin Delany, the black abolitionist from Virginia. Using Delany's novel *Blake*, Gilroy forcefully contests ethnic absolutisms, black and white, and urges that *Blake* provides an appropriate provocation to

> move discussion of the black political culture beyond the binary opposition between national and diasporic perspectives. The suggestive way that it locates the black Atlantic world in a webbed network, between the local and the global, challenges the coherence of all narrow nationalist perspectives and points to the spurious invocation of ethnic particularity to enforce them and to ensure the tidy flow of cultural output into neat, symmetrical units.[31]

These claims may be more true of Gilroy's work than Delany's, but they provide some vital lessons for the present project. By analyzing a reformulated structure of feeling that characterizes what is called "the inner dialectics of diaspora identification," Gilroy is able to elaborate significantly on the double consciousness of black thought. In Gilroy's text, which argues away from ethnic definitions of racial authenticity, the Atlantic reemerges as an imaginative space of contestation, a rhizomorphic plenitude that defies its conventional geography. Similarly, the metatheoretical articulation of the Atlantic zone of flow resists the "tidy flow" of theoretical output into "neat, symmetrical units" (because the space that it implies cannot be guaranteed by the oscillations across it). Again, this is indicated in "flow's" excessive etymology, but such excess has often been conspicuously absent from the indexes of theory's central texts. That is to say, the production of theory itself has not escaped forms of ethnic absolutism in terms of sources or indeed ideological purview.[32] The answer is not a politically correct theoretical smorgasbord in which theorists dutifully select from a well-policed version of the ethnic platter. I am urging a greater awareness of the internal logic of exclusion/inclusion that structures the movement of theory toward a *logique métisse* better equipped to understand its dialogic pulsions.

This term forms the title of Jean-Loup Amselle's provocative *Logiques métisses: Anthropologie de l'identité en Afrique et ailleurs.*[33] His analysis of culture as a "structured field of relations," as a fluctuating context (*ensemble mouvant*), provides a conceptual understanding for the Atlantic I describe, as well as a polemical rejoinder to summary notions of hybridity and syncretism. The notion of *métissage*, or originary mixing, challenges hegemonic interpretations of multiculturalism (which themselves depend upon prior ideologies of unitary culture); but it also helps to demystify the homogenizing tendencies in theoretical circulation that suppress the internal differentiation of this theory or that (Ahmad's discussion of the reductionism of "Three Worlds" theory provides just this kind of demystification).[34] The more one considers the fluctuating context, or oscillation of theory, the more one confronts the internal and external limits of its articulation. (There was Marxism before Marx, but what augments his possibility? There was poststructuralism before structuralism, but what specifies the moment of its emergence?) The logic of time, or chronologism, is not adequate to this task (a theory of history, however, is not to be disparaged) because, although it might foreground different temporalities, it cannot account for their simultaneously different localities, their discrepant situatedness. This is precisely the challenge of Gilroy's remapping of the Atlantic because he details in a comprehensive way how "transcultural reconceptualization" explains not just the "diasporic intimacy" he reads among many black artists of the present but also the historical formation of black consciousness traversing the ocean. The Soul II Soul hit Gilroy cites, "Keep on Moving," is also a comment on his perception of the *ensemble mouvant* of black communities.

Theory is not, however, the equivalent of what Gilroy describes as the expressive counterculture of the black diaspora, and it would be both romantic and colonizing to suggest as much — materialism does not need a theoretical equivalent of postmodern primitivism. There are, nevertheless, serious political and epistemological implications to the kind of decoding, recoding, and transcoding that Gilroy attempts. The main problem is that theory remains a manifestly minority pursuit in the negative sense, in that, as cultural capital, it almost always circulates between and among elites (which, however marginal, have contributed to a harmful institutional status quo precisely to the degree that they have not fundamentally transformed it). Of course, this view offers another form of romantic image by way of compensation, that of the revolutionary, but even as I hold on to that utopian desire, the sense here is on responsibility, or Bakhtin's answerability in the broadest interpretation of social engagement. The contingency or the phantomatic realities of the public sphere do not exempt theory's or theorists' responsibility in constructing it. Gilroy's explorations provide a trenchant sense of the difference that riddles the Atlantic's cartography in terms of what is called "the difficult journey from slave ship to citizenship." But it is clear from his narrative that the emerging "politics of transfiguration" he describes is not the monopoly of the black Atlantic even if that remains its most insurgent instantiation. Theory too is being politically transfigured as the Atlantic zone of flow opens out in a new metamorphosis. The evidence for this could be elaborated, as I have indicated, in an examination of the displacements that have occurred along the hegemonic flow between the United States and Western Europe, but there are other significant disruptions within this discursive field. I will review some of the discrepant reformulations of the Atlantic before concluding on the politics of space in Atlantic oscillation.

The Caribbean produces a salient polemic that what drives the epistemological flux of cultural theory is not just the new social movements but the legacy of colonialism that, while it guarantees what Edouard Glissant calls the Caribbean's "irruption into modernity," also means that its production of theory is as forceful if not more so within the "periphery" (or between what Glissant notes as "the periphery and the periphery") than it is in its respacing in the hegemonic flow between the United States and Western Europe. There are many examples of this unique theoretical positionality and potentiality (including Kamau Brathwaite's nation language, the "patwah" of the Sistren collective, and the articulation of Creoleness by Jean Bernabé, Patrick Chamoiseau, and Raphael Confiant),[35] but I want to note two particular attempts to theorize Caribbean cultural space beyond the formulas provided by the colonial adventure. Antonio Benítez-Rojo's *The Repeating Island* and Edouard Glissant's *Caribbean Discourse* (*Discours antillais*) both make space their central concern precisely because it has been produced by the violent epistemes of transatlantic trade.[36] That is to say, theory's zone of flow is inscribed by the dislocation of the slave trade, the middle passage that produced a plantation belt from North to South America. The Atlantic itself, especially in Benítez-Rojo's account, is a direct product of colonial expansion, a plantation machine through which Europe copulated (as he puts it) with the Caribbean (then later with Asia). The machinic discourse is derived from Deleuze and Guattari (who also figure in Glissant's work, although, as Gilroy notes, the connection has been excised in translation)[37] and creatively respaces their anarchic sense of borders and territoriality. Through this Benítez-Rojo constructs the complex metaphor of the repeating island (a term that is fettered neither by repetition nor by geography — it is a principle of chaos, the cultural underbelly of thermodynamics).[38] The Atlantic zone of flow looks very different from this perspective:

> [W]ithin the sociocultural fluidity that the Caribbean archipelago presents, within its historiographic turbulence and its ethnological and linguistic clamor, within its generalized instability of vertigo and hurricane, one can sense the features of an island that "repeats" itself,

unfolding and bifurcating until it reaches all the seas and lands of the earth, while at the same time it inspires multidisciplinary maps of unexpected designs. (3)

While Benítez-Rojo's analysis does not quite bear the weight of this exuberance (for his text itself is a text because it is not a rumba or a carnival, key elements of centrifugal turbulence), the movement he describes is effective testimony to the politics of transfiguration, in this case, in the space of theory. For Benítez-Rojo, the Caribbean is a "supersyncretic referential space" (270). There is no "Là-Bas" (as in Barthes's essay on Japan), except as the recognition of textuality (182); therefore Benítez-Rojo takes postmodernity and poststructuralism at their words. He provides a reading that takes the epistemes of contemporary Western theory and "floods" them with "a poetic and vital stream" — the languages of the Caribbean text. The Caribbean itself is a meta-archipelago with neither a boundary nor a center; thus, there is no original island, just tropisms in series — a repeating island. In a sense, the Caribbean prefigures the theoretical production of postmodernity and poststructuralism since its articulation signals the emergence of the modern. What Gilroy calls the counterculture of modernity (251–52) is, in Benítez-Rojo's text, actually what makes modernity possible, and so, although a margin in Euramerican "post" scripts, the Caribbean signs back along the Atlantic flow that would deny it. Antillanité, for Glissant, is also a reevaluation of the moment of the modern, in which the double consciousness of the forced laborer continually decenters. He asks, "What is the Caribbean in fact? A multiple series of relationships" (xxxix). Again it is this seriality that disrupts the circulation of theory in the Atlantic zone of flow with its somewhat tidy exchanges across its northern tier.

An important lesson of the work of Benítez-Rojo and Glissant is not that the integrity of their Caribbeanness depends on a knee-jerk absolutism where Western theory is concerned, but that they both (in different ways) de- and respace the latter so that their Caribbean confounds the logic that reduces the otherness of the archipelago to an economy of the Same in Western philosophy. The stand against marginality is also one against separatism, however, and in this light "the repeating island" and "the poetics of relation" both challenge the epistemic isolation of the Caribbean vis-à-vis the Atlantic. If the black Atlantic transfigures the cartography of culture, Caribbeanness redraws the zone of flow. For both, the impulse for transformation does not assume the consciousness of that space.

As Christopher Miller's *Theories of Africans* has emphasized, and indeed Neil Lazarus's critique of Miller's contribution,[39] Africa is no less a contradictory space vis-à-vis the Atlantic, but the implications of the invention of Africa for a spatial conception of theory's travels are vital. "Africa" is as ambivalent in theory as it was at its low point in colonial ideology where generalizations swerved between abject inscrutability and pure transparency. If one detects critical vacillation in the thought of someone as important as Fanon (about which Miller and Lazarus strongly disagree), it is in part a legacy of the contradictory Manichaean logic that sought to render Africa simultaneously inside and outside European space in the first place (here read as inside/outside hegemonic articulations of the Atlantic). Around the question of "nation" colonial spatiality is particularly complex; here I would say only that it is limiting theoretically and politically to view every glimmer of nationalist thought as the unreflexive colonization of the "non-Western" mind. The spacing of nationalism within African decolonization is certainly in evidence within Fanonian formulations: the value of Lazarus's critique is that it foregrounds the de- and respacing possible within the same paradigm.[40]

Kwame Anthony Appiah suggests that "Africa" cannot stand in for the diverse histories of precolonial times (nor can it for the complexity of colonial experiences), but that does not mean that Appiah rejects the notion of "being African": he is, however, strongly resistant to what he calls a "bogus basis for solidarity."[41] Africa, as an invention, has several modes of signification, most infamously as the "dark continent" whose traces still permeate the colonial unconscious of the West. But, importantly, it can also function as a phantasm in black thinking, as Appiah shows in the first chapter of his book *In My Father's House*, where he challenges the racialism of Alexander Crummell, the nineteenth-century African American intellectual. Once more the point is not about origins necessarily, but about deployment, circulation, and space in the Atlantic zone of flow. Appiah's target, like Gilroy's, is ethnic absolutism, which in this case produces a specific form of Pan-Africanism dependent upon precisely the metaphysics of race that European modernity "invented" as a legitimating discourse for racist practice. Appiah therefore rejects the latter, but also African theory that, ironically, spaces such tenets within an Afrocentric economy of difference (he provides many examples, including those of Cheikh Anta Diop and the work of Chinweizu, Onwuchekwa Jemie, and Ihechukwu Madubuike).[42] Rather than deny African identity, however, Appiah argues for its multiplicity, fluidity, and combinatory potential. With the despacing of racialist theory, metaphysical philosophy, and essentialist mythology, the critical crossing to and from Africa might articulate a continent beyond the ruse of its invention.

V. Y. Mudimbe, however, provides an important contrast to this view: he interprets invention as a construction in the same manner of multiple identities, as a fact of discourse. On the one hand, there is a "primary, popular interpretation of founding events of the culture and historical becoming" (this corresponds to what Appiah calls the mythological);[43] on the other, there is a secondary discourse of disciplinary knowledges that inscribe the first discourse as a rational field, as a "regulatory frame," as an invention. The invention of Africa occurs at this second level but comes with a significant indemnity: namely, that "African second-level discourses have been silenced radically or, in most cases, converted by conquering Western discourses." Mudimbe continues: "The popular local knowledge has been subsumed critically by 'scientific' disciplines. The process meant not only a transcending of the original locality, but also through translation (which in reality is transmutation), the 'invention' of Africa" (981–82). It is along this second level of discourse that the Atlantic zone of flow invented and colonized a subject for theory. Yet by Mudimbe's own admission, Western discourses themselves have been converted, or respaced, as in his creative "misreading" of Foucault and Lévi-Strauss, which provides a significant portion of the conceptual apparatus for Mudimbe's book, *The Invention of Africa*.[44] The narrative of that modification is, for Mudimbe, provided by a third level of discourse, "one which, in principle, should be critical of the second level discourses, and interrogating their significance and objectives; and, at the same time, by vocation, autocritical."[45] This, I would argue, also describes the metatheoretical outlook of the Atlantic zone of flow that, by interrogating the logic of theory's circulation, seeks to understand the production of cultural theory in exchange.

Metatheory, despite its autocritical inclinations, courts a sometimes less-than-ambivalent totalizing philosophy. Mudimbe's impulse, if not Appiah's, is to deploy the metadiscursive as a dissembling corrective, whether the philosophy at issue is European or African (this has led more than one critic to describe him as a "weak thinker" in Vattimo's sense). Of course, historically the Atlantic has been produced by a will to totalize, but the desire to trace that geopolitical expansion is not synonymous with it, just as it would be idealist to think that theories of modernity themselves complete modernity's project. The point in emphasizing these examples is to underline that the space of theory is not the theory of space in some Lefebvrian gesture or the discrete transatlantic crossing of yore (which was never that in reality) but a heterogeneous and contradictory zone that transfigures the theoretical apparatus available and possible. The space of theory is perhaps a "practiced place" in Michel de Certeau's interpretation, but lacks its quotidian geography.[46] As for the tendency to view intellectual migration and technological change as evidence of a smaller world, the space of theory suggests that the rapid implosion of discourse along the hegemonic flow has been conducive to a concomitant explosion within the epistemological range of the Atlantic in general (interestingly, Edouard Glissant terms his Caribbean contribution an "exploded discourse"). But while it is difficult to provide a map of the depth of this discursive transfiguration (the process at this stage is in deconstructing the maps available), I do want to indicate, by way of clarification, some approaches to the conceptual knot the zone of flow presents.

If Said's method is limited it nevertheless argues persuasively for a spatial understanding of theory on the move. My qualifications or additions are merely meant to suggest an apparatus consonant with the contingencies of the present and, I believe, an alternative materialist framework. Clearly, the Atlantic zone of flow looks different according to the evaluative hierarchies of interest applied. Aijaz Ahmad, for instance, has noted the alarming tendency for diasporic intellectuals to foster a theoretical antinationalism once they have secured the fruits of metropolitan largesse — as if those centers guaranteed a critical distance on nationalism's contradictory inscriptions at the margin. Ahmad's work in particular offers more than a salutary warning about the politics of position in theoretical articulation.[47] A second warning may be found in the complex politics of translations, whose relations go far beyond the methodology required to turn source into target language. In a multibillion-dollar industry that is driven by the dictates of business, the translation of theory is a drop in the ocean, but even a cursory discussion of the Atlantic zone of flow shows a stunning complicity of the logic of one with the exchange of the other. Mudimbe, for instance, whose African languages include Swahili, Sanga, Kikongo, and Lingala, writes and publishes theory in French and English. And, about Ngũgĩ's decision to write in Gikuyu, Mudimbe comments that it is politically sound but technically romantic. Yet, although the medium of exchange reflects the perquisites of the hegemonic flow, the question of language does not, in and of itself, adequately characterize traveling theory (even as one could complicate the issue by examining what, say, Glissant or Abdelkebir Khatibi or Assia Djebar does to French that renders it a translation to itself).

There is already a rich tradition of feminism engendering the space of theory (Gloria Anzaldúa's work on "borderlands" has been more influential in this regard than any of the deterritorializing spatiality of Deleuze and Guattari). Yet it emerges as a significant pause for any metatheoretical account of the Atlantic zone of flow. There has been significant doubt for some time that just as feminism theorized a gendered subject, certain kinds of theory destabilized subjectivity altogether (if the subject cannot be male, then it must be schizo to borrow from schizoanalysis once more). Similarly, just when feminism problematizes place and location (in the constitution of the "home" but also in manifestations of traditionally held "public" space), nomadism strikes the hegemonic theorati as entirely prescient. "Flow," which is itself an intensely contested gender metaphor, would seem to be complicit with just these kinds of lines of escape that, when linked to theory, compound the suspicion that whenever masculinism is at stake theory has to move or be caught in a web (Charlotte's, presumably) of gendered location.

As Kamala Visweswaran has noted of Arjun Appadurai's "global ethno-
scapes," avid transnationalism often elides the location and constituency of
its participants[48] and therefore the engendering that prescribes and inscribes
its possibility. Janet Wolff's criticism puts the point succinctly: "For all these
metaphors, there *is* a centre. In a patriarchal culture we are not, as cultural
critics any more than social beings, 'on the road' together."[49] Wolff's comment is part of a longer argument about the explicit link between theory and
travel as a compromised metaphor of masculinism. Yet she argues in the end
for a "reappropriation" of such metaphors if gender critique itself is to "keep
on moving." Clearly, however, the Atlantic zone of flow must not "escape"
the engendering of its space if it is to facilitate the mapping of the politically
possible. This is one way of reading Gayatri Chakravorty Spivak's recent "re-
visiting" of French feminism, where she cogently respaces the "international
frame" of an earlier critique by introducing the intervention of Marie-Aimée
Hélie-Lucas's insurgent internationalism — a poignant and vital disruption
of the flow that "takes" French feminism to North America.[50]

The Atlantic zone of flow depends upon a network of institutional affiliation and logic of dissemination. There is no doubt that the mode of
answerability is overdetermined by institutional constraints or flexibilities that
inexorably inflect the process of spacing, respacing, and despacing I have invoked (Spivak signals this in her reference to the "teaching machine" itself).
The familiar move here is, "Well, there you have it. Power saturates the socius; *pouvoir/savoir* delimits every transaction; so let's get on with the game
and stop worrying about the rules." But this Gordian knot is not the vital
issue. If the concept of the university is subject to the same discursive aporia celebrated by its rebellious deconstructors, then it is not just the space of
theory that cannot be guaranteed but also the institutional shape in which it
is taken up. Again, while one must ultimately reject the notion of cultural
theory *as* politics, this does not mean that it cannot speak to the political.
Oddly, the spatializing of theory might support Lukács's point that the production of theory itself can fight reification and commodification rather than
simply being an expression of such processes.[51] Thus, the Atlantic zone of
flow is not a geography that marks off theory as a medium between institutions but in effect challenges the logic of connection and destination in that
journey. The onus if not guarantee of transformation therefore lies in the alternative lines of force, for instance, between Fort-de-France and Montreal,
not because they are trendily marginal, but because their very marginality
was/is produced by the epistemic violence of Western modalities of modernity. Perhaps that is also what makes the margin a more viable source for
what Bruce Robbins has termed comparative cosmopolitanism, accepting the
contradictions that riddle such a term.[52] The breakdown of colonial and imperial logic crossing the Atlantic continues, but space will tell what new shape

will emerge in the social imaginary. The difference of that space will mitigate against the barbarism that produced it, and theory's minor role will have been to earn what Terry Eagleton calls "significance" within it.

There is a somewhat easy shorthand that connects theory to its material "outside" (say, from Plato to NATO), but it is only relatively recently that this has been connected to a logical suppression of space in the politics of theory itself. To be sure, this has only ever been a convenient suppression, for certain orders of cognition (the colonial unconscious for one) have been busily mapping all along. If there has been a "cartographic anxiety" (as Derek Gregory calls it), then for much theory it has been induced by its own culpability in the production of real spaces of exchange and exclusion. By reimagining these spaces postcolonial theorists, for instance, are not playing the theory game (despite the lure of that interpellation) but are blasting the assumption that conceptual space does not have a geographic correlative. Edward Brathwaite can indicate this just by the term "*slave* trade winds," which emphasizes in a polemical way how barbarism drew the Atlantic. But this does more than oscillate materialism's blindness to its logic of mapping. Counterhegemonic conscience of space now promises to destabilize the borders of space in its national "natural" confines. Such arguments are "spaces of representation" (in Lefebvre's terminology), each with its logic of reconfiguration. This is the difference, as Glissant pursues it, between a "return" and a "diversion." The former (*le retour*) seeks the unity of the Same, the "one" — an oscillation that returns to itself and thereby attempts to confirm the integrity of its space. The latter (*le détour*) articulates a cultural and linguistic diversion, detour ("La langue créole est la première géographie du Détour" [Creole is the first geography of the Diversion] [32]), which exceeds the geography of its inscription. Glissant explains, "Le détour est le recours ultime d'une population dont la domination par un Autre est occultée: il faut aller chercher *ailleurs* le principe de domination, qui n'est pas évident dans le pays même" (Diversion is the ultimate resort of a population whose domination by an Other is hidden: it then must search *elsewhere* for the principle of domination, which is not evident in the country itself) (32). The politics of this tactic rests in the specificity of Martinican space (the object of Glissant's example), but there is a general lesson to the oscillatory, diversionary urge in Glissant's theorization. The principle of domination rests in many theories, but particularly those that hide their exploitative territorial embrace. As Gilroy suggests, the Atlantic can be a heuristic device in accentuating such modes of domination, but it can also provide an alternative "counterculture" of space — a transatlanticism that deconstructs the parochialism of theory itself. And, for materialism, this offers an equally important political prospect: a space of theory that can counter the current transnationalism of global capital.

CHAPTER FOUR

FETISHISM (OF SHOES)

The Indonesian worker only exists in the sole of my shoe.
— AMITAVA KUMAR

If the study of ideology is an enduring (and oscillating) theoretical legacy of Marxism, the analysis of commodity fetishism has become so naturalized as to be transparent. Indeed, according to this formulation, the ideology of the commodity is so successful it is the dominant axis of production in forms of capital while at the same time being the most assumed object of critique. In a bizarre twist in regimes of desire, what is coveted in the process of fetishism is the very structure of commodity exchange, its most "public" expression. And, for the same reason, what is invisible in the fetishism of commodities actually allows Marxism to "disappear" (the compulsion of one is the presence of the other). Balibar describes Marx's theory of commodity fetishism as "one of the great theoretical constructions of modern philosophy,"[1] but because of its close relationship to its putative "object," it is also the linchpin of materialist oscillation in global critique.

For materialism, fetishism is *the* example of a concept that is dependent upon a logic of vacillation to maintain its explanatory power. The "real" of commodity exchange is underwritten and stamped (in Lacanian parlance) by an abstract ambivalence, one that Marx elucidates by linking the sensible with the "suprasensible" through the fantastic and the uncanny. This structural wavering is something of the truth of oscillation as a concept. As Deleuze and Guattari note, "Philosophical concepts are fragmentary wholes that are not aligned with one another so that they fit together, because their edges do not match up."[2] The oscillation in fetishism is afforded by the nonalignment of the edges of the sensate and psychic overinvestment in an object — the borders of two different fields of conceptual inquiry. In his book on the history of the concept of fetishism, Alfonso Iacono has described the consequences of this nonalignment as the ground for a great misunderstanding (*un immense malentendu*), symbolic both of a tremendous philosophical quandary in Western anthropological discourse (a structural misrecognition of the other) and of an impasse that is intrinsic to the logic of the concept itself.[3] By contrast, W. J. T. Mitchell reads this misunderstanding as a revenge on Marxism that, bound by the extravagant, ill-fitting tropes assigned by Marx to both ideology and fetishism, continues to disable its knowledge in a profusion of inappropriate iconology.[4] The characterization of Marx's vacillation is accurate, but obviously I do not read this as a steady descent from hypertrophy to atrophy. Mitchell does not sufficiently consider the relationship between the iconic confusion in Marx's discourse and the historical mode in which such muddled illusions and reality are precipitate (nineteenth-century anthropological discourse, for one). My interest here is primarily in the consequences of this vacillation for materialism now at a moment when the theory itself mimes, through effacement, the naturalized emptiness of the commodity. The name for this cruel analogy is not obsolescence, but *globalization*. The latter now constitutes a primary reality in which the fetishism of commodities can "appear."

There are many ways in which this narrative might be explicated, from the micropolitical focus on the culture of the everyday (the fetish not as a radical excess but as a posited norm — recent analyses of fetishism as style fall under this category)[5] to the macropolitical intricacies of the commodity in international exchange. In what follows I tend to emphasize the latter while implicating it in the logic of the former. Just as I have used space to frame the discussion of theory on the move, here I consider a particular form of the commodity within the globalization of capital. The tension of the local and global, of course, has the familiar inflection of the dialectic, but this cannot be separated from the theoretical limits already enumerated and the function of the theorist in materialism's sway. And because globalization now means the proletarianization of women as never before, the time/space, or chronotope, that I will detail is always already a psychic compulsion in a specific cartography of masculinism. It is no coincidence that Lacan and Granoff articulate fetishism in terms of oscillation and vacillation ("something that the patient cannot face without vertigo"), for the anxiety at issue is a certain wavering of masculine desire (distinguished from a crude monopoly of the male).[6] Desire and disavowal must be specified within the history of capital, not simply to make materialism "visible" but to understand how commodity fetishism came to characterize a hegemony without naming it. The case study that follows will give a moniker to this regime of ongoing contradictions — vacillations — between the sensible and suprasensible: let us call it the chronotope of the shoe.

Marx suggested that "[a commodity] is a very strange thing, abounding in metaphysical subtleties and theological niceties."[7] A social history of the shoe would show as much, for there is no commodity in modern history with a greater capacity to confound thingness and spirit, use value and exchange, desire and displacement, and production with consumption.[8] The commodity stands in for Being where Being itself threatens the logic of the commodity form. The shoes (for they come in pairs) deconstruct the binaries that bind while yet confirming the convenience of their duality (the commodity status of shoes makes their use and their function as objects of desire both separable or collapsible within a marketing machine). Rather than elaborate the social history implied above, I am more interested in the contemporary logic of space and time that links culture and capital in the aura of the shoe. In the manner of Deleuze and Guattari, one could state that the aura of the shoe spreads, rhizome-like, across the globe as an (almost) metaphysical index of desire in capital (indeed, to be "over the shoes" is an expression of desire). But while this allows an understanding of the theological and theoretical inside/outside of the shoe, it does not coordinate the affective points of responsibility that (as Kumar reminds us) leave the trace of a Jakarta woman shoe worker in a rubber sole and, as we will see, a working-class African American male dead in the streets of Chicago with his shoes removed.

To chart this chronotope I will elaborate the *pointure* (in Derrida's interpretation, to be discussed in detail below), or pricking of the shoe in theory, and the rise of a particular commodity, the athletic shoe. The aim throughout will be to map the "metaphysical subtleties and theological niceties" of commodity culture as it currently confers aphanisis on the workers of the world (even when, or precisely because, the workers are positioned between the earth and the people who use them).[9] I have three modest claims that are central to this critique: first, a materialist understanding of transnational capitalist commodification is not simply a problem of totality, but one of imagination;[10] second (but a point that is, in essence, inextricable from the first), time/space compression in transnational commodity culture offers an abstruse simultaneity that necessitates a reevaluation of the conceptual oscillation in the fetish and fetishism;[11] third, commodity desire is no more inevitable than responsibility (both desire and responsibility are produced within regimes of truth that are irreconcilable); their contradictions are themselves an index of the world system.

The chronotope of the shoe invokes a Bakhtinian framework of affective responsibility — a means to understand the logic of the commodity by foregrounding the time/space coordinates that naturalize its circulation.[12] The chronotope for Bakhtin was multivalent, a complex constituent feature of his developing "historical poetics" that could link recurring literary devices across cultural history.[13] Yet this immediately marks Bakhtin's chronotope as a contradictory concept. If, as Bakhtin argues, literary chronotopes develop from and respond to specific extraliterary contexts, then how can these chronotopes be manifest transhistorically? Michael Holquist suggests that we distinguish between chronotope as a device or category of narrative and the principle of chronotopicity itself. The latter refers to time/space relations that structure the always already mediated condition of art and life.[14] As Bakhtin notes, "Out of the actual chronotopes of our world (which serve as the source of representation) emerge the reflected and *created* chronotopes of the world represented in the work."[15] While chronotopicity is not a stable bridge between art and life, it nevertheless draws attention to the mediatory functions of time and space in their interrelation. Beside its transhistorical inclinations, however, there are other obvious weaknesses in Bakhtin's articulation of the concept. For instance, the concrete forms of everyday life that Bakhtin summons draw attention to the situatedness of *his* critique, from which one must ask — What would it mean to specify "the actual chronotopes of our world"? Would one not be forced, by the very terms of Bakhtin's exegesis, to particularize quite radically what is "ours" in that phrase? And what are the processes by which "our" world gets generalized so that in a chronotopic economy "our" world might stand in for others? Again, one must distinguish quite carefully the "worldliness" that Bakhtin advocates, despite and because of its correlations with the transnationalism of the commodity form. My point is this: if, as Katerina Clark and Michael Holquist contend, the chronotope is "a concept for engaging reality"[16] then we would do well to examine the chronotopes of that world and not just their artistic or literary correlatives in isolation that are the hallmarks, for better or worse, of the "world" about which Bakhtin wrote in "Forms of Time and of the Chronotope in the Novel."

When we are in life, we are not in art, and vice versa, as Bakhtin muses. But, of course, chronotope, like dialogism and exotopy, is a bridging concept that links these autonomous yet interdependent worlds: "However forcefully the real and represented world resist fusion, . . . they are nevertheless indissolubly tied up with each other and find themselves in continual mutual interaction; uninterrupted exchange goes on between them, similar to the uninterrupted exchange of matter between living organisms and the environment that surrounds them."[17] Bakhtin is recalling the thought of Ukhtomsky, from whom he first heard and used the word "chronotope" in 1925. There is little use in transposing directly these comments on uninterrupted exchange with the production of value in exchange represented by the commodity form. Can they be coordinated or tied up within cultural critique, however, without losing the specificity of either? And if the aura of the shoe, the athletic shoe in particular, is enabled by what Jameson calls the cultural logic of late capitalism — indeed, is symptomatic of its transnationalism — can these terms be interrelated without inexorably reproducing the inclusionary fantasy of worldliness that most transnational corporations (TNCs) tout as the very integer of their success?

Here, the chronotope is a story of a shoe and the worker to which it refers. The invocation of the shoe, however, does not build a world picture of culture and capital at the end of the twentieth century (for representation itself will remain the problem and not the provider), yet it can implicate cultural critique in the fate of the increasingly absent or disappearing worker whose labor "disappears" in the commodity form but now also vanishes in the commodification of theory itself. The strategy I recommend is not only to inscribe the shoe within a metonymic chain of affective being, but also to elaborate the shoe within a code of affective answerability. The shifting registers of the symbolic of the shoe are less about the capabilities of the cultural researcher than about the abject culpability of the same. The aim is not the production of guilt (however some may revel in the discourse of victimhood); rather, I seek the production of a counterlogic, one that challenges the tidy knowledge that the trail of the shoe might leave. Cultural critique cannot, as Kumar knows (following Gayatri Spivak's powerfully argued notion), make the subaltern (Indonesian) speak beyond her confines in his footwear, but it can attend to a geopolitical imagination that challenges the production of that "existence" on a world scale.

The shoe is magical, within both the history of the commodity and the psychological compulsions of modern "man." The shoe is *the* emblem of the fetishism that links the commodity to desire. And the most magical shoe of all is the athletic shoe because it is simultaneously a symbol of cultural capital, physical prowess, self-esteem, economic and psychic overinvestment, and crass economic exploitation; in fact, it epitomizes late capitalist flexible accumulation *and* continuing masculinist regimes of desire and disavowal.[18] Although Donald Katz has a different argument in mind, he states the case quite nicely: "The name-brand athletic shoe might seem an unlikely seminal artifact of these last years of the twentieth century, but that is clearly what the shoes have become."[19] One brand in particular demonstrates the aura of the shoe for Katz, and that is Nike — named after the Greek goddess of victory, and now a company that marks the triumphalism of transnational corporate élan.[20] This "seminal artifact" conjures the chronotope that is our chief concern and runs from the culture of consumption to the international division of labor and the critical methods that must be answerable to both.

What is the magic of capital for late capitalism? In 1962 Phil Knight "faked out" a Japanese athletic shoe company and became their distributor in the United States under the name Blue Ribbon Sports. Ten years later Jeff Johnson, an employee of Blue Ribbon Sports, sat bolt upright in his bed one morning and blurted the word "Nike." Phil Knight was looking for a new name for the company and its sports shoes. In just twenty years the epithet of the winged goddess of victory has become synonymous with the success of American transnationalism in recreational footwear, enough to produce nearly $4 billion of annual sales and profits of $365 million in 1994 alone (a year in which Nike sold two hundred pairs of shoes a minute).[21] The story of

Nike has become a legend in American capitalist history, a lesson in tremendous company growth, and a benchmark for savvy marketing tactics.[22] To underline the latter, one should note that Nike is not really in the business of making shoes: what it does is market shoes. The shoes themselves are made through contracting and subcontracting in twelve- to eighteen-month production cycles outside its major market, the United States. Nike harnesses the metaphysical subtleties of the shoe with a godlike touch that few have matched. Yet who is vanquished in Nike's "victory," and what other rendezvous of victory is possible in the nexus of culture and capital? Seen in this light, Kumar's comment is not mere cynicism: it is a challenge to the culture of criticism itself.

For some time now cultural theory has been able to integrate levels of economic and aesthetic interpretation within what we may broadly term "cultural logic" (Fredric Jameson's analysis of postmodernism or Arif Dirlik's interrogation of the postcolonial resonates, albeit in different ways, with this possibility). Among other requisites, this has meant developing an increasingly sophisticated and complicated theoretical apparatus to unfathom the apparently unfathomable or nontotalizable: global economic and cultural difference. The problem is not just that "going global" can mime the neocolonial urge of contemporary transnational capitalism, which wears, as its badge of honor, all the flexible positional superiority that Edward Said once attributed to the cultural logic of Orientalism;[23] the problem is that the power of imagination required is very close to fantasy, an illusion that masks the authority of comprehension. The desire to map cognitively is compromised by imaginary maps that exceed or deconstruct cognitive intelligibility. This is the fix of a materialist analysis of the commodity within the terms of fetishism. We understand quite well the power of position in the production of knowledge (who is the "we" of this sentence, who speaks for whom, from where, at what time?), but much less the logic of imagination that emanates and returns to it. If materialist cultural theory is to avoid the apparently endless reproduction of the inclusionary fantasy ("We are the world" slogans, Benetton multiculturalism, etc.), it must do more to rearticulate or reconceptualize the time/space coordinates of imagination that are intrinsic to its operations. The cultural logic of late capitalism depends upon a simultaneous suppression of critical imagination coupled with an overinvestment in the fantastic metaphoricity of the commodity form (typified by advertising). The danger is that a critical imagination can collapse back into the fantasy that the commodity itself enacts. Given the compulsory conspiracy of inclusion, can the world not just be imagined, but imagined otherwise?

In *The Geopolitical Aesthetic*, Jameson attempts to extend the critique of postmodernity provided in his 1984 essay and subsequently revised for his book on postmodernity in 1991. While his interest in the more recent volume is primarily the techniques and technologies of contemporary cinema as a representational quandary, the subtext is an extended critique of culture in the world system. The geopolitical aesthetic is not the geopolitical chronotope of the present discussion, but it shares several significant features that require elaboration. Jameson underlines that attempts to "map" the world system often end up as caricatures because they fail to engage the "non-visual systemic causes"[24] that, together with their figurative representations, are constitutive of social totality. Obviously, the "cartography of the absolute" that Jameson offers does not carry the risk of responsibility that, I would argue, prescribes and destabilizes the imaginative power adequate to that task (that is, the way in which oscillation is immanent to the theoretical approach). Yet self-conscious reflection is not beyond Jameson, who is aware that world-system analysis at the cultural level does not resolve itself into the "Third World" national allegories he initially proposed. Now, by invoking a geopolitical unconscious, Jameson hopes to "refashion national allegory into a conceptual instrument for grasping our new being-in-the-world" (3). But if the idea of national allegory was too narrowly defined, the geopolitical unconscious comes with an indemnity of equally alarming sweep: namely, "that all thinking today is *also,* whatever else it is, an attempt to think the world system as such" (4). As with every overstatement in Jameson's oeuvre, however, this one comes with a brilliant insight. If capitalist relations permeate dominant culture to the core and its everyday "reality" is sutured, however imperfectly, by ideologies that rationalize its nature, then awareness, or what Jameson fondly recalls as "self consciousness about the social totality," is going to be harder to find or trace than its unconscious correlative — that which cannot be simply matched and marked by the representational compulsions that lie beyond it. The trick, as it were, is that this unconscious is indeed manifest in everyday life but not in the form that one would expect it (if it were, it could be commodified and colonized by capitalist social relations as easily as any other object). It comes as no surprise that in Jameson's model allegory reemerges as the unconscious mode of articulation, yet seemingly stripped of the parochialism (and essentialism) of its earlier "national" configuration: "On the global scale, allegory allows the most random, minute, or isolated landscapes to function as a figurative machinery in which questions about the system and its control over the local ceaselessly rise or fall, with a fluidity that has no equivalent in those older national allegories" (5). The allegory is "beyond the landscape" of conventional representations of the world system, yet strives to stand in for its unmappable integration.

Jameson's formulation is useful in its emphasis on absent causes as no less causes for all that; the worldliness of seeing within media technology in fact plays out the shortfalls of its desire to represent. The problem remains the line of fantasy between this desire and the alternative globality of the unconscious, which apparently does not have a form in which to express itself. The political consequence is that the former is taken for the latter, and history marks time rather than makes it. It is as if historical depth is on pause while allegory, as a spatial concept, measures the evacuation of the temporal. This paradox is shared by Bakhtin's articulation of the chronotope that ostensibly represents the time/space connectedness in certain literary expressions but often elides the history that informs it. The modernist moment of Bakhtin's creativity, however, does not exhaust the richness of his authorial point of view. Yet the paradox of the universal in the particular remains, since one could fairly easily recode the micrological aspects of the forms of time Bakhtin elucidates for the exceptionalism now called "postmodernity."[25] This returns us to Jameson because a literary formulation, allegory, is itself performing a double function in Jameson's theory: first, within an analysis of the artistic processes of contemporary culture; and second, as a touchstone for a geopolitical critique of capital. But the allegorical mode extends to the very process of critique itself so that capital provides a surface meaning under which one can find the nitty-gritty cultural correlatives that are the heart of the matter. The story of capital appears almost incidental or arbitrary alongside the artistic playing out of the allegorical mode. Like Bakhtin, therefore, Jameson displays a tendency to prioritize an aesthetic universal in the face of an inscrutable reality. And for literary criticism this has always been an entirely natural reflex.

Jameson realizes, however, in a way that Bakhtin did not (except, perhaps, in *Marxism and the Philosophy of Language*), that the universality of aesthetic categories like allegory does not inexorably entail the aestheticization of the political. Nevertheless, the danger remains, just like fantasy's relationship to imagination. This is not just the inherent risk in deploying the terms of classical aesthetics: it is also the ineluctable hazard of tracking the way capital structures commodity desire on a world scale, since consumption must begin with the subject who perceives — the commodity must be sensed to be consumed as a function of desire (Marx's sensible/suprasensible once more). The chronotope of the shoe, then, is interlaced by desire and the claims of answerability (an ethical dimension to the mode of commodity desire). Like Jameson, I will eschew the easier representational labor of the "landscape" this might offer; unlike Jameson, however, I will focus on the commodity *as* the scene of capitalist culture and not the symptom of the commodification *of* culture. This will emphasize the actual process of commodity production (which still seems to require labor) rather than its realist representation or the critical process used to describe it.

The time/space coordinates of capital and culture today present themselves in dizzying plenitude: a multiplicity that is at once both concrete and abstract. The concreteness is often seen to lie only in the tactile presence of the commodity form in all its manifestations (even the image is "touched"), yet of course its abstraction lies in this very same thingness: the object that is an expression of being. There is no definitive outside to this commodity form: there is no space or place where the commodity itself empties out the content of being. Why this is the case is not a product of capital's nefarious saturation of global economic relations, despite the earnestness and compulsion of its embrace, but because the process of capital consistently denies or disavows any and all logics that attempt to disconnect the naturalized sublation of being in the commodity and its "possession." Delinking from capitalist logic is nothing new — it has often formed the constituent desire in a number of sociopolitical movements, from Marxist and socialist revolutions to those of postcolonial nationhood and the more recent challenge of the "Greens." But the problem has taken on an increased urgency in light of the collapse of "actually existing" socialism around the globe and the end of the Cold War. The inevitability of capitalist social relations seems all the more "naturalized" even as its dysfunctional operations are still more apparent. The tendency is to aestheticize this moment, this bizarre *interregnum* in which various forms of capitalism compete not just with each other for accumulation on a world scale but with real and imaginary agents who might spell their collective demise. There are, however, significant lessons to be learned from reading the processes of the commodity against the grain of aesthetic formalism.

The chronotope of the shoe immediately invites questions of desire (the projection of the fetish and its disavowal) that are more than a subtheme: they describe the limits of the geopolitical at this historical juncture. Thus, the worker "exists" at the nexus of economic integration, spatial differentiation, cultural globalization, *and* masculinist disavowal. While the notion of existence as aphanisis follows Marx's analysis of the commodity to a certain degree, it also imbricates the fate of the worker in contemporary forms of engendered power. The financialization and transnationalization of the globe are partial (despite the triumphalism that their proponents proclaim) but significant enough to throw into relief the patriarchal and capitalist ideologies that inform their mode of accumulation. These must insistently be made answerable to the being of the worker, however decentered that self has become. The task is not to make visible that which has been transmogrified beyond recognition (for that visibility is also often at man's behest): the point is to understand the contemporary processes (psychic, social, economic, political) by which workers must be rendered a convenient abstraction — the shoe for the flesh.[26]

Nike makes shoes in Indonesia.[27] Indonesia is a country that needs no "national allegory" to understand its integration into global capitalist and cultural relations (here I agree with Aijaz Ahmad's cogent critique that Jameson's characterization of the "Third World" text is an exercise in "positivist reduc-tionism").[28] Indonesia's contemporary links with the world system begin in 1965, first with a military coup, then with the overthrow of Sukarno and his populist regime and the subsequent crushing of the Communist Party (PKI) by the Western-backed sources of Suharto, himself recently ousted.[29] Suharto's "New Order" meant several things: a political system that continu-ally steamrollered any and all forms of opposition to its "beneficence" (what was left of the PKI was outlawed in 1966, and periodic social unrest, like the riots of 1984 and 1996, was quickly "remedied"); a foreign policy that was not beyond a little old-style colonialism to maintain hegemony in the Indonesian archipelago (the process of incorporating East Timor has cost several hundred thousand lives to date); an enforcement of constitutional rule that meant a narrowly defined interpretation of the Pancasila (the Five Principles originally devised by Sukarno as a basis for the modern Indone-sian state);[30] and an opening to foreign investment that undoubtedly raised living standards in many sections of the population but did not fundamen-tally address the root causes of systemic inequalities that attract transnational corporations in the first place. Development in Indonesia has meant this and more.

The periodic World Bank country reports on Indonesia make for dry and clinical reading.[31] The studies appear to have been prodded by the typical traumatic stress associated with massive foreign investment and the exploita-tion of Indonesia's natural resources (including large oil reserves, a factor that has clearly spurred growth but, because of the geopolitical significance of oil prices, has often meant internationally produced austerity programs). The piles of statistics on poverty rates in Indonesia are a measure of the World Bank's own vacillation about investment strategies.[32] Not surprisingly, poverty rates are highest in the agricultural sector. Families are generally big-ger, wages lower, and living conditions substandard compared to their urban counterparts, especially those in Jakarta. In several reports the concern is about the social and political consequences of fostering a large and generally poor underemployed population (Indonesia's population is now the world's fourth largest). And, of course, the economics of development strategy are closely tied to this. The Suharto regime, mindful of any IMF or World Bank attempts to influence the internal politics of the state, nonetheless generally followed the advice of these reports and the examples of other Asian "mir-acle" economies like Taiwan, Malaysia, and South Korea by drawing surplus labor into other segments of production. But industrialization has raised not only real wages but the specters of class division, on the one hand, and en-vironmental disaster, on the other. Both now threaten to drive transnationals away, but in the early years of the New Order these considerations were distant, to say the least.

Indeed, it is tempting to say that Indonesia still garners importance not because it makes shoes but because it was made for shoes, which is of course merely to underline that transnational capitalism is not that interested in what Indonesia might otherwise "represent."[33] The political, social, and economic circumstances of Indonesia after 1965 increasingly made it ripe for exactly the mode of light-industry, low-tech, labor-intensive development symbolized by shoe production. Yet this capitalist desire is simultaneously a masculinist desire, both a product of the search for higher profit margins in the process from production to consumption *and* a symptom of global fetishistic disavowal. The shoe stands in both for the desire that compels it and the actual conditions that inform it. This means not only the feminization of the developing world through the rubric of transnational market "penetration" (such language is not marginal but part of the very texture of the socioeconomic relations that accompany it); it also means the internationalization of markets has attempted to efface the psychic inscriptions on the commodity form by exporting the nonrepresentation of the worker to the farthest corners of the globe (farthest, that is, from the object of the commodity's production — the consumer).

What starts out, then, as a conventional narrative about the onward march of late capitalist "development" in the newly industrialized countries (NICs) in the thrall of TNCs becomes a web of complex synergy that the commodity presents as its natural apotheosis. To be sure, the roots of this process of commodification of relations on a world scale can be found in Marx's reading of industrialization, but there it was seen as the rallying point of a unifying labor movement conscious of the world that left it underfoot; now, however, it is the mark of amnesia and aphanisis — the great complexity of commerce that precedes the arrival of the commodity is repressed (disavowed). The commodity appears in its advertisement, not in the hands of shoemaker or rubber molder twelve thousand miles away. Of course, a capitalist has never showed the immiseration and inequality built into the production of the commodity as a way to sell it: that is one of the meanings of capitalism. But it is only now, in the transformed time/space relations of global capital, that even criticism of this process seems beyond the powers of the cognitive. Even radical approaches to knowledge like cultural studies inadvertently buttress this point of view by hypostatizing the subversive meanings of the consumer — what the consumer does with the commodity. The worker either is an old shoe or has disappeared, except as an ironic integer of her continuing absence from the realm of social, economic, and political power.

Again, a different sense of time/space critique does not solve that absence, as if a chronotopic imagination alone might disarticulate the logical consistency of superexploitation. Yet the internationalization of cultural critique, with all its dangers, may be a necessary evil if one is to understand culture's implication in the order of things and thingness at this time. The story of Indonesia in the twentieth century is one of colonization, occupation, revolution, independence, counterrevolution, development, integration, and so forth. That it is also the *disjecta membra*, the refracting shards of Western capital and culture, is not a coincidence, however specific that narrative must be. It is the real foundation of the chronotope of the shoe.

No shorthand version of Indonesian politics and economics will provide an adequate understanding of the tremendous changes wrought on society by the New Order's version of modern statehood.[34] The transmigration program of relocating large numbers of people to outlying islands in order to ease the burdens of population explosion in Java would itself serve as a case study of the disjunctions of Indonesian "development" (during and after colonization). And, of course, given the rapacious sway of transnational capital, some comparison with the business practices of the Dutch East India Company in the preceding centuries would also shed light on the differences in the extraction of surplus value from labor today.[35] From the above, three characteristics, however, have particular relevance to Indonesia's recent integration into the global economy: an excess of labor suitable for labor-intensive, low-wage, light-industrial production; little or no organized labor infrastructure; and an authoritarian regime that routinely disregards the nominally democratic nature of Indonesian statehood epitomized in the Five Principles in order to smooth the flow of capital in and out of the country.

In terms of the Asian economic miracle since the end of the Second World, this adds Indonesia to a metonymic chain that has included Taiwan, Malaysia, and South Korea. As transnationals move around Asia (and that obviously includes Asian transnationals, particularly those of Japan), competition for cost effectiveness has intensified. Interestingly, as the Asian markets seek out cheaper production costs, many of the companies that were subcontracted to boost production in places like Taiwan and South Korea are now subsubcontracting in other emerging economies. This is certainly true of Indonesia, and it appears to be the case in China, which is rapidly becoming the metonym to supplant all others in this process. Focusing on Indonesian shoe production is not meant to stand in unproblematically for developments of this kind elsewhere in the region but rather emphasizes what elements disrupt an otherwise tidy metonymy. In the end, it is not simply desire for cheaper labor in accordance with the appropriate prerequisites that produces these changes but the logic of desire itself — that which does not favor mere cause and effect, but abstruse simultaneity.

The chronotope of the shoe articulates: a psychic compulsion linked simultaneously to gender hierarchization and commodity fetishism; a narrative that comprises the actual production of a shoe within regimes of capital; and a tale of the embodied labor of a shoe worker here interpellated in the Indonesian economy. The shoe is a particularly useful way to understand the chronotope of culture and capital because it accentuates the process of desire intrinsic to the logic of global circuits of production and consumption. The importance of the shoe relates simultaneously to its status as a commodity and to its function as fetish. In Freud's famous formulation, fetishism is a masculine prerogative — a reflex to the "horror of castration" produced by the boy's belief in the woman (the mother) having a penis.[36] The boy does not repress the contradictory evidence of this projection so much as disavow it (*Verleugnung*), a process that more properly describes the function of a fetish as an external reality. Why the shoe emerges as a fetishistic substitute for the "absent female phallus" is only hinted at in Freud's explanation: he avers that the young boy fixates on the shoe or the foot at the very moment of disavowal as the boy glimpses the woman's genitals from below. In the absence of the phallus the boy fantasizes its presence: the shoe, particularly the woman's shoe, becomes the metonym for something that it is not — namely, the belief that the being of female is male.

More of a sketch than an essay, Freud's thoughts on fetishism have produced a plethora of interpretation. Indeed, recent discussion would seem to underline still further the importance and the controversy of this piece.[37] The psychic significance of Freud's formulation is accentuated by its ambivalent relation to its cognates in political economy, anthropology, and literary theory in which its critical function alternates between touchstone and gravestone. Marx preempts the Freudian turn to a certain extent by associating fetishism with the general aura of the object as a commodity. Behind what Marx refers to as the "hieroglyph" of the product lies value, which he explores as the social character of labor, precisely what the money-form's relationship to the commodity must erase or deny. In Freud's theory, the object arises as a presence for something that was never there; for Marx, the commodity stands in for a real absence, the social labor that produced it. In *Feminizing the Fetish*, Emily Apter explores a "curious compatibility" between these readings, a space where the commodity's "secret" and the "strangeness" of consciousness form (and here she quotes from Michel Leiris) an "affective ambivalence, that tender sphinx we nourish, more or less secretly, at our core."[38] Apter persuasively theorizes ambivalence as a "third term," as the space where fetish, fetishism, and theories of fetishism ("the fetishism of fetishism") seem to mutually deconstruct — and is thus a place where "feminizing" becomes both necessary and ineluctable, as long as one limits its function to literary narrative (the textual examples that Apter provides). Whatever the ambivalence of Marx's own tropes on fetishism,[39] the "metaphysical subtleties" of the commodity do not stand in the same relation as Freud's fetishist to the fetish. Not quite.

Within commodity fetishism the social relations in exchange between commodities substitute for the social relations of those human beings who have labored to produce them. The illusory aspect of commodity fetishism is that the value of the commodity appears inherent to it, whereas its value is not natural, but social. Yet it is important to emphasize that this is a *real relation*, not simply a representational fallacy. One can easily accept Baudrillard's exegesis of simulacra on this point, but not the overhasty displacement of the economic onto the signifying chain for the very same reason. Thus, commodities can simulate one another without reference to an actual original (which never existed, hence the link to psychic fetishism), but labor value does not exist as an imaginary referent to the commodity even if it is presented as such. In addition, in the rush to find equivalence between Freudian "affect" and commodity effect, it is easy to overlook that commodity fetishism is specific to the relations among things (that is, their exchange value), but fetishizing the shoe or foot is a displaced relation of subject and object, not two shoes' *danse macabre*.

One could examine the possible category errors in much more detail (which would have to account, for instance, for the precapitalist realities of the fetish), but here, at the risk of "fetishizing the fetish" as Apter warns, I wish to push the historical confluence rather than conflation of such phenomena in capital and culture. For instance, it is entirely prescient that the cover of Jameson's *Postmodernism, or, the Cultural Logic of Late Capitalism* features Andy Warhol's *Diamond Dust Shoes*.[40] In the opening chapter, the veritable Ur-text for materialist analysis of the postmodern, Jameson includes a valuable discussion of several "shoe paintings." Jameson sets up a series of polemical contrasts between Van Gogh's *A Peasant's Shoes* as a "Utopian gesture" and Warhol's "glacéed X-ray elegance" (9). For my purposes two orders of the shoe are operative — two chronotopes indeed. In looking at Van Gogh's painting, Jameson stresses that one should reconstruct the "initial conditions" of the work in order to understand its symbolic act — "as praxis, and as production." The raw materials he elucidates include "the whole rudimentary human world of backbreaking peasant toil, a world reduced to its most brutal and menaced, primitive and marginalized state" (7). Jameson is waxing allegorical once more, for he knows that the reproduction or inert objectification of the painting about which he writes itself describes capital's commodification of culture, which remains his central concern. Counterpoised to this is his own reconstruction, the stunning "mental restoration" of hermeneutics:

> I will briefly suggest... that the willed and violent transformation of a drab peasant object world into the most glorious materialization of pure color in oil paint is to be seen as a Utopian gesture, an act of compensation which ends up producing a whole new Utopian realm of

the senses, or at least of that supreme sense — sight, the visual, the eye — which it now reconstitutes for us as a semi-autonomous space in its own right, a part of some new division of labor in the body of capital, some new fragmentation of the emergent sensorium which replicates the specializations and divisions of capitalist life at the same time that it seeks in precisely such fragmentation a desperate Utopian compensation for them. (7)

This reading is every bit as effervescent as Heidegger's famous interpretation, which Jameson paraphrases in his own argument. Heidegger imagines the world of the peasant woman who wears the shoes and the more general being that they signify but, unlike Jameson, does not fathom the materiality of the art (the paint, which is Jameson's point) in reconstituting its origins.[41] Jameson claims that high modernism can function in this way, interrupting the order of the commodity form by compensating, in a Utopian fashion, the deracination of modern life. The comparison with Warhol could not be more stark. If the shoes represented by Van Gogh invoke a vaster reality of meaning and possibility, Warhol's deathly assortment of women's pumps seems to close off that hermeneutical avenue. Of Warhol's picture Jameson opines, "[I]t doesn't really speak to us at all" (8). The denial of this larger lived context naturally fascinates Jameson, all the more so because of Warhol's biography (which includes the fact that he once illustrated shoes for the fashion business and designed display windows for shoes). Jameson makes several points that can be briefly summarized: in highlighting the commodity fetishism of late capitalism, Warhol does not appear to provide strong political critique of it; the stridency of modernist expression is in Warhol answered with "depthlessness"; and the death of the world of appearance typified by the shoes signals the now-famous "waning of affect" in contemporary culture. Art has finally succumbed to the regime of commodification that it has incessantly opposed. Where the first chronotope offered utopia in the midst of alienation, the second displays defeat through the contradictory celebration of fragmentation.

But of course, as several critics have pointed out,[42] the examples that Jameson uses do not necessarily support the sharp contrast he draws. There is no logical reason, for instance, why one could not argue for Warhol's *Diamond Dust Shoes* performing the same compensatory move as Van Gogh's painting, albeit on this occasion by answering the busy commodification of the world by accentuating its flatness, depthlessness, and forbidding homogeneity. Yet this suggests a further point: that the all-too-brief critique of Heidegger's view of shoes nevertheless marks an affinity with its subtext in a form that is every bit as compensatory as Van Gogh's — nostalgia. In Heidegger's essay the nostalgia is most pointedly for the rootedness, the organicism of peasant life (which, of course, is also a foil), but although this is at some distance from Jameson's invocation of the social, the latter can also be read as a nostalgia for a utopian spirit that may, or may not, be the object or aura of Van Gogh's painting.

The relevance of the Van Gogh example is the shoes. For Heidegger, the painting is almost incidental to the thingness of the shoes, but that "almost," that space between, is what allows him to distinguish the "product" from the "thing" and the "work" (of art). The shoes are a "thing-as-product" and not any old thing, but their being-as-product is not available to them simply because they are "equipment" in Heidegger's parlance. It is art itself that calls forth this truth in being, the *aletheia* or "unconcealment of being" that is the very mark of its origins. There is a sleight of hand (or eye) in Heidegger's argument here, since in bracketing the function of the author in the origin of art, he allows the critic much more sway on the imaginative terrain. The work can reveal the being of a product in a way that the product itself cannot, but the world, or the worlding of the world, that Heidegger invokes is not grounded by the work of art, sui generis. The cognitive map of that world also resides in a consciousness adequate to its perception. The world of the peasant woman whom Heidegger ties to the shoes in her absence in Van Gogh's painting is only available to her in the usefulness of the equipment, the shoes themselves; whereas the truth in being of the shoes is something revealed to the critic in his perception of its representation in the work of art. This is a crude reading, but no more crude than Heidegger's suggestion that the shoes in Van Gogh's painting were the peasant woman's in the first place. The metaphysical subtleties of the process of commodification begin to unravel there, in the matter of fact of the incidental ownership of the thing itself.

But these are shoes, and I do not believe there is something accidental in their choice by either Van Gogh, Heidegger, Warhol, or Jameson. The point is not that the fetishism of the commodity is simply a masculine prerogative (even as this must be underlined) but that the symbolic of the shoe describes an intricate field of desire and disavowal that links the past to the present and the moment of transnational capital. Van Gogh's shoes, like Heidegger's reading of them, are avowedly modernist: the *Stöss*, or shock, of the work of art is an alienation effect about the depersonalization of the modern world. The shoes do not represent a community "in a moment of danger," to borrow from Walter Benjamin, but mark their own insufficiency to the object world that is penetrating every aspect of the forms of representation available. To this extent, the shoe is a phallic presence but one that certain artists and critics must otherwise deny.

But how can Van Gogh's shoes help us with the moment of capital today, the moment, indeed, in which Being is built into a transnational sole? Before returning to the affective responsibility that links the shoe worker in Indonesia with the "world" campus in Beaverton, Oregon (the "home" of Nike), we must resole the philosophical disposition of shoes. Jameson casually mentions a point by Derrida that Van Gogh's shoes are a "heterosexual pair," but perhaps he underestimates the usefulness of Derrida's 140-page essay on Van Gogh's shoe paintings to his argument. One could be more severe and say that Derrida's critique deconstructs Jameson's in advance (and is therefore disavowed), but I want to maintain a complementary materialist *pointure* of the latter, despite the ingenious convolutions of the Derridean text. Certainly, the philosophical niceties, like the shoes themselves, are not just the *parerga*, or ornaments of the chronotope; they are intrinsic to it (and therefore *parerga* in the sense that Derrida reads Kant). Derrida's interpretation stages the problem of Being not only for Van Gogh's shoe painting but for the athletic footwear that now, in a fundamental way, supersedes the question of art that the painting foregrounds.

The form of Derrida's essay, a " 'polylogue' (for *n* + 1-female-voices),"[43] is not an exercise in intricate and elliptical wordplay but a measure of criticism's inadequacy to its object. One of the reasons critics often write conversations ("dialogues") when invoking Bakhtinian dialogism, for instance, is to highlight who or what is excluded in the critical act. For his part(s), Derrida deploys the polylogue to intervene in something of a pseudo-exchange between Heidegger and Meyer Schapiro over the attribution of the shoes in Van Gogh's painting. As both Heidegger and Schapiro are aware, and Derrida underlines, Van Gogh painted a lot of shoes (Derrida includes black and white facsimiles of at least five such paintings). Once Derrida asks "Why these shoes?" the text becomes an elaborate graft on "pointing" (*pointure*), which is how the truth gets stitched.

Using Derrida's essay, I want to raise the question that he does not ask in elaborating the problem of the restitution of the shoes to "their rightful owner" (258). While it is certainly true that the magic of the commodity within capitalism depends on the psychic investment in possession (which extends even to the exchange of Heidegger and Schapiro — "the desire for attribution is a desire for appropriation" [260]), it also rests on the annulment of the producer. In today's shoes the subjectivity of the worker is marked only by a geographical referent ("made in"), but for both Nike footwear and Van Gogh's painting the chronotope of the shoe depends upon the suppression of a question that the commodity must hide: Who made the shoes?

To the extent that Derrida examines the process of restitution in terms of attribution of ownership he elides the material conditions of the object's possibility. Van Gogh could have imagined any kind of shoe in order to produce *a* painting, but could he have painted *those* shoes in particular had they not been made? If the point is moot, it is only because the maker has been rendered mute. Derrida calls the shoe "the lowest degree, the most subjective or underlying level of culture or the institution" (264), but he bases this observation on the philosophical problem of the wearer (who is absent in Van Gogh's paintings), not the maker who is absent even when the shoes are "filled." The double-subject of the painting whose truth in *pointure* Derrida untangles or unknots is the "subject-shoes" of the wearer and the shoes as subject in a painting; yet, I would argue, the economy of the fetish works to exclude precisely the double-subject of the labor that makes the shoe possible. The worker is a double-subject because of the specific relationship of labor to the commodity form — a relationship that, as Marx explained, depends not upon the material properties of the object but upon the value in exchange. It is the disavowal of the latter as a property of labor that allows commodity fetishism to proceed. The shoe, in particular, foregrounds both the principle of the commodity and its changing form in late capitalism. That this finds or interpellates woman as a primary worker in the newly industrialized zones of the world is not a matter of convenient coincidence in the psychic aura of the shoe but is the very logic of transnational capitalism at the end of the twentieth century. For Jameson, the paradigmatic shift from Van Gogh's shoes to Warhol's is in the waning of affect whose ideal subject is the schizophrenic (a subject who is "easy enough to please provided only an eternal present is thrust before the eyes" [10]); for Derrida, the will to restitution in the *pointure* of the shoe is the delirium of modern philosophy: "These shoes are hallucinogenic" (273). Yet for neither critic does the subject of shoe paintings invoke the problem of the commodity form for its makers (the "thing" with "grotesque ideas," as Marx notes).[44] Here philosophy conspires with the systemic logic of elision that the commodity wears in order to circulate.

There are, however, several aspects of Derrida's essay that may help us find our feet if not the shoes that fit them. First, he is careful to distinguish the "paradigm of the shoe" in Heidegger's *Der Ursprung des Kunstwerkes*. Initially, Heidegger discusses the "being-product of the product" with reference to shoes but not, as Derrida astutely points out, in terms of art, or Van Gogh's art in particular. Yet the product occupies a position that mediates between a thing and a work (its "being-product" appears in the latter). The artwork, then, bears a relationship to the thing but is enhanced by the presence of a being-product that, in turn, allows perspective on both the thingness of the thing and the origin of art. The distinctions are valid although, by themselves, they do not clarify the symbolic of the shoe (for instance, would not Marx's conception of the commodity cancel through all three components of Heidegger's critique?). Derrida puts Heidegger's paradigm to work in order to ponder the specter of truth that haunts presentation and representation (while undoing the attributive compulsion in both Heidegger's and Schapiro's reading of Van Gogh's shoe painting — here, truth be told, Schapiro comes off worse). The object, of course, is not the shoe as product or the being-product of the shoe in a painting, but the truth of truth, on which any theory of representation must be based in the first place. Not surprisingly for readers of Derrida, this truth gets laced up by the law of the *parergon*, "which comprehends everything without comprehending" (343). To fathom the shoe is also to understand the "hallucinogenic fictions" (375) that gird, or envelop, theories of truth. In this way, Derrida finds a usefulness for Heidegger that Heidegger himself does not locate in the example of the shoes. What Heidegger discovers is the reliability of the product — its *Verlässlichkeit*. The reliability of the product is a condition of its usefulness, the way it belongs to the world it invokes (the peasant world of Heidegger's example). Again, this is not the equivalent of product reliability in capitalism (or, indeed, of built-in obsolescence), but its proximity is not irrelevant. The problem is that the proximity is displaced. Neither Heidegger nor Derrida (nor, for that matter, Jameson) is overly concerned with the specificity of the shoe as a commodity form; they are more concerned with it as a symbol of the way the truth gets told in art. The advantage of such an approach is that it can avoid the lure of crude empiricism (the attributive mode of Schapiro's argument) and the hasty equivalence of shoe production and the production of shoes in art. The disadvantage is that art can be read less as a specific site for the revelation of truth in being and more as the only locus for such sublimity. Kant is kept at bay but is somehow tied to those who distance him.

Derrida's polylogue reveals, despite itself, the conditions of possibility that the regime of the commodity provides. In this regard, the shoe functions as a complex metaphor that allows Derrida to turn truth inside out without simply negating it. But the *pointure* of his approach resists stitching the shoe to the context that informs Derrida's discourse "four times *around* painting," including that of commodity fetishism. This is the space/time or chronotope in which the shoe is precipitate. To take Derrida's use of *pointure* seriously will pitch us forward once more to the contemporary commodity form. Derrida likes the confluence and undecidability of meanings in *pointure* — the fact that it refers simultaneously to the art of pricking or pointing in printing a page as well as the punctures made in the stitching of gloves or shoes. "Pointing" is a somewhat polite and inaccurate rendering of *pointure* in English, or at best a feminization of the process invoked (in needlepoint for instance). Here, the *OED* betrays that the staid eloquence of *punctura* in Latin was almost always upstaged by the brute abruptness of "prick" in the history of English. The significance of prick and pricking to the subject of the shoe should not be underestimated.[45]

In the twentieth century, the culture of pricking or stitching shoes has changed dramatically. Van Gogh's paintings feature shoes that had been stitched or nailed for the most part. Today's athletic shoes, however, would find such technology cumbersome and not cost effective. The uppers of such shoes are so thin and light (leather is sometimes used, but in the main the materials of choice are synthetic, like "Durabuck" — a staple of Nike shoes) that stitching can be done very easily and quickly. But the soles are not stitched at all: they are glued. Nevertheless, the culture of pricking remains in shoe manufacture as an index of the function of masculine desire in capitalist production. Here, the truth of truth is not for all time, but is the truth in a certain mode of fetishization that offers the image of an attachment (another being-product) that it must always necessarily deny. Van Gogh compensates for the deracinated world of the peasant by celebrating her ever-threatened absence in the "out-of-work" (as Derrida puts it) image of shoes; later, in Indonesia, the peasant woman goes to Jakarta to work in a factory making shoes that she cannot afford to wear. Between these two moments a whole regimen of production and exchange has been transformed. And this is, by the way, why Warhol's shoes give up the ghost of compensation, or a certain form of restitution.

Although Derrida's critique tends to be most effective in the way it unpicks modernist nostalgia for the function of art against the rage of technological progress (a facet that finds Van Gogh and Heidegger in the same aesthetic if not philosophical shoes), he also pricks the conscience of contemporary logic by defamiliarizing its gendered suppositions and dubious oppositions. Briefly, Derrida quotes himself in the "Double Session" talking of the points of the ballerina — that "each pair, in this circuit, will always have referred to some other, signifying too the operation of signifying" (264). He remarks that "prior to all reflection you reassure yourself with the pair" (265), and this, in essence, is the problem of restitution in the associative chain of Van Gogh/Heidegger/Schapiro that Derrida painstakingly (de)constructs. But the pairings that occur (for instance, Schapiro "will see the 'face' [la figure] of Van Gogh in 'his' shoes" [266]) emphasize a masculine attachment, whereas the single shoe, as an abstraction, is the fetish object of that which never was, a woman's penis.[46] The inside/out of the shoe, as Derrida notes, insistently collapses the logic of opposition in this fetishistic fantasy, for while the outside form of the shoe intimates the phallus, the inside invokes the vagina (when Cinderella is shoed with the glass shoe, the double economy of inside/outside becomes palpable).[47] The production and consumption of athletic shoes does not just play out this contradictory pairing and doubling — it is its contemporary apotheosis.

If one links the processes involved in the production and consumption of athletic shoes, several familiar patterns begin to emerge. To think these simultaneously within the chronotope is itself, as I have suggested, something close to fantasy (something hallucinogenic in Derrida's usage), but is nevertheless the first circle of affective responsibility. Within production there is primarily a woman worker. She is hired because she is cheap and because she is dexterous (she has to be able to work inside and outside the shoe with great speed).[48] With increasing unemployment on the land, the woman worker is lured from the village to the emerging urban centers in Indonesia. Nike moved to Indonesia from the middle of the 1980s at the same time that this labor force was itself emerging in the Indonesian economy. Light industry of this kind continues to be crucial for the Indonesian government in picking up the slack in industrial development caused by the reining in of its oil business in the international market. As noted, the World Bank has played a large role in this "retooling," and some $350 million of foreign aid poured into Indonesia over three years in the late 1980s for light-industry development, including shoe factories.[49] In 1988 Indonesian athletic shoe exports stood at $4 million, but by 1993 this had risen to $1.5 billion. For Nike, the switch to production in Indonesia became more attractive at this time both because of almost nonexistent government oversight in this form of business and because labor costs in South Korea and Taiwan in particular were beginning to eat into profit margins. Since Indonesia was seen to lack a sufficient managerial class, Nike imported its own managers from other parts of its Asian operations — a move that often caused friction with the Indonesian workforce (and occasional strikes). In 1991, for instance, the *Far Eastern Economic Review* reported a woman line worker for Nike in Indonesia protesting that "they [the Korean managers] yell at us when we don't make production quotas and if we talk back they cut our wages" (quoted in *J* 172).[50] While working conditions for the women have improved, athletic shoe production is still a harmful business. The solvents used to glue the soles of these shoes are highly toxic, and even when the extractor fans are working well the women constantly breathe fumes. Interestingly, the cofounder of Nike, Bill Bowerman, often made shoe prototypes using similar glue solvents and was eventually crippled by them. He developed narapathy, a degenerative condition often experienced by shoe and hat makers that gives us the popular phrase "mad as a hatter." Nike opens and closes factories with such speed in its search for cheap labor that its workers are probably spared most of the long-term effects of glue sniffing. But the narapathy remains in transnational exploitation itself.

To be sure, Nike's labor practices in Asia are unremarkable for late capitalist transnationalism.[51] Subcontractors scour emerging economies for the usual characteristics mentioned above, and sufficient infrastructure to get raw materials in and the finished product out within the requisite business cycles. Some of Nike's shoe lines require more skill than others (Air Jordans, for instance, were still made in South Korea at the Tae Gurang Industrial Company's factory called "T2" long after most of the other production lines had been shifted to Indonesia and China). In the main, however, the price of the shoe is connected to its image much more than the cost of the skill required to make it. Where the artwork, Van Gogh's shoe paintings for instance, might invoke the product-being of a whole community, the image of the athletic shoe provides a status in excess of the performance provided by the shoe's design. Nevertheless, the truth in *pointure* shares much of the epistemological form of the truth in advertising where shoes are concerned. To maintain the responsibility at issue one must continually reconnect these elements of the shoe's aura — that is, the sheer weight of marketing mystique with the object of superexploitation in the developing world, the woman worker.

The condition of women workers in Indonesia is overdetermined by several interlocking factors that facilitate the Nike "miracle." Among those mentioned so far, the authoritarian nature of the government is vital. Despite the violent resistance to the newly restrictive Pancasila from the moment it was drafted into law in 1984 (which resulted in the Tanjung Priok massacre of protesters by the New Order in September of that year), in general the fate of women in the workforce is guided by the Pancasila's democratic absolutism. Women must know their place as wives and mothers, but, when interpellated by the dictates of light-industrial need, they must further submit to paternalism in the workplace.[52] Although this does not completely negate the possibility of industrial action (there have been strikes against Nike in Indonesia), it minimizes the risk by making protest appear as against the foundations of continuing Indonesian nationhood. This limit on worker solidarity is not the monopoly of Indonesia; it is, rather, the unimaginable of contemporary regimes of time/space in capital. The limit always appears to emerge elsewhere.

One of these highly regulated women workers in Indonesia is Sadisah. In 1992 Jeffrey Ballinger displayed one of her pay slips in *Harper's Magazine* to make visible, in an obvious way, the cost of Nike's business in the Asian market.[53] In April of that year Sadisah's wage was 14¢ per hour for a total of $1.03 for a 7.5-hour day — significantly less than the government's figure for "minimum physical need." Sadisah, like the other 114 workers on her Nike line, was forced by material need to work long hours of overtime. Ballinger reports that an International Labor Organization survey found that 88 percent of women workers in Indonesia on Sadisah's wage were malnourished. Sadisah herself has come from a peasant community to make Nike's shoes and now can afford to rent a shack without electricity or running water. The cost of her labor to make one pair of Nike athletic shoes is about 12¢. In the American market these shoes will sell from $80 to $150 a pair. When Derrida writes of surplus value in his shoe essay he does not consider the maker, not even for a sentence, in the production of surplus value. To raise this specter (of Marx, and more besides) is not simply a question of restitution — to somehow claim or appropriate these shoes for their rightful owner, the shoemaker. Sadisah, on the contrary, remains with the shoe, in its stitching and gluing, just as the shoe stays with her, in her poverty and in her body (the effects of both the vapors and long-term exposure to the purple lights that illuminate the glue used in the soling process). She exists in the shoe in a way that the capitalist cannot. Where the shoes in Van Gogh's painting leave a trace of the subject as owner, as user, the shoe itself is always already the embodied labor of its maker (yet without the laborer's body). Air Max, Nike's most successful running shoe, illustrates the presence of this being quite succinctly. The sole is see-through, like Cinderella's shoes, but here it is so that the consumer can see and show that "Air is real," as one commentator puts it,[54] that you are indeed walking on compressed air. There is the being of Sadisah, there, where she is entirely absent, see-through, invisible. Her labor is to be walked upon because she is there, in her absence. Note, this is not a realistic representation of embodied labor that must, necessarily, remain abstract. The Being of Sadisah is an abstraction; whereas "Air is real" is an imaginary resolution of this real contradiction (in the Althusserian formulation). But, occasionally, the shoe worker reminds the owner as consumer of her absent presence, for her pricking can chafe the foot, or the sole can burst, leaving the owner disconsolate but aware, briefly, that the air-to-be-seen was a product-being out of sight: the shoes had been made.[55]

In April 1992, Sadisah earned $37 net for her month's labor. Ballinger, an AFL-CIO researcher, notes an alarming disparity between this figure and that of the earnings of Michael Jordan. Jordan, the linchpin of Air Jordan marketing, received $20 million from Nike in 1992 for endorsing the shoe that bears his name. It would take 44,492 years for Sadisah to earn this amount based on Nike's payments to her. The disparity lies in the power of the image, in the mystique of "branding," in the unfettered circulation of commodity culture.

But the obviousness of such statements does not do justice to the complexities of corporate culture, so here we will oscillate briefly from Jakarta to Beaverton, Oregon, the production machine of Nike's "global imagery" and a "corporate Xanadu" as Katz calls it. "Nike World Campus" is a key node in the geopolitical imaginary of the chronotope. Of Nike's over six thousand American workers, most are based in Beaverton. It is an extraordinary think tank devoted to the magic of the commodity form, to the marketing of image. For instance, in the mid-1980s, Nike was big but had not yet become a transnational "player" like MacDonald's or Coca-Cola. Then, in 1984, the company signed Michael Jordan to its roster, and there began a marketing partnership that would give Jordan name recognition beyond belief and Nike global brand power. Consider the "Jordan Flight" TV commercial developed at Beaverton in 1985. As Jordan glides toward the basketball rim, the soundtrack emphasizes the roar of jet engines. The image is slowed down to enhance the fact that Jordan is in flight; indeed, he stays in the air for ten seconds. This human impossibility is precisely the point: Jordan has become the equivalent of the goddess whose name graces the ad. He can fly. Just before his retirement in 1993 (he has since made a comeback), Jordan noted: "What Phil [Knight] and Nike have done is turn me into a dream." Here there is a bizarre correlation with the immiseration of Sadisah somewhere offscreen in the shoe factory, as if the hyperreality of Jordan's flight is inseparable from the phantom in Air that the worker represents in Nike's sole. It is only in Beaverton, where Adam Smith's old invisible hand is still at work, that these complementary components must be kept apart, unlaced and unglued.

The Nike World Campus at Beaverton is a world removed from Sadisah's factory. Responding to Katz's questions, Nike employees said the campus was "like being in a playground" and that it was "a factory for fun."[56] The workforce is young (but not as young as the women workers in Asia) and often displays a highly motivated sports mentality.[57] The corporate identity of Nike is predominantly white and male even if the sportspeople who endorse its products are not (buildings are named after Nike success stories like Alberto Salazar, Bo Jackson, and Joan Benoit Samuelson). While this is unremarkable for American capitalism, it cannot be separated from the implications of Nike's global reach. The interior walls of each building are drenched with sports paraphernalia and associated imagery (Katz compares the buildings to frat houses). This, however, goes beyond the trappings of jock culture: it is part of the very fabric of corporate life that makes up Nike's "matrix" structure. To read book-length studies of Nike like *Swoosh* and *Just Do It* is to understand that transnational corporatism itself depends on a working logic that is thoroughly masculinist. The activities at Nike management retreats (called "Buttfaces"), corporate parties ("Nike Nites"), and the annual Nike "Beer Relays" are perhaps the most obvious symptoms of the Beaverton mind-set. But the dominance of testosterone in Nike activities has still more glaring "high" points: for instance, in December 1979, when the company went public (and Phil Knight became superrich to the tune of $178 million), no women employees were offered stock in the company (even Carole Fields, one-time "controller" for Nike and nicknamed "Dragon Lady," got nothing from the stock options). Similarly, even after the decision to move into the emerging and lucrative market for women's aerobic shoes in 1987, it was several years before women were invited to "the boys' club in Beaverton" (as Katz calls it) to take a more active role in this marketing process (incidentally, this was a financial success, and by 1992 Nike was the leader in the aerobic niche).[58] In the playground, however, the fun is mostly male and insistently so.

The matrix structure at Beaverton must acknowledge the material force of the Asian women workers even as the images it creates are the material reality that denies this link. While "exposing the technology" might allow one to "see the Air," it also belies the stark contradiction and dependence between two material forces of production, the physicality in the fetishism if you will. Both aspects are integral to the time/space coordinates of the shoe. They are, in Bakhtin's terms, "the knots of narrative that are continually tied and untied" in an apparently empty continuum. Inside the Nike World Campus the designers, consciously or not, wrestle with the implications of this ineluctable link. While they all have a "license to dream,"[59] the designers must work with the contractors and subcontractors to render their imagination profitable.[60] The cost of the material components is one consideration, and Nike has, over the years, developed a highly integrated system for bringing together materials made in different parts of the globe. The production of air pockets or sacs, the air that can be seen, is not trusted to the Asian market: the heart of Nike's "technology" is produced in the United States by a company called "Tetra," then shipped to Asia for assembly in the shoe itself. Lightweight leather substitutes like Durabuck are made by a Japanese affiliate (Nike came up with Durabuck while its lab technicians were working on Michael Keaton's Batboots for *Batman*). And the designers must also take note of regional variations in color tastes around the globe even though preferences among youth culture often change at rates that are out of synch with the production process. Of course, Nike advocates a high degree of homogenization (a mainstay of economies of scale), something facilitated by the power of the brand, but augments its "branding" with what it calls a "psychographic" view of the marketplace. When Nike designers are indulging in "free association," they are also targeting particular psychic profiles. This is one of the ways that masculinism (and other logics of being) gets built into the shoe.

Cultural critics find the hard-edged rationalism of marketing anathema to cultural understanding, and yet it seems to me we seriously misapprehend the cultural logic of capital by suppressing the realities of corporate culture while celebrating somewhat traditional symptoms of art in the marketplace. What the Nike psychographic approach attempts is a breakdown of market segmentation in any one production cycle. This is represented as a triangle whose apex is dominated by Nike's leading profile target: the "hardbody" male "sports driver" between the ages of sixteen and twenty-six. The fetishistic impulses of this group set the standards for the rest (including the women's segments). These young males (again, the primary market is in the United States, but global sales continue to expand) will shell out the $80 to $170 for "top of the line" models (even this last word is in step with the overall logic). This segment is designated "Max," although it is not reserved solely for the Air Max line. The next segment is called "Perf" (performance) and targets athletes and aspiring athletes who might actually gain from the design technologies in the shoe. Beneath this is the "Core" segment, which is also called the middle or "kill" zone, where Nike makes most of its sales. The Core identify with Perf and Max yet usually lack both the body and the psychological investment to make as much use of Nike's high-profile shoes. Eighty percent of Nike's shoes are not used for their intended purpose (Nike always contests this figure, but gradually and grudgingly "fashion" has pushed aside "athletic" in the symbolic of the shoe that Nike presents). At the base of the Nike psychographic triangle is the "Entry" segment, those people who must be weaned onto Nikes by an incessant combination of peer-driven, price-driven, and advertising-driven campaigns. While brand loyalty is difficult in the ephemeral life of an athletic shoe (Max, for instance, may choose another line precisely because Core and Entry are choosing theirs), the psychographic approach is also beholden to the paradox of commodity fetishism in general: the consumer must be made to sustain his or her private fantasy even though he or she covets an object or image that is traded publicly. The savvy theorist has an answer to this dilemma, but then so too do Nike's marketing gurus, like Jim Riswold, who says of the psychography: "[I]t never appeared to me as part of some grand strategy. I mean, it's not nineteenth century philosophy."[61] Quite. Commodity desire gets a lot more help than Marx (or Freud for that matter) could envisage. The magic of the fetish requires the magic of money. In 1993, Nike spent $250 million on promotion.

Most of Nike's shoe lines play to and reinforce conventional definitions of masculinity. Just as the Greeks used Nike to symbolize victory in war (at one point they clipped her wings to keep "victory" in Athens), so Nike laces the sports profile with the language of aggression. Featured shoe models have included Air Assault, Air Barrage, Air Force, Air Magnum Force, Air Raid, and even Air Stab. Other companies in the business market shoes like Run'N'Gun, Predator, Marauder, Shooter, and Slasher. This association of sport and violence is not surprising, but it has other repercussions along the chain of affective responsibility than the epistemic violence that produces the superexploitation of Asian women workers. Before considering that in more detail I want to say more about the design process of a typical Nike shoe.

The Air Carnivore was first dreamed up by Bill Worthington in 1992. The path from idea to actual shoe is laborious: Nike employees once sketched out the process of a shoe's development, and the resulting map, cognitive or otherwise, was sixty feet long. Even then, the designer is weighed down by doubt. Worthington muses, "The question now was whether the consumer would be able to appreciate the technology inside the shoe, or to understand its true personality" (*J* 159). This is something of my own approach in stressing the chronotope of the shoe. Worthington, however, stops short in his assessment of Air Carnivore's time/space coordinates: "People will tell each other about the Carnivore. They'll say, 'Here's a shoe that represents the aggression of sports'" (*J* 159). The aggression takes on another meaning in Pusan, South Korea, where the Carnivores were made. The Carnivores would be one of factory T3's last production runs in 1993 as Nike moved still more production to Indonesia and China. The name of the shoe is a fitting metaphor for Nike's labor practices: by the end of 1993, thirty-five hundred T3 workers, mostly women, had been laid off. The graffiti on the factory walls included the demand: "We want to be compensated for working our brains out!" (*J* 165). They were not.

Meanwhile back in Beaverton, a price structure was worked out for the shoe. Before they were fired (and disavowed in my schema), the T3 workers were paid about $4.50 for every pair of Carnivores made (this labor cost was considered too high alongside the margins available from workers like Sadisah elsewhere in Asia). Nike paid the subcontractor about $29.50 for each pair of Carnivores (60 percent of the price went for product materials). "Landing" the shoe in the consumer market would take another $7.40 (including duties). After taxes and another $15 for running the operation at Nike World Campus, the company would have a $5.50 profit built into the shoe. The retailer would pay about $70 for the Carnivore, the consumer up to $60 more than that depending upon demand and promotions (if the line becomes coveted, the price can soar — a little retail hoarding can exacerbate this effect). While the women in Pusan look for employment in the emerging service industries, Nike will chase "nations farther down the developmental ladder" (*J* 168) — places where a $130 pair of sneakers can still be made, not worn.[62]

The Air Carnivore looks like it could eat jobs and dollars as fast as it creates them. It is predominantly green (when the shoe was first pitched at an annual sporting goods show in Atlanta, the Nike salesperson barked: "Vegetarians beware") and appears to abjure the natural contours of a foot. The bulkiness of the shoe is an illusion, since the synthetic materials used render it quite light. The sole is purple and black and deeply striated into "pods" of supporting rubber. The upper of the shoe is deformed by several straps of Velcro that, like the advertising images, hold the shoe together around the foot. These straps are part of an "anti-inversion" collar that is heavily indebted both to technobabble and to a desire to prevent the ankle from turning should this cross-trainer actually be used for cross-training. The top of the shoe is dominated by a third Velcro strap that sticks, rather than stitches, the subject in the shoe (to complicate the metaphor so heavily analyzed by Derrida and the series of allusions I have made thus far). The inside of the shoe sports a Neoprene sock. This "Dynamic Fit Sleeve" allows the foot to

move and breath inside a shoe whose outside suggests completely the opposite — anti-inversion indeed. We are far removed from Van Gogh's peasant
shoes here, but other peasants are not completely erased: in the belly of the
Air Carnivore a tiny label testifies "Made in South Korea."

The belly of a shoe? Worthington, the designer, is unequivocal: "This shoe
is like an animal. It's like a living, breathing thing instead of an inanimate
consumer product" (*J* 127). Just as the Greeks anthropomorphized a symbol of military success, so our young designer gives life to the fetish of his
desire. And what inspired this fearful symmetry? Worthington, like other
Nike designers, is a self-professed "culture pirate," and, unlike most others
at the World Campus, the designers often draw their imagery from outside the world of sports. The Air Carnivore owed its animal nature as much
to the films *Jurassic Park* and the *Alien* series as it did to man's "natural"
aggression (when Katz interviewed Worthington, the latter's office featured
stills from *Alien*). Worthington also drew up a cartoon character to "image"
the shoe's effect on its owner. An average kid, "Bert Starkweather," becomes
"Bolt Stingwater" (Luke Skywalker?) in his Carnivores and proceeds to "win
drag races on foot and step on people's faces" (*J* 128). Could it be that this
creativity never leaves the shoe but becomes part of its affective image, its
aura, its product-being?

Obviously, the suggestion is not that merely by buying into the image one
becomes the character that the designer projects, but nevertheless, if the main
point of such consumption is not in fact the practical utilization of sporting
technology for sport, then how the shoe is made and marketed stands in (and
contradicts) a corporate claim that is otherwise "ethically neutral." In contemporary capitalism, the violence of representation is also, and always already,
the violence of production and consumption. To separate off the moment
and malevolence of image from the being in production and consumption is
to collude with precisely those avatars of this epoch who claim that image is
everything and representation is, in itself, the sole arbiter of debates about
the mode of production in and outside culture. The chronotope of the shoe
suggests that the time and space of athletic shoe production across the globe
curve toward simultaneity but in fact maintain context-specific criteria that
appear to render them incommensurable. The inside/outside of commodity
production, like the inside/outside of the shoe itself, is indeed inseparable,
but how easy it has become to reduce the sign of worker presence/absence
in production to a label tucked away from view. Two examples may elaborate
the cycle of violence that is endemic to the production and circulation of
commodities at the moment when fetishism must disavow its responsibility
to the Real, and indeed reality.

Nike is taking greater control over its production and distribution operations in Asia as a result of the bad press it has received about the labor

practices it fosters. Yet responsibility is a very relative state of mind in Nike's corporate ideology, since when accused of crass exploitation of its Asian workers, Nike — through its spokespeople — maintains a dogged moral neutrality.[63] This line of argument proposes either that problems occur because of the nature of the market or that Nike can hardly be held responsible for the internal socioeconomic (and political) conditions of the countries where it bases its production operations. The record, as I have already implied, underlines that Nike, like many TNCs, actively seeks and supports conditions of this kind. In addition, a program Nike describes as "Futures" exacerbates poor labor relations because, by securing future orders from retailers six to eight months in advance, the tendency is to speed up production quotas in Asia and reduce flexibility in the hours of work on the line. Other spin-off practices within this mode of production include the nightly confinement of young women workers to the dormitories within the factory grounds.[64] The apex of these violations is, of course, the wage itself, and here violence begets violence. In Serang, near Jakarta, in 1992, Nike workers went on strike and demanded a 15 percent pay increase. While this may sound excessive to some, in fact it amounts to only 24¢ a day at 1992 exchange rates. When the local subcontractor, a South Korean, refused to bargain, the women workers smashed windows at the factory and overturned furniture. Obviously, this is not the only form of resistance available to Asian women workers (as Aihwa Ong has pointedly elaborated in her study of Malaysian factory women);[65] nevertheless, on this occasion, it made the point. Rather than jeopardize the production cycle, the owner caved in.[66] But, as the Korean workers in Pusan testify, workers take a risk with such activity: Nike can "just do it" elsewhere. In the five years leading up to this strike the company had closed twenty of its Asian factories and opened another thirty-five. And anyway, the TNC can say that any industrial action is the result of the contractors' malfeasance, not the company that pulls their strings.

But if the violence of production has material effects on workers like Sadisah, then there is a concomitant violence in the culture of consumption that accompanies it. Nike's psychographic approach to the market has another valence in the symbolic of the shoe: for American inner-city youth racked by unemployment and the lure of drug culture, the athletic shoe offers *status*. Again, the athletic shoe company will claim that the imaging of a particular desire is not an endorsement of its consequences, which are, in the first place, overdetermined by a host of other causal factors. But when Nike's cofounder, William Bowerman, proclaims that one should "play by the rules, but be ferocious," the difficulty is believing that the second emotion can be contained by the civic duty of the first. Nike itself has not "played by the rules" to the extent that (according to *Swoosh*) it has used bribery in the past, kited checks, and avoided custom duties. And, if Nike's labor practices are anything to go by, the rule in athletic shoe production is that there are no rules, at least none that need strict compliance. One reason the slogan "Just do it!" is so enticing is surely that it imagines a world virtually without rules, a world in which "being ferocious" is some Darwinian compulsion. Do we really believe that the slogan "Just do it by the rules" would have the same effect in the competitive frenzy that is the athletic shoe market? And even if the desire to win in athletic competition can be characterized as "ferocious," is that the same desire communicated in such Nike models as "Air Stab" and "Air Carnivore"? The goddess of victory is smiling.

In 1989, Michael Eugene Thomas was strangled to death by his friend David Martin for his $115 pair of Air Jordans. The same year Johnny Bates was shot to death for his Air Jordans, and Raheem Wells was murdered for his Nikes. In Chicago in 1990 there were, on average, fifteen violent crimes committed per month over athletic shoes (up to fifty a month if one includes warm-up jackets and other sports-related garments).[67] Jordan and Spike Lee have been singled out in the past for their Nike advertising campaigns of the late 1980s in which "Just do it!" became a street knowledge that dovetails with the "ferocious" reality of urban crime. In their defense, Nike played the race card by suggesting that it was typical of race bias in the media that African Americans were being blamed for contributing to the violence already heaped at the doorstep of low-income African American communities. To the extent that white celebrities are not routinely criticized for their contributions to cultures of violence (dozens of Hollywood names immediately come to mind), Nike's point is well taken, but the company's race relations contain their own history of bias. As we have seen, while Michael Jordan makes $20 million a year for footwear endorsements, Nike's predominantly white American marketing managers pit Asian workers against one another (Korean versus Indonesian, Indonesian versus Chinese) in a game of wages tag in which the only defining qualities of racial esteem are the profit margins that accrue to their location. In the United States, Operation PUSH, the Chicago-based civil rights group, mounted a campaign against Nike because of its poor record in minority hiring in the United States and because of its failure to provide support in the communities where a disproportionate amount of Nike products are sold (disproportionate in terms of income to sales, not total sales). PUSH also discovered that, at the time, Nike had no African American executives and did not use a single African American–run company to promote its products. Nike was cashing in on the image of African American athletes while cashing out on any responsibility to African American communities in general.[68] Naturally, Nike's public relations department has worked on these issues. (TNCs usually have philanthropic programs — which in some cases provide tax breaks — to ward off the accusation that they are in the business of economic exploitation. And, as mentioned in note 63 to this chapter, the hiring of Andrew Young as [image] consultant is supposed to negate the criticisms of groups like PUSH.) Nevertheless, the larger issue remains, whether a transnational corporation should be held accountable for the forms of identification with its "global power brand."

The fetish is a lure. Nike spends millions of dollars each year to cultivate an "emotional tie" (as Phil Knight describes it) to the athletic shoe but disavows this connection at the point where its psychography facilitates an irrational logic of possession. Yet this is intrinsic to the commodity form and does not resolve itself in fine-tuning an image attached (with Velcro) to it. To murder someone for their Nike shoes is irrational in the extreme but is symptomatic of, among other socioeconomic factors, the culture of possession in general. Van Gogh's shoes may well have symbolized the eclipse of valorized peasant communities (certainly this is Heidegger's belief), but the fetishistic overinvestment in the athletic shoe is no less significant: it conjures the madness and malevolence of a particular form of globalism that is itself deracinating peasant communities in different parts of the world *simultaneously and in the same affective space.* In the chronotope of the shoe, pricking stitches Sadisah to Thomas: the maps must be redrawn to account for this.

Commodity fetishism is not the same as the psychological compulsion sketched by Freud, but the centrifugal aura of the athletic shoe within contemporary transnational capitalism shows how one may be dialogically implicated with the other. Branding accentuates this overlap in the psychic and economic coordinates of the newest world order — a relationship that is crucial to athletic shoe culture. Violence, epistemic and real, is not an accidental by-product of the matrix of contemporary commodity production but is vital to it, while the "costs" of production and consumption are necessarily rendered invisible or inconsequential. For Nike, the desire to expand sales far outweighs the use value of its athletic shoes. In 1993, 77 percent of American young men said they wanted a pair of Nikes (even if they could not afford to buy them); some knew more than a dozen of the models available that year; others even knew the stock numbers. In the "teenager to young adult male" bracket, Americans owned more than ten pairs of sporting footwear *each.* And every year another seventy million pairs of athletic shoes are sold in the American market alone.

Michael Haines has a Nike obsession. When interviewed by Katz he had already collected almost forty pairs. Interestingly, his "fetish" (as his mother calls it) began in the early 1980s when he first spotted the see-through air sole of the Air Max. His desire, piqued by the appearance of absence, became at one point almost uncontrollable — he was forced to hide new pairs around the house, and, when that aroused suspicion, he persuaded his father to buy them instead. Most of the shoes have never been worn and are revered almost solely for their associative effects. To read what Haines has to say about his shoes is to face the superaddressee of commodity production: "They have to face backward on the shelf because they're so much more...beautiful from behind"; "...if I could have a new pair every day...I still love to come home during school breaks and come up here to open the doors" (of the cupboard that houses his collection); "I love them. I love thinking about opening the box for the first time. I love taking them out. Just talking about them gets me...I don't know..." (*J* 262–63). The sexual dynamic of Haines's attachment may be exaggerated, but few CEOs in the athletic shoe business would be upset by a desire directly connected to a company's advertising machine. How much commodity desire is enough desire? Can this be calibrated, or is the love of these shoes incalculable, such that the violence of the sweatshop and the street is an inadvertent by-product for which responsibility is an empty concept? Nike does not merely satisfy a need for athletic footwear; it deliberately creates a need far in excess of what is necessary (this, of course, is one of the meanings of capitalism). Yet conventional wisdom would have it that Haines hurts no one by coveting his shoes. In truth, his personal fixation has been purchased, and in that exchange his desire is globally localized (to borrow once more from contemporary TNC lore), just as Sadisah's labor has been interpellated in an international network of capital exchange. The names and the products may change, but as long as the logic of these connections remains predominantly unimagined, then the commodity fetish will continue to be naturalized: the ontology of the commodity, the Being of the shoe, will present itself as a normative Being of culture. And what seems like an adjunct to cultural discourse is in fact what silently defines it.

Sadisah does not speak to us in these pages, and neither do the shoes (although, on this point, the Nike designers are close to the philosophy of art proposed by Heidegger, Jameson, and Derrida).[69] The athletic shoe will pass out of TNC production exploitation not because people will stop running but because the "victory" invoked is not about running.[70] Indeed, the chronotope of the shoe is only about the essence of the shoe at all to the extent that such a commodity is a narrative about the international division of labor. Similarly, Indonesia is not miraculously mapped (even as it is integrated into global circuits of commodity production and exchange) by the affective points of time and space that I have sketched above (and no handy reference to shadow theater will wrest it from that chiaroscuro).[71] But to imagine the links in the aura of the shoe is what must be risked if criticism is to be responsibly positioned in global analysis. For the specular commodity, the chronotope becomes something of a heuristic device, "the place where the knots of narrative are tied and untied," but a place that is always displaced by the logic of desire in the marketplace and by the desire for a logic that is not stitched by authoritarian regimes of truth. The imagination required is less sure-footed not only because the product-being of the contemporary commodity is dispersed fantastically, but because there is no language adequate to the global representation of the worker. While Nike has global imagery there is yet no global imaginary that can transform the developmental ladder that the TNC typically exploits. And merely by detailing the deaths that result from a psychic overinvestment in the commodity one does not break the production of desire that informs it. What, then, is the point of chronotopic critique?

I have borrowed chronotope from Bakhtin as he borrowed it from Einstein, "as a metaphor (almost, but not entirely)"[72] to draw together seemingly disparate elements of the world system attached (artists, workers, philosophers, inner-city youth, and cultural critics alike) by affective responsibility. We have no alibi for this responsibility (the boycott of selected consumer items is besides the point) because, as Bakhtin reminds us, we cannot claim to be anywhere else but where we are in Being. Materialism must do much more than express concern for the wasted humanity of capitalist production (a somewhat sentimental, humanist answerability) by making the deracinated Being of the commodity form imaginable. But this responsibility is also about meaning, which Bakhtin suggests can become part of our social experience only when it takes on "the form of a sign." The shoe is not perhaps the "hieroglyph" that Bakhtin had in mind, and that is partly why his formulation has been refigured in my argument by the "hieroglyph" that Marx identified. Just as our philosophers overlook the maker, so Bakhtin's fetishization of the novel placed formal limits on the range of social experience imaginable. That the novel can conjure the world of commodity culture is undeniable; the test of a geopolitical imaginary is whether it can imagine how the commodity can conjure in the opposite direction. This is not ultimately about the cognitive abilities of the cultural critic (or his or her humanist inclinations) but, more importantly, about forms of collective reciprocity disrupting the aura of the commodity that anxiously purports to embrace a world economy. To imagine the world otherwise continues to be the challenge, not by individual volition, but by alternative forms of socialization. Only then will the shoe be on the other foot.

The "chronotope of the shoe" suggests that materialism must take an imaginative and cognitive risk in elaborating the logic of commodity circulation. In part, this is in the spirit of Marx's own attempt to imbricate a theory of the objective and subjective in fetishism. As Balibar has noted, the risk for Marx was a theoretical "confusion" (of science, metaphysics, and morality). There is no doubt that I have maintained some of that confusion here, not out of a blind allegiance to Marx's procedural errors, but out of a belief that the logic of the commodity demands an intense negotiation of its subjective and objective Being. There will always be an element of confusion to this extent, but each time it is specifiable within the history of the commodity form. The confusion is a function of the generalized equivalence that the commodity requires in order to circulate, but the form of that equivalence will mutate according to specifiable coordinates within an otherwise chaotic theoretical vacillation. It has been my argument that those coordinates are now driven by globalization, even if this does not represent the panoply of capitalist production. Ultimately, this does not end the theoretical vacillation produced in the doubled moment of subjective/objective articulation; rather it intensifies it by showing how the globalization of fetishistic desire and dis-avowal now threatens the logical integrity of what has often been the ward of social ideology — namely, the nation-state. The aura of the shoe in this example doesn't just question the aphanisis of the worker but throws into relief the structural compulsions of the state as it struggles with its own os-cillation — an economic and social wavering produced by the eruptions of the world system. Materialism's quandary between ideology and fetishism is now writ large in the hesitation between the commodity and the state. For materialism it perhaps comes as no surprise that the worker is kicked by both sides. But the politics of resistance must be reimagined at the moment when that violence is imagined into obsolescence.

CHAPTER FIVE

(   ) OF GHOSTS

I do not believe I have ever spoken of "indeterminacy,"
whether in regard to "meaning" or anything else. Undecidability is something else again. While referring to what I have
said above and elsewhere, I want to recall that undecidability is always a *determinate* oscillation between possibilities (for
example, of meaning but also of acts).   —JACQUES DERRIDA

Capitalism as a world system is haunted. One hundred and fifty years after
Marx and Engels's celebrated invocation of the specter haunting Europe, it
torments the world. Derrida opines that there is no *Dasein* of the specter,
and this, he believes, is why a Marxism that eschews the eschatology and
ontology of Being must always return — must remain, in spirit, to haunt
the contradictions of capitalist rationality.[1] It is an intriguing proposition and
one that will certainly lurk in the pages that follow. One wonders, however,
whether the ghost that Derrida conjures — the spirit of a Marxism internally differentiated (or *différantiated*) by the equivocation of the "event" of
revolution (deferred then, within a structure of oscillation) — is a compensatory mechanism. It is not a personal compensation (Derrida always has an
easy answer for that) but a conjuring wrought by the stunning absence of
the event interpellated by Marx and Engels. Where there is no communism,
what is left but to inure the spirit of its absence? A millennial materialism
begins with this fact (as startling as ice cold water on a face quick from
slumber): the claims of "actual existence" (of socialism, of communism),
the bulwark of a traditional ontology in Marxist thought, lie almost completely disgraced across the landscape of history. And this is why the spirit of
Marxism, the specter that haunts, is a problem of philosophy, a philosophy
that struggles to articulate a process of political practice without succumbing
to the mystique of interpretation, the dead-end that the eleventh thesis on
Feuerbach explicitly warns against. Marxism oscillates now most forcefully
around and between the elements of a philosophy that must remain dubi-
ously inchoate and incoherent. "Without doubt" this sounds like the worst
politics of all — a quagmire as deep and muddy as the state bureaucracies of

"actually existing socialism" had become. Yet it is precisely the reinscription of this philosophical problem (What is the philosophy of Marxism?) that traces the differential space of the political in millennial materialism. The vacillation of the moment is an index not of the teleology that must be but of a constellation that *is*, an architectonic of what structures contemporary reality. Thus, the ghost is manifest in the way the philosophical problem is posed, and not simply as a projection of spirit onto an otherwise foreboding political situation: the absence of "actual existence."[2]

Oscillation as a concept elaborates a philosophical trace in the forms of praxis meant to subtend it. The restlessness is the spirit that looks over the shoulder of the forms of the political now possible. This ambivalence, a philosophical compulsion, is more pronounced in moments of crisis or, as I would contend, in *interregna*. But it is not just philosophy that marks contingent possibilities. As I tried to emphasize with the chronotope of the shoe, the worker within the logic of transnationalism is confined to spectrality as never before — these billions of ghosts who live and breathe but who do not devolve into classes, and yet whose concrete individuality cannot corporealize except through abstract conjunction. We will not sentimentalize the once-occurrent Being of the workers of the world, as if that injunction might realize the "Unite!" of the *Communist Manifesto* — which was only ever, and can only be, a provisor (no *Dasein* indeed). But "the time is out of joint," as Shakespeare/Hamlet/Derrida tell us, and philosophy speaks to the break in that continuum, to the specificity of the worker's unrepresentability now unhinged from the state's ardent and arrogant delegation — those phantom states, as Derrida terms them, that have "infiltrated and banalized themselves everywhere" (*SOM* 83).

Similarly, as my exegesis on the body has indicated, the incarnation of a body subject — one that disarticulates the decorporealization of capitalism, the empty flesh of value extraction — oscillates within the history of materialist theory as a conceptual shade of the historical agents it attempts to recorporealize. It is not mindless metaphoricity or torpid tropism that puts these spirits into play, but the oscillations of materialist thought itself. When Balibar boldly declares, "There is no Marxist philosophy and there never will be,"[3] he draws attention not only to Marx's antagonistic relationship to traditional philosophy (the Hegelian dialectic, etc.) but also to the nature of Marxist critical faculties, its dynamism with respect to historical determination: it cannot resolve itself into a philosophical system qua philosophy. Indeed, with respect to philosophy within Marxism (as Balibar shows on the question of ideology), Marxism is beside itself. Its systematicity is bound, paradoxically, by a spiritual double, an other Being that constantly troubles or undermines the philosophical underpinnings of its social prescriptions. The specters of Marx are not just the workers who do not have a social form for their socialization or realization, but the philosophical ghosts that Marxism cannot simply put to rest within its critical framework without collapsing it.

What follows is a philosophical answer to the double entendre of the ever-more-prescient question, Whither Marxism? In the ghostly presence of philosophy in Marxism, Marxism itself opens out onto different plains of social explanation. The danger, or vacillation, comes with the tenor of philosophy (which is why Balibar's statement must be closely observed) whose very language mimes the floating signifier's metonymic dance. I do not wish to save materialism from a certain irreducible play in language (it is social praxis itself that exceeds the linguistic predilections of discourse), but I do want to outline some of the conceptual instabilities that sign back across philosophy's semiosis of the social. On one level, to acknowledge the ghosts of Marxism is only to reincarnate the founding spirit of Marx and Engels's injunction; on another, to take seriously the spirit of the letter is to address the Being and the space of Marxism now. The question Whither Marxism? does not necessitate fatalism: it requires an exorcism.

Specters of Marx and *Whither Marxism?* are two volumes that came out of a conference conceived by Bern Magnus and Stephen Cullenberg at the University of California, Riverside, in 1993, and, to be sure, Derrida's spectral philosophy in the first volume haunts the collection of essays that compose the second book.[4] These are not, however, "companion" volumes as the editors contend. Derrida's contribution is in the spirit of the question posed by the collection and the conference, but it is also "out of joint," to use the epigraph that Derrida borrows from Hamlet and interrogates within his text. In the haunting presence of the Derridean mode, *Specters of Marx* fulfills two practical aims: first, it "proves" (and there is always already a beyond a "reasonable" doubt) that Marx, like Derrida, was fascinated by the history of ghosts (*Gespenstergeschichte*), a penchant that begins and permeates the materialism in his prose; second, Derrida's interpretation functions as an ambivalent shadow of the arguments entertained in the collection of essays, something that is less a "companion" and more a principle of "nonidentification." That this is in step with the general trajectory of deconstruction is obvious; what is less clear is whether it is the logic of Marxism, the *philosophies* of Marx as Balibar puts it, that draws or conjures the spirit of deconstruction toward it. In a strange way, what keeps coming back is the tendency that Michael Ryan identified almost two decades ago: that the kind of Marxism that deconstruction disables is the kind that deserves to be disabled.[5] Nevertheless, this ghostly return, this *revenant,* does not make deconstruction the autocritical function of Marxism, as some might wish, for if poststructuralist theory has deservedly pounced on the more flagrant examples of essentialism within materialist theory, then Marxism (from Ryan's position of "critical articulation" to Spivak's, Jameson's, and Eagleton's various disarticulations) has passionately resisted the idealism of textuality and textualism. My point is that the relationship is not resolvable in the way that two "companions" might embrace one another after sustained disagreement. The impasse is intrinsic to the methodologies at issue. In this sense, the ghostly metaphors that animate the prose of Derrida and Marx are not stylistic trivialities: they mark the conceptual difficulties of the "*philosophies of Marx.*"

Now, to the extent that Ryan has already demonstrated the undecidability written into the conceptual terrain of Marxism, the problems posed by Derrida in *Specters of Marx* are quite literally prescribed. Ryan's discussion of the law of value, for instance, preempts in a rigorous way Derrida's somewhat casual reading of *Capital* on the question of the table as an example of the commodity form.[6] But, as I hope the analysis of the aura of the shoe has confirmed, there remains a mystery in the commodity that the hyperreality of the present does not simply sublate. Derrida addresses new contingencies not just because the ghost is his primary touchstone (which nicely expresses the paradox of its deployment — it is immaterial and cannot be touched) but because the nature of the relation articulated has profoundly changed in light of the events of the late 1980s and early 1990s. What may have been read as a prediction in Ryan's uneasy rapprochement is now a condition of the present. The ghost of philosophy, of a certain spirit in philosophy, has become almost worldly in light of the collapse of communism's social mandate. The era is not necessarily one of philosophical reflexion, however (except to the extent that reflexion remains part of the problem — According to what logic?), but is one where philosophy may speak to the process of spiriting away that some Western ideologues seem to foster (and thus, fear a return in Poland, Russia, Hungary, etc.).

I will not focus on all of the implications of Derrida's text (precisely because they might conspire to conjure away a politics that must be rethought, not rejected), but I do want to consider in some detail how "thinking the ghost" might reanimate materialist critique. I will do this obliquely in a number of ways. First, I want to examine the status of "class" among the specters of Marx that Derrida invokes and read this, not into the "companion" volume of the conference, but into Balibar's essay "From Class Struggle to Classless Struggle?" (which, coincidentally, also begins with the question, "Whither Marxism?").[7] I will argue that, far from going away or disappearing, the dislocations of the present have *incarnated* the question of class in a historically specific manner. Second, if as a concept oscillation partakes of a deterritorialization of space (and is what Deleuze and Guattari describe as a geophilosophy in that regard),[8] what is its relationship to the worlding of the world as world system? I have already pressed the issue in terms of imagination, which makes class and class subjects like Sadisah less a cognitive fantasy; but what if the desire to imagine such a world is itself implicated in the philosophical systematization of subjection? This is not simply a question about the specter of Marxism's roots in the Western Enlightenment, but addresses what the consequences of global integration are for a materialism that must learn from its conceptual oscillations. To think globally one must sense the world differently from the synaptic largesse of capital. Here, politically, what comes back to materialism is the ghostly apparition of "freedom" or "emancipation," which was an assumption that became dogmatic in some of its expressions, but now returns in the form of a different philosophical dilemma, as something that cannot yet be thought of except in ghostly fashion. Jean-Luc Nancy has suggested that this requires a revolution in thinking itself, but only if we free this call from the voluntarisms of yesteryear.[9] Finally, "thinking the ghost" will bring me back to ideology, the oscillation with which I began. Here, however, the exorcism is on the order of production and will register a materialism caught between its thought and consequences. Lest this sound too much like the familiar theory/practice binary I should add that I will read this against the philosopher's tendency to hypostatize this moment as a discursive dead-end. In oscillation, all roads do not lead straight back to the signifier: reality keeps making detours and providing alternative intensities. This remains the trajectory if not the answer to the specters that haunt us.

Class is the most ghostly concept within Marxism, and I will not rehearse that history (history back in its hearse?) in order to justify its centrality. Class, of course, is not a thing but a concept of relation (something with enough tempero-spatial import to connect it with our chief conceptual tool), which has made it all the more easy, apparently, to spirit it away according to the dictates of hegemonies of various kinds. As Balibar notes, quoting from Spinoza: "There is more than one way to perish."[10] If we have indeed produced social orders that construct classes and class divisions, then those systems and their classes are condemned to expire at some point in history (that is to say, they are historical systems). But there lies the trick of the spirit of class, and one that resists the eschatology that seems synonymous with such statements. The death of a world system does not correspond to the hasty analogy of our fated selves. Class does not live in the same way as its breathing constituents. This is why we must separate class from its experience or identification. The lack of the visibility of class is quite widespread today, but that is different from the object of class for science, or for Marxism for science. But surely, this does not make class a ghost.

Indubitably so. Class cannot be thought as a ghost; it is an example, however, of how to think the ghost. For Derrida, the scrupulous philosopher, the thingness of the ghost is its relationship to the Thing, not its identity as a thing. The distinction is important, not least because it helps to separate identity from presence. The specter is a special kind of ghost, for it appears as a "stealthy and ungraspable visibility of the invisible" ("la visibilité furtive et insaisissable de l'invisible" [*SDM* 27]) — let us call it the spirit of the Thing. Thinking the ghost is precisely this coming to grips with the ungraspable. Deconstructive practice is founded (and founders) on this difficulty: it is a calculation without rules between the incalculable and the calculable. It seems to me that although Derrida once said that he had found no "satisfactory protocols for reading Marx,"[11] those protocols seem to have found him; they have come back; they keep coming back first as a dimly remembered utopianism and now as a fully fledged critical approach. The specters of Marx are the materialist injunction of iterability. But does class, like communism, return in this way?

Here Derrida is less useful. He tracks the Marxist invocation of the specter in the *Communist Manifesto, The Eighteenth Brumaire, Capital,* and *The German Ideology* in a variety of ways (he is particularly jubilant about the Stirner/Marx conjunction), but his critique is also a symptom of the "out-of-jointness" of our time by eliding the importance of class to the spectrality he otherwise quite forcefully presents. Note, it is not the primacy of class that is at issue, but its constitutive role in modes of socialization. Nevertheless, the implications of Derrida's approach must be engaged and/or otherwise extended, not least of which because the theoretical question he addresses cannot be answered by Marxism alone (a protocol that says that a philosophy cannot adjudicate its own meaning). This much Balibar admits when he asks the question "Whither Marxism?" but this is also why he attends to Marxism's philosophical disposition in *The Philosophy of Marx* by using the following formula (between the calculable and the incalculable):

> L'activité de Marx, ayant rompu avec une certaine forme de philosophe, ne l'a pas conduit vers un système unifié, mais vers une *pluralité* au moins virtuelle de doctrines, dans lesquelles ses lecteurs et ses successeurs se sont trouvés embarrassés. De même, elle ne l'a pas conduit vers un discours uniforme, mais vers une oscillation permanente entre l'en deçà et l'au-delà de la philosophie. Par *en deçà* de la philosophie, entendons ici l'énoncé de propositions comme des "conclusions sans prémisses," ainsi qu'auraient dit Spinoza et Althusser. (*PDM* 6)

> [Having broken with a certain form of philosophy, Marx was not driven by his theoretical activity toward a unified system, but to a virtual *plurality* of doctrines that his readers and successors have found perplexing. In the same way, it did not lead him to a uniform discourse, but to a permanent oscillation between "falling short of" and "moving beyond" philosophy. By *falling short* of philosophy, I mean

stating propositions as "conclusions without premises," as Spinoza and Althusser would have said it. (*POM* 4)]

If it seems as though I am moving Marxism in and around deconstruction, it is only because the latter, in spirit, moves to and within it. As Ryan notes, "Marxism, as a historical mode of theory and practice is, from the outset, undecidable, that is, open to extension according to what history offers" (21). But iterability has almost always given way to irritability where Marxism and deconstruction are concerned. Where the latter disagrees wherever it finds eschatology and positivism, the former deplores a vacuum of tropology where social theory should be. But Balibar, nevertheless, offers a vision not just of a Marxism beset by the weight of its contradictory theorizations, but of one whose ambivalent relationship to philosophy, "short of and beyond," calls it into question in such a way as to open out its concepts into the realm of the political. The oscillations of Marxism are therapeutic for philosophy in the sense that they are homeopathic. And this is as true for philosophy with respect to Marxism, as long as we keep in mind that in the Pharmakon of ideas the line between poison and cure is itself an undecidable ("an oscillation between possibilities").

I have written about Derrida's use of Hamlet's quip "The time is out of joint" elsewhere as a suitable if problematic description for the disjunctions and dislocations of the present.[12] Central to this out-of-jointness is the diminution of class within materialism. Within theory, much of this can be placed at the doorstep of cultural materialism (a doorstep that already has tripped up a good many residents on their way in). But, of course, it is the objective conditions of the world system that have been pivotal in this regard, and this is why class goes away and comes back as a ghost in Balibar's critique (this is what is so odd in Derrida's speculative and spectral investigation: class is the ghost who is precisely not addressed). Most of these factors are well known: the deindustrialization of large sectors of Western Europe and North America accompanied by the burgeoning of service industries, de-skilling, and "acceptable levels" of unemployment (which has often meant recalculating the figures until an acceptable level is found!); the transnationalism and flexible accumulation strategies of major corporations that have decentered (or obliterated) traditional communities of opposition (attributable both to location and to organized resistance — unions, for instance); the financialization of capital circulation aided and abetted by technological advances and outright speculation that has denatured traditional class discourse; the rise and fall of nation-states that have both nurtured and malnourished consciousness of social position (to think the ghost is already to imagine one's community otherwise); and the emergence of several competing political discourses that have, if not turned the world upside down, made it imperative and possible not to think in the same way about social change. These factors are only viable causes for the diminution of class as they are articulated simultaneously at the social, political, and economic levels of theoretical analysis. This is indeed part of Balibar's approach, but, as we have noted, the first line of reflection is focused on the conceptual ambivalence of class as it is developed in Marx's writing.

When Balibar notes that classes have lost their "*visible*" identity (his emphasis), we know that it is visibility itself that is in question. Marxist critique depends on "grasping" the visible of the invisible — that the illusion of classlessness is a reality of the concept of class, something *both* historically determined and intrinsic to its ambivalent formulation. On one level, thinking the ghost means understanding the incommensurableness of the concept with its instantiation (again, the space between the calculable and the incalculable); on another level, it means separating a theoretical invocation from a historical conjuration. At a séance one may be predisposed to receive the spirit one desires, but in history class comes and goes (as Derrida notes, the specter always "begins by coming back" ["il commence par revenir"] [*SDM* 32]) according to a more complex pathology.

Balibar approaches the problem in two ways, by examining the contradictory logic of proletarianization and by picking away at the structural identity of capitalist class formations. In both cases he roots the conceptual instability in a reading of Marx, but the problem then becomes whether the present conjuncture provides an exit to the various kinds of impasse he identifies or whether these ambiguities are intrinsic to the methodology at stake. As I have tried to indicate throughout this study, much depends on the interpretative gambit here, overdetermined as it is by the intense oscillations that characterize if not define contemporary existence. I will provide a couple of brief examples from Balibar, but in the main I am interested in pushing the implications of his critique a good deal further than the first circle of his inquiry. It is only in this way that the Marxism he elucidates might be seen to haunt even the unlikely discourses of contemporary philosophy.

Following my exposition of the different interpretive levels of oscillation, it is clear that the initial conditions for the theorization of class in Marx's works (and subsequently, therefore, in Marxian extrapolations) are riven by contingent fluctuations so that we see a stark difference in formulations between what Balibar calls the "historic-political" writings and *Capital* itself. In Balibar's view, the former "suffer indirectly from the circumstances of their writing. The pictures they paint are like an adaptation of a basic historical scheme to the peripeteia of empirical history (for the most part European history), and they oscillate constantly between a posteriori rectification and anticipation" ("Class," 159). In these documents, the immediate conditions of theory produce what Balibar describes as personification, which makes it strategically easier to array one class against another as a series of symmetrical agents. This means plugging in the theory to examples that tend to render the characteristics of class ambivalent (think of the personification of Louis Napoleon for instance). *Capital* never quite lets go of the strategy of personification (to this extent, it too partakes of the "peripeteia of empirical history") but, crucially, presents a class struggle in fundamental "dissymmetry." Whether bourgeois or capitalist (these terms themselves are in oscillation) the ruling orders in *Capital* do not constitute *one social group*. In contrast, argues Balibar, the proletariat or working class (as we have seen, another oscillatory scission) appear always already constituted in the valorization of capital and capital accumulation. In a sense, suggests Balibar, there is only one class in *Capital,* and that is the working class (indeed, Marx says as much in his postface to the second edition).[13]

Certainly, the large sections of *Capital* devoted to the processes of proletarianization (the appropriation of surplus value, the expropriation of working skills, and the production of insecurity through competition) support Balibar's contention regarding dissymmetry. But, in personifying the capitalists and depersonalizing the workers in order that the latter might be more properly recognized for their group characteristics, Marx presents this dissymmetry in a contradictory form, one that comes with a significant risk. In *Capital,* the processes of proletarianization are not identical with a subject of those processes. What the processes do is produce effects that provide the character of class without its subject. Ironically, the dissymmetry that Balibar identifies has an opposite implication: *Capital* is about one class that is unrepresentable.

That labor is indeed nonidentical with itself is a function of capital: that is what it does to workers. But Balibar attempts to explain this identity in difference (or the indifference toward an identity) by giving some order to the oscillation he has so deftly revealed. Thus, for instance, the ambivalence of class is predicated on "an oscillation between economism and politicism" ("Class," 165), but then the revolutionary proletariat comes in as "a unity of contraries": a correspondence between the "working class as an 'economic' class and the proletariat as a 'political subject.'" On the one hand, this is precisely the conceptual limit of the dialectic that says, as Balibar does, "this oscillation cannot be preserved"; on the other, it opens class identity to a range of presumptive discourses that ceaselessly announce then stand in for the unity that the dialectic desires. I would argue that there is another way to understand the ambivalence at issue and that is by using oscillation as an *operative concept* for the logic that Marx sketches out rather than viewing it as an aberration, that which is remedied by a form of willed stasis. Balibar suggests that "for the theory to be intelligible and applicable, it must be *fixed* at one point or another" ("Class," 165), but this could be done as a function of oscillation itself rather than as its dialectical sublation. I have already suggested that oscillation as a concept encompasses such a point, in Adorno's homeostasis for instance, but here it might relieve the tendency (epitomized in the incidence of "actual existence") to hypostatize a revolutionary subject as a handy agglomeration of a ceaseless equivocation. If the "last instance" arrives, it is internally structured by the ambivalence that provides its very possibility. This is why the proletariat "appears," but at the moment of its annihilation (in the sense that its self-identity is the moment of transformation from capitalism). That the dialectic necessitates a limit is not incompatible with the conceptual range of oscillation, but one must maintain a sense of dynamism in the model or risk deemphasizing the processes at its heart and the openness to new evidence, the eventness of events. In light of the "end" that readings of the Cold War now encourage, this is not an insignificant theoretical endeavor.[14]

Ultimately, this is what Balibar attempts in his formulation of class and class struggle as a "process of transformation without pre-established end" ("Class," 168), but only after granting the opposite inclination precedence. In essence, what he identifies as speculative empiricism necessitates the spectral empiricism I advocate here. Although Balibar's approach is at one with the general premises of oscillation as concept, he draws back at those moments when oscillation might seem to threaten the logical integrity of his materialism. This, I believe, is a methodological error. This is true both at the interpretative level, the search for theoretical symptoms of oscillation, and at the conceptual level — that oscillation constellates an array of strategies that do no resolve themselves into a closed system. To some extent, this is indeed a "Marx beyond Marx" (the term that Balibar borrows from Negri's reading of *Grundrisse*), a materialism at or beyond the borders of its normative claims. It is, more specifically, a Marxism beyond Marxism because it suggests that some of the interpretative claims of the materialist tradition have themselves been overreached (although, for philosophical reasons, this is not a case of simple transcendence).[15] This is not only a basic reaction to the frenzied transformations of late capitalism (many of which are a mask for otherwise good old-fashioned plodding exploitation), but also a proactive theoretical strategy that haunts the dynamism of materialism itself. That this dynamism is part of the machinery of capitalism (as some examples from Marx below will emphasize) is undeniable, but one must keep the principle separate from its purpose. If, as Balibar contends, one of Marx's key discoveries is that societies are based not on general interests but "on the regulation of conflicts" (and thus form a history of class war), then materialism must not mimic capitalism's regulative desire but disrupt it (in terms of both its model and application). While the term is flamboyant, "oscillate wildly" is a condition of such disruption.

Marx certainly details the oscillatory compulsions of capital. What Balibar does is elucidate, symptomatically, the conceptual oscillations of Marx's approach, and, as I have maintained, this is a service to materialism much greater (and usually more sincere) than the incarnations and voluntarist embrace of the "new" or non-Marxist in theory (on this point at least, Ahmad's contribution undeniably recommends itself).[16] But the next step is a more nuanced understanding of the underpinnings of such conceptual sway, one that recognizes an integrity in oscillation that incoherence would seem to deny. This reading, itself caught between the calculable and the incalculable, is the space where ghosts return, the spectral becoming that cannot be laid to rest by the regulatory oscillations of capitalist logic.

The reason class is absent from Derrida's proto-Marxist text and entirely central to Balibar's symptomatic exegesis is because of the status of philosophy in their approaches. It is a question not of choosing between the two on this occasion (although there are significant political consequences at that level) but of understanding the spectrality marking that difference and, I will maintain, mutual imbrication. In part this is a function of the texts deemed appropriate to the reincarnation of Marx and Marxism for the next millennium. Derrida concentrates on the exchange with Stirner and *The Eighteenth Brumaire* primarily because there the spectral is, as it were, manifest in the content of the discussions (the latter is so chock-full of ghostly references that it is a veritable founding text of *Gespenstergeschichte*). For Balibar, the ghosting occurs at the conceptual level by reading Marxist principles beside themselves, as part of a theoretical process that does not quite congeal (as he notes, "[T]hat doctrine does not exist" [*POM* 117]). Whether through representation or through implication, both share the same unspoken creed: class is ethereal.

But in Derrida the ethereality of class does not take place just in the representational paradox of the specter (the visibility of the invisible): it is also produced in the form of his reading. The shadow of class in Derrida's approach is manifest in both the texts he uses and the displacements he enacts. When he foregrounds Marx's discussion of money, for instance, Derrida is drawn to its apparitional status in capital's "movement of idealization" (*SOM* 100). Paper is rendered as gold in a process of magical simulacra that Marx insistently links to the logic of capital itself. This would be enough indeed to take seriously the symbolic structures of capital, but of course in Marx's argument (chiefly *Capital,* volume 1), he accentuates what is crucial in money's "illusion" for capital: what it can purchase in terms of labor power. In other words, the symbolic structure of the criterion returns to the question of the worker and then to the process of proletarianization itself. The magical conversion of paper into gold is an equivalent of money's transformation into capital but with one key difference: the spectrality of the latter has a direct, fleshly embodiment (e.g., "[L]abor power exists only as a capacity of the living individual" [274]; or "[T]he owner of labor power is mortal" [275]). The use value of labor power is its real manifestation (*Äusserung*), just as necromancy might profit from the tissue of the living. Again, the importance of this step is not that humanity comes into play (and therefore, by association, humanism), but that the possibility of class resides in this commodity exchange, money for labor. Thus, Marx is less fascinated by the symbolic exchange qua symbol — the visibility of the invisible — than by elaborating its implications for socioeconomic formations. And in that direction Derrida gives up the ghost.[17]

Similar displacements occur in Derrida's discussion of the party, the state, and revolution. In each instance, the agency and actualization of opposition remain appropriately specular but unspecified, ghostly but unalloyed. The specter haunting Europe takes shape in the party that embodies the precepts of the *Communist Manifesto,* but does that mean that the Communist Party itself is the most feared form of those principles? Tactically, of course, the time called for this alignment, but in subsequent prefaces to the document both Marx and Engels suggest that its original conjuncture does not exhaust the possible manifestations of the specter.[18] And this spectrality is a product of the nature of class struggle, not the name of the party that takes such struggle as a central issue. The *Manifesto* answers the "nursery tale of the Specter of Communism" with a revolutionary document, but it is class struggle, not the party, that constitutes the spirit of the specter, the spectral grounds of ruling-class fear. The same displacement occurs in Derrida's invocation of the state, which is read as a "correlative" of the party in this context. This is the bad side, or the bad ghost, of communism whose manifestations have often produced a malevolent instantiation of state practice. But once again, this is not a "correlative" of the specter that haunts. Parties and states will die, but how can the specter of communism according to Derrida's approach and indeed according to the reasons for Marx and Engels's characterization in the first place? Derrida is surely right to underline the "equivocation of the event" (*SOM* 104) that is revolution (and not just because this is a function of oscillation in the social), but why has he no place for class and class struggle in the elaboration of that event? The specter of unity that ends the *Manifesto* is not about parties or states: it is about a force of history that will keep coming back as long as certain forms of economic exploitation depend upon its suppression. This is the difference between a specter and an empty space.[19]

For Balibar, the ethereal in class is entirely dependent upon a principle of historicity: class struggles and class identities are conjunctural.[20] According to this thesis, "class struggles organized as class struggles" are rare equivocations that themselves have been spectralized (as a historical motor) alongside "a more complex and *ambivalent* dialectic of 'mass conflict'" (xx; emphasis added). It is easy to see why this might be read as a logic of defeat. In a historical conjuncture when the forms of class politics have been recoded almost beyond recognition, the "equivocation of the event" finds class struggle itself a margin within a margin. Class struggle may inform a politics of opposition in the present, but it does not drive it. The problem can be formulated in the following way: class struggle in history, like class struggle in theory, is not self-present with the moment of its perception or inception. Ideologically, class struggle can be interpellated and foregrounded as a central cause, but its true nature lies in its conjunctural effects. What can be read as a rationalization of defeat is simultaneously a recognition that forms of struggle are historical through and through. Thus, the spectrality of class struggle is not undermined by the claims of its "disappearance" from the map of the political: the specter persists as an integer of the forms of its possibility.[21]

But all this ghostly (and ghastly) metaphoricity is not really about class, is it? Surely we are trampling on Marx's concept of class by troping it. The invocation of the specter by Marx in his writing (in the *Communist Manifesto, The German Ideology, The Eighteenth Brumaire of Louis Napoleon,* etc.) is part of his politics of theory. Materialism is not just a theory of materiality but also about processes of materialization and dematerialization (or corporealization and decorporealization, as we saw earlier). It is a theory (philosophical and more) about "becoming." Marx makes the conjuring of ghosts a symptom of the materialization of theory. It is not some idle image but an active component of his explanatory critique. The point is not to collapse back this theorization into the discursive trope that is its possibility, but to understand the trope as an operative logic in the model proposed. The reason class comes back is because of the spectrality of its composition, not because it can be crumpled into a ball and carelessly tossed into the dustbin of history (despite the claims of "endists," class is not disposable in this way). Yet its understanding is thus rendered ethereal and as ambivalent as the identities of class that might otherwise be affirmed as its perfect distillation.

To return to *Capital,* chapter 1, for a moment (the scene, already, of fetishism's phantasmagoria), the specter is both a trope of criticism and explanation. Marx attacks dominant forms of political economy for precisely their faulty spectrality; they do not understand, do not "think," the ghosts that they array:

> Political economy has indeed analyzed value and its magnitude, however incompletely, and has *uncovered the content concealed* within these forms. But it has never once asked the question why this content has assumed that *particular form,* that is to say, why labor is expressed in

value, and why the measurement of labor by its duration is expressed in the magnitude of the value of the product. (173–74; emphasis added)

Needless to say, there can be no adequate knowledge of the process of class formation (or in this instance, proletarianization) without an assessment of value in the moment of commodity exchange and elsewhere — without an understanding, therefore, of labor's embodiment in the commodity form. Here, Marx assails the political economists for identifying value as an abstraction but then refusing its implication for real knowledge. In the critical mode, then, the specter becomes the place of misrecognition or illusion. Thus, in a footnote, Marx details how such a misrecognition creates a contradiction in political economy that will later permit Marx to define his own position by contrast:

> We ... find that economists who are entirely agreed that labor time is the measure of the magnitude of value, have the strangest and most contradictory ideas about money, that is, about the universal equivalent in its finished form. ... Hence there has arisen in opposition to the classical economists a restored Mercantilist System (Ganilh etc.) which sees in value only the social form, or rather *the unsubstantial ghost of that form.* Let me point out once and for all that by classical political economy I mean all the economists who, since the time of W. Petty, have investigated the real internal framework of bourgeois relations of production, as opposed to the vulgar economists who only flounder around within the apparent framework of those relations. (174–75; emphasis added)[22]

Unlike his contemporaries in political economy, Marx is not satisfied with the representation of an illusion as a fiction: he seeks to establish the grounds of a social form in such an illusion (for better or worse, this remains at the heart of the labor theory of value and, indeed, Marx's analysis of the commodity in general). But this means coming to terms with the "good" ghosts as well, and there Marxism remains predominantly hostile to the function of the metaphor for Marx. Without doubt, this has proved to be a major political and theoretical stumbling block. In a far-ranging argument, at once critical and enabling of materialist critique, Jean-Marie Vincent reads the confrontation of Marx with political economy as the process through which Marx's own principles are overreached to a significant degree.[23] The bounds of Marx's theoretical project are continually pushed back by the new contradictions his concepts face in political economy so that, for instance, Ricardo can be seen as an ally regarding absolute value (in *The Poverty of Philosophy*) even as Adam Smith cannot. The crucial point for Vincent is the acceptance of a logic of transgression within Marx's concepts (again, the Marx beyond Marx

["Marx au-delà de Marx"]), one that gives up a false dichotomy between the real and illusion in his theorization. Thus, the ghost story of value for labor is one where ghosting, or doubling, is not merely misrecognition (the attack mode) but part and parcel of the process of articulation. Vincent writes:

> It is particularly important to move beyond the simplistic opposition between the "spellbound" [*ensorcelé*] world of value and commodities on the one hand and the "authentic" world of material and sensible metabolisms on the other. Each pierces the other, and represents and asserts itself through the other. In this sense, real abstractions function in such a way as to assure a route from one level of reality to the other, even before becoming barriers to an overall perception of processes. The flows of production and exchange, as material-sensible combinations of transformations and transfers, find meaning and direction in the codes and signs which impart coherence to the market relations between equivalent values. In the same way, dialectical relations between forms of value are fueled by the material displacements and changes set in movement by people, although they reveal themselves to be in opposition to people's interests. Constant permutations and substitutions transfigure the social scene with optical illusions, quid pro quos and telescoped images and the like, in which reality is always disguised and appears in double. (97; translation modified)

Much as we want to keep the "spellbound" and "authentic" apart, critical explanation demands an understanding of their interrelation — how one is imbued in the other (overdetermined as they are by the constant oscillations of the social). We can say that, particularly where value is concerned, the doubling is not a simple disguise that one can peel off (or replace) according to one's theoretical perquisites. If we follow the logic of Vincent's claims for materialist practice, the double nature of political economy is written into Marx's formulations so that the spellbound or enchanted can indeed be manifest in the claims of authenticity.[24] When Marx sees the ghost in other political economists, he recognizes the specter in his own discourse. Another example from *Capital* (volume 1, chapter 1) will clarify this critical symbiosis.

By comparing two commodities Marx seeks to elucidate the quality that allows them to be equated in quantity (different quantities of two commodities can be expressed as the same value). Every commodity, according to Marx, can be addressed in terms of the doubled nature of quantity and quality. But once Marx seeks to detail the logic of this process he quickly moves away from the empirical attributes of the commodity form: "This common element [the quality] cannot be a geometrical, physical, chemical or other natural property of commodities" (127). If exchange value allows use values to be exchanged for other use values, it is a quality of commodities that cannot be expressed in terms of the physical attributes of the commodity. And yet, of course, it haunts every moment of commodity exchange, which strikes Marx (and many others since) as an altogether appropriate way to convey (to make visible the invisible) the suprasensible constituents of such exchange. To think the ghost, therefore, Marx asks us to imagine these two commodities stripped of their use value: minus not just their sensuous char-acteristics — the useful characteristics of the commodity — but also minus the kinds of labor, the different forms of labor, embodied in the commodity. The residue, as he calls it, is the quintessence not of an individual com-modity but of commodification itself: it is *gespenstige Gegenständlichkeit*, or ghostly objectivity. Take away the sensuousness of the commodity and the useful labor in it and one is left with "congealed quantities of homogenous human labor" (128). Now what do we see? Marx underlines that what is left is the human labor power expended to produce the commodities: human la-bor has actually accumulated in the commodities, but not as a human, only as a ghost (the ghost of objectivity). To put it still more bluntly: the nature of commodities is the nature of ghosts.

Marx is able to explain the process of exchange only within a spectral economy of difference. What seems like a mixed metaphor or an oxymoron, a congealed or jellied spirit (like ectoplasm), is the necessary conjuration of the spirit of capital: for what remains, remains to come back. Because this ghostly quality is dependent upon a chain of difference, deconstructionists have often been Marxism's ally in articulating the theory of value (see Spi-vak, Ryan, and Keenan for instance).[25] My point is less that the labor theory of value provides a topic for deconstruction, but more that Marx's protocols themselves depend upon a conceptual spectrality much greater than the odd reference to specters. And whenever one hears recourse to positivist and es-sentialist definitions of proletarian Being, this spectrality must be conjured once more.

But is not what remains, this jellied residue, itself an essence, a trace of Being that might yet confirm a certain ontology of Presence? Certainly there is an essence of labor in the exposition that Marx provides that would seem to mark value in labor's image. Yet it is not labor that offers up this essence (it is not labor's essentialism) but a capital relation that links labor to value in commodity exchange. It is an essence without Being; it is a law that it is as variable as the market itself. This is a troubling form or ground for subjectivity, one that paradoxically permits varying degrees of objectification (by capital in the constitution of value, and by a Marxian reflex that places the labor theory of value above a complex of values in social formation — and is, therefore, a "fetish of labor," as Vincent terms it) and subjectification (in the sense that capital requires a subject for subjection but only as an object or effect of social relations themselves). The ghost of labor is phantomatized in the interstices of what must be calculated according to capital (the cost of labor from a labor value, its quantifiable function) and is yet incalculable (the fantastic form of autonomous commodities that Marx elaborates in this section of *Capital*). Should we be surprised that a ghost of labor predicates a ghost of labor politics, one caught between advocating agency, the praxis over forms of subjection, and a more dispassionate scientificity that says that the laws of history will unravel these unreconcilable contradictions?[26]

Although eschewing all traces of philosophical smugness (which is what he ridiculed in others, Feuerbach to name but one), Marx tended to displace the practical and philosophical implications of his analysis of value and labor for class. As Balibar has argued, a significant part of the legacy of Marx rests in the confrontation with the dilemmas that Marx articulated ("humanity cannot abandon a problem that it has not yet solved" [*POM* 119]). For materialism such a confrontation cannot be deferred: it is part of what comes back in the oscillations of its theoretical components. But materialism is impatient with philosophy. Materialism wants the good clean concepts that stir the soul: "Get rid of those chains, you still have to win the world" (as if these slogans were/are not as much a part of state ideology as they are the culture of advertising). Politics is the simple form of an abstract and complex social conjunction. Political praxis itself answers the otherwise aporetic formations of the social, but some of those answers emerge despite the amoebic and anemic forms that politics might take. Materialism needs philosophy to that extent — it wants a critical explanation of the unexpected and the contingent but cannot escape an attendant risk, that in coming to terms with the deferrals built into its model of analysis it opens out into a more general philosophy of deferral that it fears more than capital itself.[27]

Marx analyzes the symbolic structures of the commodity, of money, of value, of class, but this does not make his materialism a symbolic philosophy (Baudrillard, perhaps, is the heir to that tradition). It does mean, however, that he struggles with an architectonic that constantly exceeds itself in the logic of its movement and its expressions. The difficulty is in accepting the symbolic without negating the real, real contradictions, real foundations of the social and of change. The reality of class as spectral does not mean it does not exist; it means merely that one grasps the immaterial as also and always already constituent of material reality. The ghost of class is a reality of ghosts and of class. Marx's analogy is not false in this claim or that of the specter of communism. Without this immaterial materiality there would be no way to understand why such anachronisms like Marxism, class, and communism continue to haunt in the moment of their suppression or outright denial. Indeed, it has taken the collapse of "communism," the "posting" of Marxism, and the diminution of class discourse to bring spectrality into focus. The symptom preexists the event even as the event foregrounds it. This is not an ideological compensation, although it might provide some vengeful solace that it can be read as such, as an imaginary resolution of a real contradiction. On the contrary, it is more like a real contradiction in the imaginary that offers no simple resolution, but a contingent transformation that "exists" as a possible future — a future, as Derrida puts it, that comes back to the present. Or as Jean-Luc Nancy puts it: "Le *communisme*, sans doute, est le nom archaïque d'une pensée encore tout entière à venir" ("Without doubt [there, once again], communism is still the archaic name for a thought entirely to come").[28] It is easy to see why some may transpose the symbolic structures that Marx elaborates onto the structure of sign itself. But for Marx these are not idle or playful lessons on the nature of signification in language (an expression in language does not mean that all is reducible to language): they are the tissue of a certain reality that continually exceeds the ability of language to adequate it. But there are other ways to think the ghost.

To a great extent, what has exploded the discourse of materialist theory is not the discovery of the nefarious signifier so much as the experience of globality. Capitalism as a world system has overrun almost every tenet of materialism that deigned to write the history of ghosts in terms of a unitary class, or a unitary nation, or a unitary state, or a unitary mode of production. As we saw with the example of Sadisah, the forms of globalization themselves are barely imaginable. They are a direct challenge to our ability, in Jameson's terminology, to map cognitively. Keep in mind that this challenge is not written univocally or monologically and certainly cannot usefully be answered that way. Marx may have understood a chain of equivalence in the commodity form (that allows for the possibility of exchange), but that does not imply that a consciousness in equivalence, an equivalent consciousness, a pure working-class consciousness is the basic cognitive tool of its sublation. Certainly working-class consciousness remains desirable, the more so for its relative absence, but that is not to say that it emerges in a singular form or mode of expression. Thus, when theory addresses a geopolitical or geocultural cognition of the global it is usually in terms of a radical heterogeneity. One answer to the process by which socioeconomic diversity yet gets integrated into the fallacy of a unitary system (global capitalism) is to foreground diversity in the moment of totalization. As Hobsbawm put it some years ago, there are "worlds of labor" and not just workers of the world.[29] The gambit remains difficult, if not impossible, not just because of the cognitive abilities demanded but because the hegemony of simultaneity built into contemporary regimes of capital delinks every connection of an oppositional imaginary at the very moment when it seems to assure it.

Let us consider the problem of the world in what returns as the specter for capitalism. The future of materialist critique depends to a great degree on how it conceptualizes the global without homogenizing it in the mirror of capitalist integration. This means understanding how the political itself is dependent upon "masking," upon both an iterability and materiality that are at once a ghostly disguise. Again, Marx resists "philosophy" to the extent that it trivializes or mistakes the real foundations of his inquiry, but Marx must attend to philosophy in order to think the determinations of his own intellectual activity.

In chapter 1 we noted a disruptive series of conceptual vacillations in and around the question of ideology. It is undeniable that Balibar's trenchant critique of Marxian oscillation describes a determinate theoretical horizon, one that cannot simply be transcended inside or outside Marxist lore. One of the difficulties is separating the constituent processes of ideology from the counterdiscourses that disarticulate it. If proletarians, for instance, are the bearers of their own ideology, how is this any less limiting than the fare on offer from Ideological State Apparatuses in Althusser's famous formulation? Engels's answer took the form of a scientific plea rather than a theory as such — a weakness that Balibar is quick to seize on. The *Weltanschauung*, or worldview, that Engels proposes in the *Anti-Dühring* is a "fantasmally constructed" concept that Balibar characterizes as a "system of knowledge" rather than a "systematic knowledge," the latter being a theory that oscillates wildly beyond system as closure.[30] The reason Balibar opposes the worldview in Engels's conception is a classic Althusserian maneuver: the scientificity of countercritique cannot be based on a promise of ideational transparency where we can enter a world in which all illusionism dissolves in the moment of proletarian self-identity. Thus, for political and not simply linguistic reasons, so this argument goes, there is no "language of real life" (as *The German Ideology* would have it): politics does not escape the masking — or the ideological in one valence — that is its very possibility. Now, to the extent that utopianism promises a purity that politics, by definition, cannot deliver, materialism must cede the intractability of the ideological. This is not necessarily the lesson of the "actual existence" of socialism, although neither were those states representative of a simple usurpation of the truth claims of worker revolution (and this continues to be the case in examples like Cuba). But it does mean that we should not be astonished if a worldview is connected to worldliness in the same way that science is attached to ideology. The problem can be stated thus: Can there be a cognitive claim for globality that is not itself an illusionary inclusionary logic of domination?

The answer depends very much on a political definition of a sense of the world. First, as indicated, one begins a counterlogic by pluralizing the totality (in very basic terms, the answers to the ideology implied in the slogan "We are the world" begin with questions like "Which world is that?" "Which 'we'?" "Which mode of being?"). But just as the concept of oscillation puts tremendous strain on the systematicity of counterlogic (a burden that must be risked, at least according to the terms of Balibar's contention above), so the sense of the world internally destabilizes the contours if not the content of the political. The "world" is problematized not just by multiplying it. It is undone and undoes the sense that senses this. Once more a philosophical conundrum offers itself, but as an example of the problem, not its obscurantist evasion. Nancy explains something of the sense I have in mind:

> The word for "world" does not have another unity of sense than this: a world (*the* world, *my* world, *world* affairs, the *Muslim* world, etc.), it is always a differential articulation of singularities which make sense in being articulated, while being their articulation (where "articulation" must be taken at the same time in the mechanical sense of joint and of play, the sense of spoken utterance and the sense of a distribution of distinct "articles"). A world is joined, played, spoken, and divided: this is its sense which is none other than the sense of "making sense."[31]

The problem is at once simple and complex, and one where materialist politics borders on the apparitional. The simplicity of singularity, different worldviews, belies the complexity in making sense of them. It is as if the different worlds articulated only make sense in the terms of that articulation, and the articulation of the world depends on the very moment of making sense. Making sense is the possibility and name for the articulation of differential worlds. There are at least two interpretations of this formulation (neither of them particularly dependent upon Nancy's exposition of singularities, although obviously sensitive to his shifting sense of sense): the first says that a sense of the world makes sense because it has been articulated; the second says that difference cancels through the articulation and renders the sense of the world unintelligible, or nonsense, to another attempting to make sense of it. The first option sounds voluntarist (I am making sense of this world and therefore the world is articulated); the second resonates of nihilism (I can make sense of the world but I cannot articulate it for you — my sense is opaque, *reductio ad absurdum*). But what if we read this philosophical problem historically, and not just within the history of philosophy? If, as Nancy (among others) argues, there is no world spirit, or something that drives it, what are the constituents for this termination, this end of a particular sense of the world? Perhaps, for materialism, it is this: the history of the senses that Marx called for (and never wrote) is also a history of meaning and judgment (it predicates it) and one that is being formed outside or beyond the constraints of a world historical identitarian formula. One can project a historical actor onto the world but only at the risk of losing sense of it (the world). The crisis of globality is both a crisis within the forms of cognition that impel materialist critique, and a more general crisis brought on by the modes of economic globalism. One end, of *the* world historical subject as proletarian, augurs another, the universality of bourgeois social relations. Thus, one's sense of crisis in the world is being made sense of by that crisis: it is rewriting a sense of the world in its complex but not impossible image. For Balibar, this worldliness changes our understanding of class struggle:

> Far from bringing about a unification of the working class, the phase of economic crisis (though it is important to ask exactly *for whom* and *in what sense* there is a crisis) is leading to an increasingly radical separation between the different aspects of proletarianization by the erection of geographical — and also ethnic, generational and sexual — barriers. Thus, though the world-economy is the real battleground of the class struggle, there is no such thing as a world proletariat (except as an "idea"), indeed, it exists even less than does a world bourgeoisie. ("Class," 178; emphasis in original)

Balibar, like Nancy, reads the crisis as an end of sorts, one that separates the process of the political from its idealization and, perhaps, its idealism. These terms must be read as the texture of the crisis although, as Balibar affirms, one would have to specify "for whom" and "in what sense" there is a crisis (this is a materialist sense that sometimes escapes the philosopher). For his part, Nancy is self-conscious about the risk for philosophy of rethinking the sense of sense, the sense of the world. It takes the form of a mania, or an obsession, one that haunts philosophy ("et qui hante la philosophie" [128]), but a haunting that allows "Le Sens" to proceed. The complexity of the world system is not made easier by "making sense" in this way, but it refuses the hasty generalizations that have left the world opaque in the past. A new sense can turn out to be non-sense — that is, a sense that is never coincident with the world that is its object. But a new sense can also be non-coincident with the world, a sense that is integrated in the world without being self-identical with the world. That this ghosting can now be part of materialist practice is not a function of metaphorical cross-referencing; it is, rather, a political imperative cognizant of the material conditions of the present, the worlding of the world as capitalist.

Here we should clarify the political permutations of ghosts and ghosting. Clearly for Marx, the specter is a political barb used to attack what he saw as a policy of demonizing communism, particularly within the states of Europe. Thus, when the pope, or the tsar, or Metternich, or Guizot invoke communism it is within a discourse of reactionary incitement. To exorcise the ghost in this sense is to eradicate its possibility. In *The Eighteenth Brumaire*, however, Marx gives the ghost a different strategic inflection. Here, the ghost is part of the spectral economy of revolution, but an "old revolution" that Louis Napoleon conjures to repeat a history that was lost. This ghost is malevolent in a troubling way, for the "old world of ghosts" seeks to impose itself on the present and replace a revolution of transformation with one of repetition (the infamous farce of history). "The ghost of the empire" haunts the present in the form of Louis Napoleon's politics, he who is "making its ghost walk again."[32] For Marx, this is a politics of despair, but one not without political potential for mass opposition. The "parody of imperialism" that the ghost represents is also an inspiration, for in the out-of-jointness of time (Derrida's Shakespearean touchstone) a reactionary spirit produces its counter, one that works to transform the reactionary force that seeks simply to spectralize the real.

This second impulse in Marx's interpretation casts a ghostly shadow on the first. As Derrida points out, the political consequences of the specter and spectrality produce a dilemma. If the "red specter" (as Marx calls it) of opposition is indeed a shadow without a body (Marx describes the people and events of the Eighteenth Brumaire as "inverted Schlemihls," from the story of a man who lost his shadow), is not this itself a function of conjuration — one that places doubt over the ghost's realization? Marx argues that when the "red specter" finally appears the political order has been stabilized, the revolution has been usurped. Now the "reds" do not represent themselves, since (like the peasants) they have always already been represented as ghosts, as specters, as a phantasmagoria. This is precisely what allows the "magician" (Louis Napoleon) to cast aside universal suffrage in the form of what Derrida terms "a perverse, diabolical, and non-apparent exorcism" (*SOM* 119). Clearly, what begins the *Communist Manifesto* in such stirring fashion is an entirely ambiguous rhetorical strategy in *The Eighteenth Brumaire*.

Yet for Marx, the logic of the specter remains a strong antidote to idealist assumptions. What he wants to do, at key moments of political and philosophical reflection, is play on the fear of the immaterial as a contingent foundation of materiality. In effect, he leaves idealism for his political opponents while exacerbating the suspicion that the fear is indeed "grounded." This is the positive meaning of the specter and one that informs the present argument where conjuration is a sign of unsettled spirits, or spirits that cannot be put to rest for historically specific reasons. As we have noted, the end of the Cold War and the collapse of "actual existence" have brought to light, once more, the spectrality of a communism to be, even as this risks (according to Marx's own deployments) the repetition of spirits of yore. The ambiguity cannot be simply exorcised, but what comes back from the future, which is also a new sense of the world and the specter, is a mode of thinking that might critically explain spectrality, the condition of ghosts for materialism.

The ambiguity is written into Marxism's relation to philosophy, and indeed to science (for history shows that certain "Marxist" claims to scientificity have themselves been forms of sorcery). But does spectrality answer the question with which we began, "Whither Marxism?" and the concept of oscillation written into it? Certainly not in any univocal way, for the logic of the spectral is also one of deferral and dialogic differentiation. It describes a principle of noncoherence rather than the hard-edged negativity of incoherence often trivialized by normative notions of the rational. The problem of the specter defies the cozy mimesis that sutures images to their objects. Hence, the aporia of class in Balibar's argument, for he shows the difficulty of socialist class and class struggle ideologies when confronted with the forms of the nation-state: a historical condition in which these state forms become introjected, mimetically, into socialist political structures. In this sense, the ghost of socialism looks over the shoulder of its state instantiation of nationalist ideologies. And this ghosting is itself a moment of oscillatory import:

> This is the uncertainty that faces us at present; namely, that to prevent the crisis of nationalism from ending in an excess of nationalism and its extended reproduction, what is needed is that the example of class struggle becomes visible in the representation of the social — but as its irreducible *other*. The ideology of class and class struggle, therefore, under whatever name is appropriate, must discover its autonomy while liberating itself from mimicry. To the question "whither Marxism?," the answer, then, is: nowhere, unless this paradox is confronted in all its implications. ("Class," 182)

From Bosnia to Serbia, from Georgia to Chechnya, from Rwanda to Liberia, from Quebec to Ireland, and from China to Taiwan, the paradox that Balibar identifies in 1987 has grown in importance. To be sure, in Balibar's interpretation the paradox comes with an Althusserian twist — that the mimetic fallacies of "actual existence" and other formations must give way to the autonomy of ideology in the name of class and class struggle. For my purposes, the other of the social is the ghost as ideology, a condition of "nowhere" that troubles nationalism in its contemporary constellations. The paradox is not necessarily the autonomy of ideology in this formulation: the uncertainty resides in the visibility of the invisible that class ideology represents. The familiar maneuver that the denial of class is itself a class ideology remains pertinent, yet the future of Marxism does not rest on the confirmation or reaccentuation of that paradox, but on a political openness to the instability written into Marxism's status as critique.

In his answer to the same question, "Whither Marxism?" Douglas Kellner picks up on this issue in a way that was possible in 1992 but perhaps was not in 1987. Here, the spirit of Marxism must be separated from its ghostly aberrations in "actual existence" (Kellner writes of the "spiritual ancestors of the modern totalitarian state").[33] This is the positive exorcism of the post-Soviet era. But it is important to maintain the spectral contours of what Kellner calls "a reconstructed Marxism" (26). When he suggests that Marxism will "disappear" when the "nightmare of capitalism" is over (or when an alternative means to a free and democratic society recommends itself), Kellner alludes to without naming the ambivalent Being of the specter that opens the *Communist Manifesto*. Capitalism wants to awake from a nightmare of history because it conjures the monstrosity of communism. Yet, ironically, the conjuring itself is seen as a means to dispose of or disavow the political and social alternative that this specter represents. A counterconjuration, therefore, is not concerned with Being as such: it seeks to elaborate why the conjuration itself cannot overcome the conditions of possibility it denies. A ghost of the past is always a troubling spirit, but a specter of the future is an aporetic apparition.

Gayatri Chakravorty Spivak's answer to "Whither Marxism?" reflects and refracts the general problematic posed by deconstruction, one where the end of *Capital,* volume 3, is itself a "blueprint of *différance.*"[34] Because of socialism's imbrication in the forms of capital articulated by Marx, it "exists" as a pushing away, or deferral, of social productivity according to capital. This is a useful way of characterizing the inseparability implied in ghosting. If we agree that socialism is an "other Being" of capital, then it cannot be expunged without exploding the very ground of its existence, its substantiality. Again, as philosophy this is a suspicious mode of argumentation (the interpellation would read: "Heh, Marxism, socialism, communism — you're not there but the condition of your existence is not-thereness, so in a sense you're always there where capital 'is' "), but the point is to maintain such *différance* as a philosophy beside itself or, as Balibar would have it, as philosophies of Marx beside themselves. It is clearer now why some pundits, including those of a nominally Leftist persuasion, might read "Whither Marxism?" as a pun, and that what we are witnessing in millennial materialism is the withering away of Marxism with its states. Such defeatism and/or cynicism is entirely natural according to the dictates of a philosophy of Being, or "actual existence." But rather than succumb to the ingenious (or disingenuous) attractions of the homonym, let us maintain a spirit of "whither" that does not depend upon second-guessing history.

Scratch the surface of "whither" as an interrogative and one finds an adjective within the discourse of oscillation. Here "whither" (as noted in the *OED*) is "a violent or impetuous movement," "a smart blow or stroke" (a *Stöss* or "shock" for and within Marxism, to recall an earlier discussion of Vattimo), "a quivering movement, a tremble," and, remembering Marx's carbuncles, "the onset or attack of illness." These meanings stand before Marxism as its specters stand before capital. Thus, as the question arrives, so too must the condition. The condition or state of oscillation does not lose the question mark that "whither" precedes: in a spectral economy the question is always there, if only parenthetically (it lurks in the space of this essay title). "Whither" marks the oscillation of theory; it is the sign of a distinct multiplicity in Marxism, the "philosophies of Marx." It is a multiplicity as instability foregrounded in the historically concrete condition of Marxism today. Millennial materialism cannot be reduced to *a* Marx, *the* Marx. Spectrality demands it. Or, as Derrida puts it, to understand the specters of Marx one must address a phantasmal imperative: *Le plus d'un* — the more than one and the no more one.

But the last word of ghosts is not just philosophical, despite these incarnations. What the ghost (*revenant*) always also comes back to is the status of science. Here Marxism has strengths that oscillation does not. Oscillation is a concept for materialism, but Marxism does not devolve, ultimately, into its constituent concepts. Yet here one faces a sharp dilemma that even "whither's" palimpsest cannot significantly displace. If, as Deleuze and Guattari propose, "A scientific notion is defined not by concepts but by functions or propositions" (117), then can one separate the wheat of Marxist propositions from the chaff of its concepts? Historically, there have been moments where this has appeared more possible (the Second International remains a crucial example), but if one accepts the conjunctural reading of Marxist theoretical formations, the process if not the actuality of those differences may now be more difficult to discern. This does not mean that such attempts are idealist or illusionist. On the contrary, work like Roy Bhaskar's identifies how materialist principles themselves can become mired in "epistemic fallacies" (the reduction of ontology to epistemology) that only a sustained critical (and in Bhaskar's terminology, realist) investigation can disarticulate as a science in the social.[35] But the ghost is neither a simple categorical error nor the reincarnation of some Hegelian absolute spirit (although, given the predilections of French philosophy, the "appearance" would be understandable). The ghost remains for science, just as a ghost of science haunts the Marxist dialectic. Here is not the place to adjudicate the truth claims of Marxism as science; I do, however, wish to counter the impression that any focus on Marx's deployment of spectral metaphors is to abjure the rational kernel for its mystical shell. If history has taught us anything in recent years, it is that the de facto rejection of the spectral in Marxism is partly what allowed utopia to congeal, then disappear, in dogma.

On the one hand, Deleuze and Guattari claim that science "slows down" variability by the use of constants or limits. A measure, or a principle of measurement, can pull reality from chaos and "suspend," however briefly, the process of the infinite. The examples they provide (the speed of light, absolute zero, the quantum of action, the Big Bang) all attempt to coordinate, to provide a scale, to provide a reference for what must always exceed them. And, not surprisingly, the sheer variability of constants produces a determinate disciplinary fear: "science is haunted not by its own unity but by the plane of reference constituted by all the limits or borders through which it confronts chaos" (119). Philosophy, on the other hand, is less troubled by the infinite as long as it can be thought consistently (philosophy, they claim, gives "the virtual a consistency specific to it" [118]). In this, science and philosophy can be linked to art: they all "cast planes over the chaos" (202). But this, of course, is an intellectual, political, and social challenge. Artists, philosophers, and scientists confront chaos not just to impose an order on it (for this alone would amount to hubris), but because a certain affinity with chaos is necessary for the crises we call change. Again, the image of this confrontation is striking: "The philosopher, the scientist, and the artist seem to return from the land of the dead" (202). And which one of these ghosts is the real Marxist?

Marxism is a science to the extent that it has developed forms of measurement (laws of motion) for the infinite chaos of socialization (in this respect, the charge of "totalization" is often a nonscientist's reaction to scientificity). These measurements (ideology, class, value, commodity, etc.) are not fictions to the degree that they have often elaborated the real contradictions that stand within and between the social and forms of socialization. But philosophy (and indeed art) is not to blame for the distortion of these measurements, at least according to Deleuze and Guattari's interpretation: it is a function of the plethora of methodologies vis-à-vis chaos. Chaosophy, as Deleuze and Guattari call it, is not for me only because I still tend to think in terms of the collective rather than the nomads who wander off into the infinite. I do believe, however, that it provides a strong antidote to knee-jerk reactions about the status of science and philosophy for Marxism at a time when "post-ality" is all too quick to dig a grave for it.

Ghosts do not make history, people do, but not under conditions of their own choosing (a point where Marx and the Shakespeare of *Hamlet* most assuredly agree). This little history of ghosts is not about the agency of the specter, but about materialism's accountability to and for specters. Derrida's bold declaration that there will be "no future without Marx" ("Pas sans Marx, pas d'avenir sans Marx" [*SDM* 36]) only makes sense within a spectral economy of materialism, a materialism that is not beholden to monologic causality but one that seeks an understanding of a material reality caught between the calculable and the incalculable, the undecidability of "determinate oscillations." Marx is dead; only the spectral can critically explain how Marxism comes back from the future. Not content with the naming of an undecidable, I have sought to interpellate Marx within his own *Gespenstergeschichte:* that is, to trace the function of the ghost, and thinking the ghost, for his materialist methodology. Millennial materialism must use this heritage not to reincarnate Marx (in the manner of a quaint religious observance) but to resist an inclination to resolve conceptual aporias merely by dogmatic statements to the contrary. The science of materialism includes its respect for the criteria of judgment, not the assumption of a universal truth in the judgment. The vacillations of class and class struggle in Marx's formulations are examples of determinate instability within the concepts and their application. What spectrality does is keep this instability "alive" at a moment when "actual existence" cannot possibly confirm or deny it.

In 1883 Engels stood by Marx's grave and predicted that "the gap that has been left by this mighty spirit will soon enough make itself felt" (an absence as agency indeed!). Yet barely a hundred years later Hobsbawm could opine that "the shadow of Karl Marx presides over a third of the human race."[36] The shade of Marx is still here, but not in the form that either Engels or Hobsbawm suggests. It exists now as a condition of possibility in a sense of the world radically different from the specters of the past, however answerable it must be to them. The ambivalence of the specter is not its virtue, only its dependence on concrete determination. And that is why the experience of freedom before us is also the space of ghosts.

CONCLUSION

THEREMIN'S TOUCH

I ended the previous chapter by noting that, after all, ghosts do not make history: people do. This much Marx affirms, but if the lessons of oscillation are anything to go by, or indeed the passage of materialism through the twentieth century, human agency cannot be counted on to fashion a realm of freedom from one of necessity — at least not as a mirror of the way that nineteenth-century political thought suggests. The uneven development of productive forces is so abstruse at this moment in history that no single "motor" or subject of history can dominate its complexity, and this is as true for capitalist classes as it is for the workers who could depose them. The argument could be made, however, and with some conviction, that all this talk of metaphoricity, all this materialist conceptual sway, is precisely what stands in the way of a more constructive agential discourse. But part of my point has been that there is no outside this circle: the conceptual vacillation is intrinsic to materialism's passage from the real to the abstract. The task for metatheory has been to track the variegations of a materialism that is cognizant of its metaphoricity and metamorphosis without sacrificing the critical explanations that it provides about forms of socialization. My position has been that unless we emphasize the historical specificity of materialist mutability, the legacy of Marxism will be little more than a disposable dogma.

When the various thinkers I have cited use oscillation as an operative metaphor in their arguments, it is rarely a conscious allusion to the word's history or current possibilities. I have taken oscillation as symptomatic of materialism's attempt to think through various theoretical aporias that are immanent to its critique. I have gone further than this, however, and suggested a conceptual framework that provides a vision of at least some of the components of a millennial materialism.[1] As my introduction stressed, it is not in the nature of oscillation as a phenomenon or concept to be prescriptive, but it can function as something of a heuristic device in understanding the logic of movement in the material world of ideas and objects. Rather than conclude with a grand synthesis regarding this logic (which would, of course, be a betrayal of it) I want to provide an excursus on the possible worlds for materialism girded by a strong sense of what oscillation as a concept can and cannot do within metatheory. Those interested in social transformation have always been optimists (at least in terms of will), and these concluding remarks will be in that spirit. That does not mean, however, that I am satisfied with the politics that oscillation implies (a pessimism of the intellect, no doubt), which cannot content itself with the mere fact of oscillation in theory and socioeconomic phenomena. The difference between oscillate and oscillate wildly must ultimately be a practical approach to the forms of the politically possible. I have tried to stress that in the chapters above, but these are not the only apparatuses in which the problem of theoretical vacillation might be investigated and/or framed.

An alternative mode of clarification is to consider some of the flaws of the general approach. From there I will move to the connection of oscillation to certain discourses in science and technology, which will not provide us with narrative closure but will facilitate a better *sense* of the motor of oscillation in millennial materialism. Indeed, I will end with a note about sense and sense perception in the moment of our not-so-wild hyperreality. The revenge of history will not be in the form in which it is traditionally conceived within materialism. For one thing, it will be nonlinear.

There are several weaknesses of oscillation as a concept and metaphor for materialist critique. I will not discuss them in the order of their seriousness, but that is not to say that some of them are not more significant than others — it is perhaps more in the recognition that materialism's answerability cannot be arbitrated by the individual critic. The counterarguments here are meant to indicate some of my own hesitation before the movement and vacillation or homeostasis I have invoked. First, oscillation is a modernist concept, redolent with that mode of fragmentation and anxiety that characterized certain forms of art at least through the middle of this century. As I have argued, materialism does not have a monopoly (thankfully) on oscillation, but the consonance with the moment of modernism is instructive.[2] Virginia Woolf, for instance, was idiosyncratic enough in her interpretation of "the materialists" to argue that materialism was not modernist enough. She urged, by contrast, that the modernist should "record the atoms as they fall upon the mind in the order in which they fall; let us trace the pattern, however disconnected and incoherent in appearance, which each sight or incident scores upon the consciousness." The "materialists" she has in mind, like Galsworthy and Wells, took "too much delight in the solidity of their fabric."[3] There are obvious problems with Woolf's interpretation (the full argument is more opposed to realism in the pejorative sense than "materialism"), but surely oscillation as I have used it is modernist to the extent that materialism has had to learn about the contradictory but significant "incoherent patterns" beneath the solidity of the modern world. Rather than see this only in the terms that modernism prescribes (for instance, the Joycean mode of the inchoate everyday overdetermined by a mythic structure of correspondence), the motor of oscillation attends to its own reinscription. The weakening of materialism is perhaps a sign of its imbrication with the project of modernity, but that is not to say that the form of oscillation remains identical to that scheme. It is to underline, however, that theory does not supersede modernity's reach merely by naming its exception to it.

If there are continuities with modernism, millennial materialism has some perspective of its difference. At the end of the twentieth century, materialist critique now understands in a much more reflexive way that the ambivalent spaces of, for instance, modernist fiction often betray anxieties brought on not just by the hubbub of "modern life" but by a confrontation with the other within the discourse of colonialism. In Mann's novella *Death in Venice*, for instance, this othering is figured literally as disease, as cholera: "But while Europe trembled with apprehension that from there [India] the specter might advance and arrive by land, it had been brought by the Syrian traders across the sea."[4] Aschenbach's "roving restlessness," his desire for travel, is bound by the conditions of this fear, and only the abjection of his desire leaves him susceptible to its consequences. Traveling theory, as I have indicated earlier, shares something of this purview, and it is by spatializing its logic that we might betray its function for modernism's orientalist discourse.

Perhaps the point might be clarified by reference to a second objection: namely, that oscillation is constrained by its structuralist tendencies. Again, there is a good deal of truth to this since, even as a concept, oscillation is recuperable within a logic of structured determination across the range of its occurrence. Balibar's analysis of the vacillation of ideology and my subsequent critique of Balibar's oscillation both owe their methodology to a belief in structural causality, one occasioned by a specific crisis in Marxist critique.[5] This respects an immanence to oscillation in materialism's legacy but does not mean that a structure (economic, social, sexual) is determined and determines in the same way. Clearly, there are hybrids of materialism that, from this view, are not materialist (Teresa Ebert has referred to one such "development" as "matterism"),[6] but the proof of millennial materialism is its understanding of the internal differentiation of oscillation, not just whether it repeats (or forgets) the structural compulsions of yesteryear. Thus, the materialism at issue is modernist and structuralist to this degree: its procedures resist the doctrinaire but only to the extent that the materiality of the modern era provides that "ground." The material, unlike an idea, is not an alibi for Being.

There are other ways that materialism breaks from the aesthetic overtures of modernism, not least of which is that it eschews individualist solutions to what are properly social contradictions. But why conceive of materialist oscillation in terms of aesthetics at all? Isn't this symptomatic of another weakness, a creeping culturalism that slowly but surely swallows up the social according to the dictate that culture, after all, is a whole way of life? The gesture toward Williams here is deliberate, for his oeuvre stages in a profound way the unresolved and unresolvable contradictions between culture and materialism. Indeed, these oscillations are so marked and complex that an entire genre of critical theory (cultural materialism) is devoted to them. In this regard, I would argue for a strategic nonalignment, for a cultural critique that maintains a philosophy of delinking from the perquisites of the university as institution. This does not purge materialism of a culturalist strain in the negative sense, but neither does it cede the cultural production of meaning to the liberal humanist tradition. Similarly, our analysis of the metaphors of materialism does not confine the consequences of critique to linguistic tenacity; rather, it emphasizes that one of the ways that materialism renews itself is through an autocritical reflexion on the organizing tropes of its methodology. Culturalism might approach theory in this way, but here a different politics is implied, and, as I tried to indicate in the chronotope of the shoe, an alternative imagination is at stake.

The charge of culturalism would seem to be particularly appropriate where a body politics is concerned, and, ironically perhaps, this is where culturalism bends back toward a modernist discourse — the care of the self. Balibar would here intercede to caution that this is what happens when you start with the Marx of the *Economic and Philosophical Manuscripts* and extrapolate from all that humanist discourse on the sensate life of a human's "species-being." Perhaps he has never suffered from carbuncles. More seriously, the metabolic realities of the human body remain a concern for Marx after the infamous epistemological break, but they are always circumscribed and articulated within a set of social problems, those in which the body materializes, for instance, according to the production and circulation of the commodity. Obviously, that Marx might mention humans does not make his discourse humanist, which is just as true of "culture's" oscillation within theories of cultural studies (similarly, the attribution of culture within a discourse does not make it culturalist). Nevertheless, the concept of oscillation remains culturalist as it names the following strategy: culture is a means to weaken the pseudo-objectivist traits in specific categories of science.

Yet another weakness of oscillation, and one that links to culturalist discourse, would seem to be its stress on ambivalence, ambiguity, and contingency. Surely all those oscillations shake materialism to the ground so that, according to some interpretations, all oscillation rehearses is antimaterialism. Oscillation, as I have used it, is a sign of structural changes in social formations with concomitant mutations at the theoretical level, changes that are much less easy to explain within conventional categorizations of the social. Oscillation is a measure of those changes even if the methodology remains less sure of their possible consequences. Like the materialism of Marx, an oscillatory approach is interested in laws of motion yet is similarly nonpredictive. If there is a crystal ball, it is suspended from the end of a pendulum.

This last point is a reminder about oscillation's playful consequences, but this is also a source of weakness for a materialism's practical politics. The seriousness of this issue requires further comment. The oscillation within a system is playful in that it measures the play of difference across that system. But this mode of critique is not interested in demonstrating such play for its own sake, or indeed for validating the efficacy of play in the critical approach itself. It seems to me that there is a much-too-easy slide between the recognition of play — in the social ("after" the social), in language, in conceptual formulations — and the celebration of the playful. For the materialist, it is the process of the production of undecidability that is at issue, not its mere phenomenological existence. But this is a warning too for materialism that jumps on any kind of play as a metaphysician's wound — and one that must be cauterized at all costs. While I believe that Ebert, for instance, is correct to criticize the ludic impulse in many of the materialist feminists she reads, her approach tends to bracket, in advance, the possibility that something as methodologically sound as Marxism might suffer from the "incoherence of the seemingly coherent" (14). Put another way, if Marxism is to maintain a crucial relevance as "explanatory critique" for feminism, it must continue to come to terms with its own abstract edges — the elisions and slippages that have often undermined its greater aims yet always by accentuating the problems and the possibilities that remain. This is a lesson for materialism in general. To describe Stuart Hall as "antitheoretical" and an avatar of "ludic postmodern cultural studies" certainly drives a wedge between him and Marxism (a wedge that has been there since the late 1950s), but it doesn't do justice to the points of continuity between Marxism and Hall's paradigmatic (as well as discursive) approach to cultural studies. Raymond Williams maintained that the materialist critic must remain open to the prospect of new evidence, and, although he did not always live up to that vigilant desire, it is a principle that can usefully be applied to the project of cultural studies. Both Williams and Hall are critics for Marxism to the extent that they urge the rethinking of its principles within radical theory. "Play" is not a useful yardstick in this regard, for it reduces the methodological impurities of Marxism to a hard line from which any deviation is summarily dispatched. Again, the analysis of ambivalence in the theoretical constructs of materialism is a way to understand how materialism changes and affects change. It is not simply the ward of the antitheorists or the anti-Marxists or the antimaterialists; it is the charge of materialism itself.

This, of course, does not let the autocritical function of oscillatory critique off the hook, but it does provide some focus on the politics of theory to which it contributes. Here the aptness and the aptitude of oscillation as concept can be argued in a more proactive way. To that end, I would contend that oscillation not only provides a pertinent allegory of the course of science this century but reconstitutes the "ground" rules for materialism at the end of the millennium. The enormity of the issue is implied in the previous chapters, where oscillation is an organizing principle of the space between critique and its object. The status of science — whose effects, as Williams reminds us, promised us progress but instead gave us the twentieth century — also marches within a narrative of trembling and hesitation. Many scientists scoff at the idea that, as here, a literary theorist might speak to the question of science, as if tropes and metaphors have not been tools of scientific critique.[7] Again, however, I am not interested in transposing the terms of science as if they might stand in for the specific modus operandi of materialism. My point is rather that the ambiguities of science's relationship to history cannot be immune to the complex trajectories of capitalism and culture — and the responsible connection of these relatively autonomous worlds remains a task of materialist analysis.

Here, the narrative of oscillation in modern science is typified by Henri Poincaré's *Les oscillations electriques,* in which he investigated and formalized some of his own research into electricity with that of Maxwell (on electromagnetic radiation — 1865) and Hertz (on radio waves — 1887).[8] The analysis of "electrodynamics" and "electromagnetics" would play a key role not only in the specific development of a scientific field, but also in making electricity central to modern technological development. Poincaré emphasizes the logic of movement in electricity in order to spatialize its understanding, to urge, as James Gleick suggests, a "geometric imagination."[9] This is the beginning of oscillation's value for modern science, and, even if a geometric imagination was rejected by the scientific establishment (particularly the mathematicians), it has returned with a vengeance in various forms of chaos and complexity theory. For the moment, I will stick with electricity as oscillation, which is a useful way to remember how Galileo's study of the pendulum lives on in the physics of the everyday.

To be sure, the recognition of the importance of electricity could be registered earlier and was relatively well known. It is notable, for instance, that Engels in his graveside speech for Marx emphasizes that the latter "followed discoveries made in the field of electricity" — although he could not have guessed its immense impact on industrialization and the reorganization of the division of labor. Even when Lenin quipped that "Communism equals Soviets plus electrification," the implications of electricity for modernity, and modern systems, remained little understood. Such references to electricity are provocative but to me are inseparable from certain developments within the

logic of science, characteristics that increasingly refract the condition of oscillation itself. Poincaré himself became identified with forms of hypothetical
science that tended toward propositions that were "neither true, nor false, but
useful" (he was more concerned with the possibility of chaos than its proof).
Meanwhile, the aura of relativity that seeps through in modernist intimations
of fragmentation and uncertainty was also a feature of scientific discourse.
Bertrand Russell, using a lens of scientific humanism, noted that a human
being's aspirations were "the outcome of chance collocations of atoms" (perhaps the ones that fall upon the mind in the order in which they fall). And
by the middle of the century Karl Popper was suggesting that there is no
knowledge in the sense that implies finality. Barely a century after Poincaré's
lecture notes on oscillation as an object for science it now describes science's
relationship to issues like "progress" as well as serving as a metaphor for an
internal dynamic of scientific change. And, as we will see, this may well return materialism to sense perception, the sense of sense as sense of the world
("Le Sens du monde" in Nancy's interpretation).

Poincaré's theories about sensitivity to initial conditions in systems analysis were overlooked or suppressed by many of his contemporaries even as
differential equations began to crop up in many usually autonomous fields
of scientific inquiry. Science played out the logic of oscillation even as individual scientists could find the metaphor reductive and misleading. And, of
course, they are right. The study of instability in physical properties does not
mean that this is simply a structural model for the fluctuation of ideas or indeed for chaotic changes in human activities. This is the difference between
human beings acting out nature and acting out *of* nature (beyond it, to recall
that mischievous preposition once more). Ironically, the Holy Grail of a uni-
fied theory (order out of chaos) recalls that architectonic for reasons sketched
out long ago by Kant ("God has put a secret art into the forces of Nature so
as to enable it to fashion itself out of chaos into a perfect world system").[10]
Given the story of the twentieth century, it is not just social and literary theorists who should be worried when scientists claim to extrapolate from that
"secret art." Nevertheless, the function of chaos within systems analysis is
provocative, as can be seen by Wallerstein's more recent emendations to his
world systems critique.

In *Geopolitics and Geoculture* Wallerstein attempts to integrate some of the
lessons of the new science for a materialist understanding of the world economy.[11] Two aspects are directly relevant for the mode of critique in evidence
earlier in this work. First, Wallerstein argues that an understanding of "geoculture" is fundamental to a critique of the capitalist world system. He terms
it geoculture "by analogy with geopolitics, not because it is supra-local or
supra-national but because it represents the cultural framework within which
the world system operates" (11). For Wallerstein, geoculture is not a super-

structure of the world system but its "underside" — something that is integral to its operations but more difficult to fathom because it is "more hidden from view." While this maintains the air of the "secret art" to be revealed, the more important emphasis is on the determinate role of culture (something that is obviously a motor of cultural studies). From the 1960s the stability of geoculture has been challenged in three ways, according to Wallerstein, which together constitute a rejection of "the universalist pretensions of liberalism." These are the focus on culture as opposed to the economic and political; the elaboration of the concepts of sexism and racism in understanding formations of the social; and the challenge of the new science that has opposed Baconian/Newtonian principles and the centrality of linear, equilibrium processes in scientific analysis. Interestingly, this last destabilizes the false opposition typified in earlier "two cultures" debates (science versus the humanities), which Wallerstein reads as a "pillar of the geocultural system of the capitalist world-economy" (13). Although this would need some fleshing out, I do not believe many would disagree with a diagnosis that reads these aspects of geoculture as a constitutive underbelly of capitalist expansionism and opposition to the same in the last thirty years. What is unusual, however, is the metaphor that Wallerstein then draws from the new science to rethink the logic of the capitalist system itself. This constitutes the second provocation of the geocultural for the present analysis:

> In brief, it is that the capitalist world-economy constitutes an historical system, which thereby has an historical life: it had a genesis; it has a set of cyclical rhythms and secular trends that characterize it; it has internal contradictions which will lead to its eventual demise. The argument is that the short-run contradictions lead to middle-run solutions which translate into long-run linear curves approaching asymptotes. As they approach these asymptotes, the pressures to return to equilibria diminish, leading to ever greater oscillations and bifurcation. Instead of large random fluctuations resulting in small changes in the curve, small fluctuations will result in large changes.
>
> The imminence of bifurcation, brought about by the fact that middle-run solutions to short-run contradictions are no longer readily available, is disastrous for the system. The collapse of Leninism is very bad news indeed for the dominant forces of the capitalist world-economy. It has removed the last major politically *stabilizing* force within the world-system. It will not be easy to put Humpty-Dumpty together again. (14)

The speed with which Wallerstein lays the logic of the new science over the instabilities of the world system is somewhat alarming, but even if we reject the convenience of the metaphor (and the optimism that results from it:

"small fluctuations will result in large changes"), it intensifies the necessity to investigate the points of contact (or what the chaos theorist might term the "fractal basin boundaries") between the dynamic systems of the cultural, the economic, the social, and the scientific. This intensity is not necessarily a sign of integration (and Wallerstein knows that the laws of thermodynamics help his analysis on this point) but does keep alive the recognition that knowledge of change is itself conditioned by the changing relations of different branches of knowledge. The study of racism, for instance, has fundamentally altered the way in which questions of imperialism, colonialism, and nationalism are construed: economies of domination cannot be seen outside the ideological modes of differentiation used to buttress them. Similarly, the ambivalence of hybridity is a fluctuation in the conditions of modes of domination that is not tangential to the laws of movement in economic systems: it is an example of its geocultural possibility. Analysis of the cultural can sustain a focus on the political even if a conventional political approach to the economic denies the complexity of those boundaries.

I have argued that oscillation is a useful concept for understanding materialist theory and its relationship to its object. Historically, one can use the concept to track theoretical oscillation/vacillation in key works of the materialist tradition that, I believe, provide the basis for strategic forms of rearticulation. In the contemporary period, the concept of oscillation is both an autocritical reflex and a bridging device for the analysis of separate spheres of intellectual inquiry — this is one of the ways that feminism comes back to Marx's body. But the third provenance of oscillation as a concept is the most difficult or abstract, and that is to understand it as a specific structural logic of contemporary theory, materialism's ghost within a spatial/temporal dynamic. Again, this is not the age of oscillation, but a crisis in the world system has intensified the possibilities of alternatives or counterindications. Thus, oscillatory critique is not just a function of materialism's quandary in light of the epochal collapse of "actually existing socialism" in Eastern Europe and the Soviet Union but a barometer of a greater instability in the system that has supposedly triumphed. One example alone, the end of the Cold War, underlines how an arguable status quo has atrophied or "unhinged" the prowess of capitalism in certain formations so that alternative lines of force now become possible. Wallerstein suggests, "Whereas, within the ongoing structural processes of an historical system, there is little role for voluntaristic 'speeding up' of the contradictions, at the moment of crisis or transformation, the role of the politico-moral *choice* expands considerably. It is on these occasions that it can be truly said that 'man [*sic*] makes his own history'" (106). This, I believe, is the oscillatory potential in the current conjuncture, one in which, as Wallerstein notes, "We have perhaps arrived now in the true realm of uncertainty."

Balibar writes of vacillation, Wallerstein of uncertainty, and Jameson of fragmentation. These are not simply examples of materialists (and/or masculinists) second-guessing, still less capitulations before a ludic embrace. On the contrary, they are instances of, as Spivak puts it, "Marxists, among other struggles."[12] This is a dominant symptom of the *interregnum*. Spivak's specific point of reference is the incorporation of Marx's econo-mimesis into feminist and anticolonialist struggles — something I have tried to emphasize in my approach to space and the body for materialist critique. For their part, Balibar and Wallerstein have made significant contributions to a new understanding of race, ethnicity, and nation, and Jameson, of course, has taken discourses of econo-mimesis into some of the furthest reaches of dialectical totality. I want, however, to draw another lesson from Wallerstein's reinscription of the new science, one that will underline that oscillation is not just about wavering but about wariness where scientific discourse is at stake.

The realm of uncertainty that Wallerstein recalls is not about the eclipse of materialist scientificity in relation to capitalism. The attraction, or one might say strange attraction, of the new science is the weakening of its own objectivist paradigms and positivist methodologies. The danger is that the social scientist or the literary theorist may believe that she or he is making "science" by analogizing from theorists of chaos and complexity. No doubt we will increasingly witness a plethora of Mandelbrot sets, butterfly effects, and Lorenz diagrams as latter-day *flâneurs* pilfer the more popular texts of contemporary science.[13] But the more important point for Wallerstein is the forms of coincidence and noncoincidence within and between the world system he details and a particular branch of science. Perhaps the data of each can be investigated through a similar paradigm, but Wallerstein knows that the capitalist world system is not a mirror of nature or natural phenomena. He sees social science and science *tout court*, however, as bound by a similar range of determinate possibilities. The calling into question of scientific premises and conventional materialist modeling is ultimately not happenstance, nor is the reason for crisis in the sciences in general. Wallerstein suggests: "It is rather the expression of this crisis, which was caused by the fact that the sciences have come increasingly to be in a cul-de-sac, as they found the changing reality increasingly incomprehensible" (121). Thus, "The confusion and uncertainty are closely linked to that found in the [social] movements, and both are products of the crisis in the world-system. All these 'crises' are simultaneous, imply each other, and can only be resolved in relation to each other" (121). The uncertainty is itself a function of structural nonlinearity in economic formations, but one that has been exacerbated in the present.

Certainly, the cultural theorist need not take this tack, but that is a question of political alignment and not just a measure of fluency in the discourses at stake. N. Katherine Hayles has been popularizing the discourse of chaos theory for the humanities for some years now, yet it is not always clear what the politics of this interdisciplinarity looks like. In *Chaos Bound*, Hayles links chaos theory and deconstruction as part of a postmodern age, but in her introduction to *Chaos and Order* this is qualified to signify what "chaotics can mean for cultural studies" (19). This shift may imply different political agendas. Hayles, like Wallerstein, maintains a suspicion of the appropriateness of chaos science for cultural analysis, but whereas Wallerstein reads chaotics as a symptom of structural crisis in the world system, Hayles limits its contextual determinations to what she calls a "cultural matrix." To some degree this is a version of cultural logic, and not just a humanist's rediscovery of the expansive play of *geist*. The correspondence between fields in Hayles's schema is isomorphic and not one of direct determination. This is pleasing to both the culturalists and the scientists, but the logic only begins to indicate the deeper context in which correspondence itself becomes possible. My stress has been on the imaginative difficulty in mapping an end to a millennium whose very condition is abstruse simultaneity (complexity minus time). The lesson of chaos theory for cultural studies so far would seem to be that it provides a metaphorics for a politics of culture that few could actively embrace. The descriptive prowess expands exponentially, but a practical consciousness withers in the face of a "matrix" of inscrutability. Is this, then, the fate of an oscillatory approach?

The conceptual space of materialism is determined by systemic crises in the object of its analysis. This does not mean, however, that minor fluctuations in the latter, say, in capitalism, lead to catastrophic convolutions in the former. The dialectic is not altogether a shadow of chaotics as currently construed. Indeed, while one must laud the critical shifts in scientific thinking in recent years, the conservatism of chaotics, its status as normal science, necessitates a continuing distinction in the forms of wavering articulated. Thus, if oscillation as a concept alludes to a history of science in its deployment, it is not a symptom of such science, but one *for* science. As we have noted, normal science, science as is, has often lashed out at theorists of economic, gender, and racial inequality as Leftist pseudoscientific poseurs. An alliance with that mode of legitimation is not just self-defeating, but undermines a belief in the structural condition of crisis (structures greater than even the posturing of the scientific community). This will mean clarifying oscillation's conceptual range even as I force a cognate in the history of electricity.

We are still less than two hundred years beyond Volta's development of the battery, but materialists generally associate the impact of electricity with an earlier stage of capitalism (let us say, capital plus electricity equals imperialism). The atomic age, the age of late capitalism, may well represent a break with conventional models of imperialism, but this does not mean that electricity is no longer a primary agent in capital accumulation. Some might argue that the atomic age ended with Chernobyl, and yet still this has not stemmed the desire for electricity (the more telling example here would be the Bhopal catastrophe of 1984, since Union Carbide remains both a major player in the processing of weapons-grade nuclear material and a transnational that routinely flaunts its responsibility to world citizenry with true postmodern flexi-local élan). And if, as Jameson suggests, the combustion engine is also a technological emblem of the imperial age, it is noticeable that currently the only viable alternative to the petrol-powered automobile is the electric car (and this was an alternative at the beginning of the century as well). For the avatars of the megalopolis, the only question is how to get electricity, not whether it is ecologically sound to do so. What I am suggesting is that electricity remains a common denominator in modern science and technology in the same way that Poincaré's experiments on nonlinearity continue to have an impact on forms of chaos science. The importance of this is not just that it betrays the uneven developments of the modern era but that we are still learning the lessons of the power unleashed by science within an earlier mode of capitalist organization. There is oscillation in space, time, body, spirit, and thought: Does this inhibit sense perception as Marx reads it, or is its intensity a prelude to the moment when the senses "become directly in their practice theoreticians"?[14]

Theremin's touch? Lev Termen (anglicized to Leon Theremin) was born the year after Poincaré published his analyses of electrical oscillation. Trained in physics (and also a dab hand at the cello), Theremin was working with an electrical device (most likely a radio) at the University of Petrograd in 1918 when he discovered that the sound it emitted could be altered according to the proximity of his body to it. Within two years he had perfected a musical instrument now known as the Theremin, and modern music has never been the same. The heart of the Theremin is the electrical oscillator (originally in vacuum tubes, but later made with transistors). By setting two high-frequency oscillators at different frequencies a differential field of electromagnetism is created that, with amplification, produces a high-pitched sound that corresponds to that difference. Introduce something that carries electric capacitance into that field (say, the human body), and the pitch and amplification can be changed. The result of the interaction between a human and the Theremin is electric music (some twenty years before the electric guitar). The Theremin was an instant success, and Leon packed symphony halls all over Europe (including the Paris Opera in 1927). Crowds were drawn not just because of the novelty of the sound but because in the history of music the Theremin was unique: it is the only instrument played without being touched. Theremin's bizarre instrument and even more bizarre life have recently been the subject of a full-length film documentary (by Steven M. Martin, 1994) called *Theremin: An Electronic Odyssey.* This odyssey, as idiosyncratic as it is, is also the story of the twentieth century.[15]

There are two key aspects to this tale. The first relates to Theremin's life and the impact of his music. Soon after inventing the Theremin, Leon was impressing music aficionados among the leadership of the Soviet Union. In 1922 Theremin demonstrated his instrument for Lenin, who approved wholeheartedly (communism equals Soviets plus Theremin?). Theremin recalls that Lenin "liked music and had some musical sense — he also tried to play my instrument with good effect." With ambitions not altogether consonant with Leninism, Theremin was quickly sucked in by the culturati of Western Europe and then the United States. Indeed, from 1928 Theremin lived for ten years in New York and toured the country as an entertainer for the upper classes (the general public was broke because of the Depression). Scientists were also fascinated by the instrument. Einstein once came to Leon's apartment and took a turn playing the Theremin (unlike Lenin, Einstein, according to Leon, "didn't have a good ear, but still he was playing it"). In 1938, Stalin apparently ordered the NKVD (forerunner of the KGB) to kidnap Theremin from his Manhattan apartment and bring him back to the Soviet Union. If this sounds dubious what is certain is that Theremin disappeared and, although Theremin virtuoso Clara Rockmore kept the art of the Theremin alive, the age of the elite concert was over. Did Stalin want to recapture the music of the first years of the Soviets? Probably not. In fact, after a long spell of "rehabilitation" in a prison camp, Theremin was set to work to develop a key instrument of the Cold War. What he came up with was an electronic surveillance device: the bug (or *buran*). This was Theremin's second major contribution to twentieth-century history (for which he may have been decorated by Stalin).

While the bug was facilitating all kinds of information retrieval during the Cold War (and who knows the precise role it played in the emergence of the atomic age), the sound of the Theremin reemerged in Western culture. In an ironic twist of history, Theremin's ingenious arrangement of electronic oscillators produced a sound that symbolized the otherworldliness (and paranoia) of postwar American society. If you watch that classic work of Cold War kitsch, *The Day the Earth Stood Still,* with the sound turned down, you will appreciate just how much of the "alien" mood of the film is conveyed by its soundtrack, which features the Theremin (*It Came from Outer Space* also used the Theremin to stir up the fear of the foreign "invader"). In the 1950s, synthesized electronic music was not just a staple of science fiction films; it was a signature of America's fragile self-identity in the face of a malevolent other. To rewrite Jameson's formulation, it was a signature of the invisible. Should one be surprised, therefore, when, in the 1960s, the Theremin was taken up as an instrument of the counterculture and antiestablishment sentiment in the Beach Boys' "Good Vibrations"? Youth culture itself had become the scene for an electronic redefinition of American identity: the amplified instrument had come of age.

When director Steven Martin tracked down Theremin in Moscow in 1991 and managed to bring him back to New York for a reunion with the ageless Clara Rockmore, a personal and political odyssey was completed. Could Theremin have reappeared but for the waning of the Cold War? Unlikely. But the symbolic power of the Theremin itself has a lesson for materialist history and theory. To see someone play the Theremin without touching it, that is, by moving one's hands in relation to its two antennae, is to witness a transformation in sense perception, one made possible by electrical oscillators and by electromagnetism in general. It is also a demonstration of how oscillation works as a different mode of the order-out-of-chaos argument. I should add, however, that there are many other examples of technology that elicit this wonder of the modern — the "difference engine" on which these electronic words appear can also be "played" without being touched — but the Theremin and its inventor epitomize this process even as they demand an alternative means of material apprehension.

First, the Theremin is a sign of a human being's changed relationship as a body in space. The field of oscillation allows the senses to interact and create beyond the normal codes of sensate experience. The instrument has its own image, which can be interlocated with the image of the human body. Again, just like the phantom limb, the Theremin conjures a liminal space in the sensorium that is every bit as "real" as a finger on a piano key. To some extent, it is a conceptual validation of Vattimo's point about the weakening of the reality principle, for the Theremin keeps disorientation alive as a measure of the shortfall between the body's sense of belonging (how it belongs and what belongs to it) and its extensions and prosthetic imputations in advanced technology. But this relationship to sense is a logic of interpretation and not simply the epiphenomenonal difference between (in Vattimo's case) the modern and the postmodern. Yes, the body matters in a different way, but its politics of materialization does not ultimately reside in a hermeneutic difference in the history of aesthetics. Marx's interest in electricity, for instance, was spurred by a fascination about what it could mean in the development of productive forces. In this sense, the Theremin stages a problem about the body's relationship to an object. It is the ghost of the commodity, its aura, that draws human sense beyond itself.

That the body is multivalent and oscillatory is clear: what materialism argues over are the forms and meanings of its mutability. For the Marx of the Paris manuscripts the body has been de-formed, estranged by capitalist forms of private property that reduce all the body's senses to the "sense of having" ("private property has made us so stupid and one-sided that an object is only *ours* when we have it" [87]). Within the vast differences that construct the body in global space the question of "having" has become more not less prescient, for "having objects" appears as the very integer of well-being. In typical declarative style Marx opines that "the forming [and, one should add, deforming and transforming] of the five senses is a labor of the entire history of the world down to the present," although it is only relatively recently that materialist histories of the senses have been attempted. In *Mimesis and Alterity*, Michael Taussig explores how the mimetic faculty itself is a utopian form in the history of the emancipation of the senses that Marx invokes. The wonder of mimesis that Taussig analyzes is that it "tickles the heels" of the very orders of representation normalized in the will to hegemony (in colonialism and imperialism, for instance). As in the carnivalesque, the constructed nature of representation as a second nature is open to replication as disjunction. And once more, the metaphor for this perplexity in movement is striking: "History wreaks its revenge on representational security as essentialism and constructionism oscillate wildly in a death-struggle over the claims of mimesis to be the nature that culture uses to create a now-beleaguered second nature."[16] As I have proposed, rather than a master trope, oscillation describes both the demastering of knowledge, on the one hand, and the intensities of socialization, on the other. This is a "nervous system," as Taussig would have it, and a "becoming" system for theories of Being, however fearful systematicity and systemic change must be. Materialism's role in this is minor one, particularly when its formulations have been complicit and complacent with movement as status quo. Perhaps only now, when grand narratives are perilously arcane, can materialism assume a more politically productive role — not by confirming the material force of culture in everyday life, but by elaborating its radical specificity at the points where its truth becomes trauma, where the body is trapped in a regulative frenzy. Most oppressive hegemonies rely upon a decorporealization of space (as Derek Gregory puts it) that is at once a contradictory and necessary move, for the body's social praxis is acknowledged in its abolition or displacement (forms of racism, nationhood, homophobia, masculinism, and capitalism depend in different ways upon positing an absence in this way). The very term "corporatism" is symptomatic of what is interpellated and effaced by its operations. As the aura of the shoe indicates, economies of desire and disavowal attempt to short-circuit the requisite imagination of cognitive mapping. And, however much a footnote in the history of the modern, the eerie sound of the Theremin is a mark of our cognitive repositioning by the wonder of technology — that which indulges our senses if only to magically destabilize the body's relationship to them.

Theremin's touch or Theremin touched? In their conclusion to *What Is Philosophy?* Deleuze and Guattari sketch a possible logic for the mind in the face of chaos. Art, science, and philosophy are compelled to order chaos but by "casting planes over it." The artist, for instance, "brings back from the chaos *varieties* that no longer constitute a reproduction of the sensory in the organ but set up a being of the sensory, a being of sensation, on an anorganic plane of composition that is able to restore the infinite."[17] This is the artistry of Theremin, who takes from the structured oscillation of the machine a realm of difference and renders it music, a sense of the body in space drawn from the nonidentity in difference of human and machine image. If this resonates with the conceptual realm of the philosopher, it is only because philosophy too draws from "inseparable variations" in producing a consistency, a reality. Deleuze and Guattari ask, "And what would *thinking* be if it did not constantly confront chaos?" Our noble chaosophers do not leave chaos as the outside of the organ of cognition (in the same way that it is not wholly outside art, philosophy, or science) but link this to the determinate operations of the brain itself:

> The brain does not cease to constitute limits that determine functions of variables in particularly extended areas; relations between these variables (connections) manifest all the more an uncertain and hazardous characteristic, not only in electrical synapses, which show a statistical chaos, but in chemical synapses, which refer to a deterministic chaos. There are not so much cerebral centers as points, concentrated in one area and disseminated in another, and "oscillators," oscillating molecules that pass from one point to another. (216)

In a move that reminds one of Deleuze and Guattari's machinic discourse, one could say that playing the Theremin mimics the brain to the extent that the chaos of oscillation can produce the order of music. Like the Theremin, the brain continually harnesses uncertainty within determinate conditions, and the possible variations are infinite. This is a lesson not only about the brain, but also about the machine. Just as Bertrand Russell considers sense data in the absence of a sensing subject/observer (the camera observes but it has no subjective state of being), so Deleuze and Guattari offer a vision of the machine that presupposes a "nonsubjective observer," that which "qualifies" in a sensory way what is otherwise a "scientifically determined state of affairs, thing, or body" (131). This is not the ghost in the machine, but the ghost *of* the machine for science. Thus, "science is haunted not by its own unity but by the plane of reference constituted by all the limits or borders through which it confronts chaos" (119). Is this also a ghost for materialism?

For materialism, Theremin's touch is the revelation of the constitution of structured orders of difference in the body's sensate being. Again, it is the articulation of an abstract space, but one that is bound by material components (and in Theremin's case, is a pertinent allegory of U.S./Soviet relations this century). The "precarious balance of subject and object" from which Adorno extrapolates must be written into the conceptual operations of materialist critique. To a certain extent, it is already there as an organizing metaphor, but now the development of productive forces demands that it be more forcefully taken up within the politics of position it implies. But this is not a lesson that swings one from relativity to relativism: it is, rather, a determined response to the changing conditions and knowledges of materialization.

Obviously, by maintaining a certain tension and continuity between the emergence of the study (and application) of electromagnetism in the modern and the present day I mean to suggest the same in material conditions. As Jameson has more recently reaffirmed, it is very possible to suspend the project of Marxism in the discourse of post-Marxism, but how long could a capitalist corporation (let us say, Nike) suspend the profit motive before it went out of business? Simultaneously, one must acknowledge that whatever the optimism in technological development at the beginning of the century, with whatever profit motive, the Angel of History now stares into the abyss of its own creation ("progress"). This ecological chaos is not quite the playing out of chaos-science logic, although it has been read to say as much, but nevertheless it reminds us that materialism must waver considerably more than Marx where science and technology are concerned.

The Theremin does not signify a "commonsense" representation of reality, just as the chronotope of the shoe does not proffer a normative time/space continuum. Both perhaps urge new categories of representation, even if the econo-mimetic faculty cannot escape its political (not to mention philosophical) contradictions. It is important to keep in mind that the ardor of oscillation does not resolve itself into a metaphorics of political economy. The point has been to track at least some of the ways that oscillation is immanent to subject and object, rather than only being a descriptor for the canny dance they make together. In this way, it is not so much the name for a politics, but more an attempt to explain the logics that are endemic to certain forms of the political. Marx's discovery of a specific law of motion in economics is pertinent to the present conjuncture only because it remains adequate to the mutations of capital as its object. Perhaps we are still only beginning to learn that the vacillations in his overall model are not fatal flaws (as if the model itself were the subject of tragedy) but are, rather, part of what keeps materialism alive — alive to the possibility of concrete change. That may be the only justification to oscillate wildly.

NOTES

AN INTRODUCTORY OSCILLATION

1. Martin Jay's use of "force field" derives from Walter Benjamin's and T. W. Adorno's descriptions of the dialectic as a *Kraftfeld*. In his book on Adorno, Jay characterizes Adorno's deployment of the term as an attempt to signify "a relational interplay of attractions and aversions that constituted the dynamic, transmutational structure of a complex phenomenon" (Martin Jay, *Adorno* [Cambridge, Mass.: Harvard University Press, 1984], 14; see also idem, *Force Fields* [New York: Routledge, 1993]). Jay goes on to suggest that the force field was the "master trope" of his Adorno book as well as, of course, being an organizing principle of his *Force Fields*. Applying it to the latter, Jay notes that "in essence . . . intellectual history can itself be seen as the product of a force field of often conflicting impulses, pulling it in one way or another, and posing more questions that it can answer" (3). This gloss on force fields is similar to my interpretation of oscillation, although Jay is perhaps less aware of its cognates in the physical sciences (the field of force in electromagnetism, for instance, is potentially a field of oscillation). Interestingly, force field crops up most often in science fiction where it is related to notions of invisible boundaries. Imagining the unrepresentable remains a focus of dialectics. The "zone of engagement," by contrast, implies a much stronger sense of external and conscious contact. Indeed, Perry Anderson's interpretation is more in step with the idea of intellectual argumentation — a form of "engagement" that he applied to Gramsci in the 1970s (see "The Antimonies of Antonio Gramsci," *New Left Review* 100 [November–January 1976–77]: 5–78). Generally, the zone of engagement provides Anderson with a critical edge on the "analytic tableau" of many a Leftist thinker. After summarizing the key notions of Gramsci, Anderson affirms that these "proved to be a condition of understanding his oscillations" (see Perry Anderson, *A Zone of Engagement* [London: Verso, 1992]). Again, the spatial metaphors organize the response. I will be giving this a political as well as literary reading.

2. Here I am using cultural materialism to describe the scene of an intense theoretical negotiation between materialism's claims to scientificity and cultural concepts that speak beyond their somewhat limited superstructural confines. The key figure in this negotiation remains Raymond Williams, and no summary here will do justice to the range and seriousness of his engagement with the problem of culturalism and scientificity. The weakness I refer to is multivalent but here refers to an overexpansive and deeply contradictory representation of culture as a primary arena of social and political change. I should add that, ironically, such an inflated representation is not in Williams's work itself, even though he has been read to say as much. For Williams's

interpretation of this question, see, for instance, Raymond Williams, *Problems in Materialism and Culture* (London: Verso, 1980); and idem, *Marxism and Literature* (Oxford: Oxford University Press, 1976). My argument on the fate of materialism "in" culture will appear elsewhere.

3. As I will argue, this moment of reflection is significant within the greater movement of materialist analysis. The content of materialist "homeostasis" after "actually existing socialism" is a key to its continuing vitality within political economy and beyond. For evidence of this autocritique, see Bern Magnus and Stephen Cullenberg, eds., *Whither Marxism? Global Crises in International Perspective* (New York: Routledge, 1995); Saree Makdisi, Cesare Casarino, and Rebecca E. Karl, eds., *Marxism beyond Marxism* (New York: Routledge, 1996); and Antonio Callari and David F. Ruccio, eds., *Postmodern Materialism and the Future of Marxist Theory* (Hanover, N.H.: Wesleyan University Press, 1996).

4. In a collection of essays, *Subject to History* (Ithaca, N.Y.: Cornell University Press, 1991), David Simpson, the editor, writes an introduction entitled "The Moment of Materialism" in which materialism maintains a certain momentum, but is not best described as momentous. Simpson concedes that materialism is "everywhere and nowhere" in his volume: partly because the processes of definition have major epistemological and political implications; partly because of the "anxiety of definition" that this entails; and partly because "materialist criticism is still very much within and between Marx(ism) and Nietzsche, unsure of exactly how much of each can be worked into the other" (25). All of these points set important limits on the will to codify a materialist methodology, but what kind of flexibility defines the "moment" remains a crucial problem in assessing the conjunctural practice of materialism (What kind of subject? What kind of history?). Indeed, one must remain committed to an analysis of the contours of materialism to make certain, as best one can, that it is ready at a "moment's" notice. This is, I take it, the implication of Simpson's Oliver Twist analogy (29).

5. During the course of this book I will provide several examples of the efficacy of this approach to materialism's situatedness. Obviously, vacillation of this kind is not the product of intention pure and simple, but is more indicative of a political unconscious bound by the material conditions of the present. It is this, I believe, that informs the mischievous question mark that is there in the *Polygraph* special issue *Marxism beyond Marxism?* but missing in the title of the book version of the same collection. Interestingly, this vacillation is repeated in the introductory essay that accompanies the latter, where the question mark disappears from the essay title only to reappear in the running heads. For some the fate of this question mark will only be a matter of editing skills, but it is entirely consonant with the logic of the introduction and indeed the collection of essays. Can there be a Marxism beyond Marxism? Are we already living its reality? Isn't the "beyond" of Marxism a function of its constitutive logic? What might make this more evident today? To reread these volumes side by side is to experience the importance of liminality to Marxist critique. See *Marxism beyond Marxism?* a special issue of *Polygraph* 6/7 (1993); and Makdisi, Casarino, and Karl, *Marxism beyond Marxism.*

6. See Terry Eagleton, *The Illusions of Postmodernism* (Oxford: Blackwell, 1996), 5. In many ways, Eagleton's opening chapters are an indictment of the attempt offered here. I would argue, however, that Eagleton himself is no stranger to the oscillatory determinants within and without Marxist thought.

7. See T. W. Adorno, *Aesthetic Theory*, ed. Gretel Adorno and Rolf Tiedemann, trans. C. Lenhardt (London: Routledge, 1984); subsequent references to this work will be given in the text.

8. The usefulness of Adorno's description here is that it shows how homeostasis itself is integral to historical process — that its fragile equilibrium cannot defend art from its imbrication in the dizzying plenitude of the social. This much is true of theory, although I tend to stress the autocritical function of its moment of autonomy.

9. See Fredric Jameson, *Late Marxism: Adorno, or the Persistence of the Dialectic* (London: Verso, 1990), 28. This is part of Jameson's general move to recapture Adorno for materialist dialectics. The case is certainly made although I obviously argue for a differential mode of "persistence" in modernity's project, if not modernism's.

10. See Eric J. Hobsbawm, *The Age of Extremes* (London: Abacus, 1995). This book has already inspired a wealth of commentary. My interpretation would begin with its stylistics. For instance, in its last section Hobsbawm beckons futurity by writing of the 1990s in the past tense. The effect is not to suggest that the die is cast as some commentators would have it, but instead emphasizes that we are at an end in which the conditions of finality remain undecidable, or to be won. The consignment to the past registers the parameters of "persistence" in Jameson's parlance.

11. Gilles Deleuze and Félix Guattari, *What Is Philosophy?* trans. Hugh Tomlinson and Graham Burchell (New York: Columbia University Press, 1994), 5; subsequent references to this work will be given in the text.

12. Friedrich Engels, *Anti-Dühring* (London: Lawrence and Wishart, 1955). See, in particular, part 1, chapter 13.

13. This is not the place to rehearse Bakhtin's hesitation before a meaning for dialectics outside the cognate he witnessed up close in the Soviet Union. I have argued elsewhere that too many critics take Bakhtin at his word regarding the dialectic, which is to say that they reproduce the terms of his reductionist critique on that subject.

14. See Derek Gregory, *Geographical Imaginations* (Oxford: Blackwell, 1994).

15. See Neil Smith, *Uneven Development* (Oxford: Blackwell, 1990), 5. Smith's argument considers, among other salient themes, the political implications of the suppression of space in modern materialist thought. Given the global pretensions of advanced or late capitalism, his intervention is crucial in resituating a materialist approach to new regimes of the production of space.

16. Wallerstein bases much of his interpretation of this branch of the "new science" on Prigogine and Stengers, who look at the philosophical implications of chaos theory. See Ilya Prigogine and Isabelle Stengers, *Order out of Chaos* (New York: Bantam, 1984). Needless to say, "normal" science finds such a philosophical disposition playfully inconsequential. I will take up Wallerstein's approach in more detail later.

17. Paul Gilroy's *The Black Atlantic* (Cambridge, Mass.: Harvard University Press, 1993) will provide a crucial touchstone for my elaboration of theoretical space in chapter 3.

18. See Henri Lefebvre, *The Production of Space*, trans. Donald Nicholson-Smith (Oxford: Blackwell, 1991). Lefebvre links this abstraction to that of labor and the moment of its alienation from the productive process.

19. This nod to Bakhtin will be elaborated in my chapter on the shoe, although I am developing a series of case studies that analyze its implications for the representation of labor in general in a separate volume.

20. Diawara expands on this point in his article "Black Studies, Cultural Studies, Performative Acts," *Border/lines* 29/30 (1993): 21–26.

21. This is a linchpin of Eagleton's claims for the aesthetic in relation to materialism. See Terry Eagleton, *The Ideology of the Aesthetic* (London: Basil Blackwell, 1990).

22. I will not attempt to summarize the extremely important work that has been done in this area. Most materialist feminists have had to come to terms with the political implications of this elision (which has been every bit as debilitating as the diminution of space). For a general but articulate argument against this tide, see Rosemary Hennessy, *Materialist Feminism and the Politics of Discourse* (New York: Routledge, 1993). For a more systematic and controversial interpretation of "body politics," see Teresa Ebert, *Ludic Feminism and After* (Ann Arbor: University of Michigan Press, 1996). For a recent attempt to reinscribe the body within a mode-of-production argument, see Donald M. Lowe, *The Body in Late-Capitalist USA* (Durham, N.C.: Duke University Press, 1995). My reading of materialist and/or "corporeal" feminism is developed in chapter 2 in relation to the work of Judith Butler and Elizabeth Grosz. An analysis of the (de)corporealization of woman as worker in the world system appears in chapter 5.

23. Spivak makes the specific argument in her *Outside in the Teaching Machine* (New York: Routledge, 1993), chapter 4. But see also her introduction and epilogue to her translation of Devi in Mahasweta Devi, *Imaginary Maps*, trans. Gayatri Chakravorty Spivak (New York: Routledge, 1995). *Doulot*, as Spivak points out, means "wealth" in Bengali, to which Devi provides an ironic and critical elaboration.

24. The answer, obviously, is not to modify capitalism to interpellate the super-exploited as consumers, for this itself would only be a further expansion of capital logic. The inside/outside logic of capital must be deconstructed (in the positive sense) to deny the ideology that consumerism itself is the apotheosis of human development. This has profound implications both for the political significance of the so-called Third World and for emerging forms of ecological anticapitalism.

I. METAPHORS (OF MATERIALISM)

1. This is evident not only in Adorno's *Aesthetic Theory*, ed. Gretel Adorno and Rolf Tiedemann, trans. C. Lenhardt (London: Routledge, 1984) but also in his collaborative work with Max Horkheimer, *Dialectic of Enlightenment*, trans. John Cumming (New York: Herder and Herder, 1972).

2. "Advanced" and "late" will be used interchangeably in the following argument, and will include flexible accumulation and Post-Fordism. The differences between such terms are significant for, among other things, registering the characteristics of contemporary capitalism. Since multiculturalism is a rather belated recognition (at least in some accounts) of the multiplicity endemic to culture, perhaps we need a similar flag or mark in economic critique: multicapitalism.

3. See Alan Sinfield, *Faultlines: Cultural Materialism and the Politics of Dissident Reading* (Berkeley: University of California Press, 1992). Like Anderson's "zone of engagement" and Jay's "force fields," Sinfield uses a spatial metaphor to elaborate the critical function of materialism. A fault line is an interesting way to character-

ize the contradictions of capitalism and, like oscillation, accentuates the importance of relational space. My only quibble would be with the somewhat pedestrian motion implied in the analogy to tectonic plates, but perhaps this is a fitting symbol for the new historicism to which Sinfield's book contributes.

4. This is something that Stuart Hall has recommended for cultural studies. As such, it is part of the general resistance to the *grand récits* of yore. The difficulty remains whether such particularism can be consonant with the global analytic that capitalism, for instance, appears to compel — that, in itself, describes an agon of the present.

5. Of course, this is not a return to economism or an orthodox invocation of base/superstructure arguments but merely a reminder (perhaps only to myself) that materialism does not *begin* from abstraction.

6. See, for instance, Sebastiano Timpanaro, *On Materialism,* trans. Lawrence Garner (London: Verso, 1975); and Perry Anderson, *Considerations on Western Marxism* (London: Verso, 1976).

7. I am developing this theme in another series of essays, some of which are already available. See, for instance, "Cultural Materialism and Material Dialogics," *Discours social/Social Discourse* 7, no. 2 (fall 1995); "Information in Formation: Williams, Media, 'China'" in *Cultural Materialism: Essays on Raymond Williams,* ed. Christopher Prendergast (Minneapolis: University of Minnesota Press, 1995); and "Cultural Studies and the Prospect for a Multicultural Materialism," *Rethinking Marxism* 5, no. 1 (spring 1992).

8. This, of course, does not mean that Williams's concepts cannot be productively reinterpreted. See, for instance, Fred Pfeil, "Postmodernism as a 'Structure of Feeling,'" in *Marxism and the Interpretation of Culture,* ed. Cary Nelson and Lawrence Grossberg, 381–403 (Urbana: University of Illinois Press, 1988).

9. Etienne Balibar, "The Vacillation of Ideology," in *Masses, Classes, Ideas,* trans. James Swenson (New York: Routledge, 1994), 105.

10. This is both a function and a symptom of theory as elitism. But this cannot be separated from a more general critique of professional specialization. For a materialist analysis of the intellectual in this regard, see Bruce Robbins, *Secular Vocations* (New York: Verso, 1993).

11. This is well-worn ground for some theorists, but part of Laclau and Mouffe's procedure is a metaphorics of materialism, ingrained perhaps in the Althusserian notion of symptom itself derived from Lacan and psychoanalysis. The slide from Marxism to post-Marxism can indeed be read within this metaphoricity, although most critics (including me) have been drawn to the argument in and around "post."

12. Gregory Elliott does this to some extent using a psychological approach in his essay "Analysis Terminated, Analysis Interminable: the Case of Louis Althusser," in *Althusser: A Critical Reader,* ed. Gregory Elliot (Oxford: Blackwell, 1994); but see also the following collections: E. Ann Kaplan and Michael Sprinker, eds., *The Althusserian Legacy* (New York: Verso, 1993); and Antonio Callari and David F. Ruccio, eds., *Postmodern Materialism and the Future of Marxist Theory* (Hanover, N.H.: Wesleyan University Press, 1996). The essay by Antonio Negri in the latter is particularly useful. Ted Benton's exposition of Althusser's thinking remains an articulate assessment that is sensitive to the historical conditions of Althusser's work. See Ted Benton, *The Rise and Fall of Structural Marxism* (London: Macmillan, 1984).

13. This usefully links oscillation to the consummate inabilities of hegemony to secure an absolute mandate for a particular form of domination.

14. I have not developed the links here with chaos theory, although that will animate a later discussion to some degree. Traditionally, the pendulum has been used to illustrate the predictability of Newtonian mechanics, but this example (and others, like that of the double planar pendulum) does not follow the assumptions of linear modeling. In general, I use oscillation in a similar way to chaos theorists in that it describes the possibility of significant variation under determinate conditions. For the chaos theorist the significance of oscillation is its unpredictability, the complexity of a dynamic system; for me, the dynamism as a function of the possibility of dramatic change remains the key. Again, vacillation may point to an impasse or to new patterns of emergence.

15. Physics, of course, is not the only scientific source for the descriptive and analytic foundations of oscillation. Similar although not necessarily complementary investigations can be found in the study of electricity, acoustics, mathematics, radiography, and engineering. In the study of electricity, for instance, a circuit containing both capacitance and inductance not only can be made to produce an oscillation in current, but if undisturbed can oscillate according to its own "natural" frequency. A more basic example is the battery, which can discharge its electricity as a function of its positive and negative poles until this oscillation is overcome by the sum of resistance to it (the battery is then "dead"). The more interesting examples occur in radiography and the study of electromagnetic fields. The general theory of electromagnetic radiation goes back to James Clerk Maxwell in 1865 (although the proofs were provided by Hertz some twenty-two years later). The whole world of radio and radar depends on the energy radiated when a magnetic field interacts with an electrical field. The signal is thus produced by electrons oscillating in an antenna and can be read by an electric circuit attuned to that frequency. Of course, television largely functions on this basis although more recently fiber optic and cable technologies have complicated the delivery mode to a certain degree. Satellite television maintains the oscillatory dependence of its forebears. The impact of electromagnetic oscillation cannot be overemphasized. Where radar is concerned, it was a crucial factor in the failure of Hitler's desire to invade Britain in the Second World War ("early warning" shifted the balance of power in aerial combat). More recently, air power has gained the upper hand, both because of the development of electronic jamming devices and because of aircraft design. Stealth technology makes radar oscillations difficult to compute because it employs materials that absorb rather than reflect radio waves, or else is made of surfaces that do not reflect waves in a uniform way. Nonetheless, despite the hoopla about the use of Stealth planes in the Gulf War their success depended more on the ability of other planes to jam Iraqi radar long enough to allow "Coalition" forces to bomb them. With Iraq's air force grounded by radar blindness, zeppelins could have conducted the bombing campaign. As with most advanced technology, the story of electromagnetism is very closely tied to the needs of a military-industrial complex. The humanitarian uses for Stealth will (like truth) take longer to develop.

16. I have already indicated some of the importance of "wavering" in my introduction, particularly in regard to Adorno's sense of homeostasis. The argument for hesitation itself, of course, presents a quandary for political discourse, and the more one investigates the psychological cognates of oscillation, the more controversial its

strategic deployment would seem to become. The *OED* (2d edition) refers to these cognates in terms of a fluctuation in mental efficiency or attention. Spearman, in 1927, for instance, describes an "oscillation of cognitive efficiency" as a function of "fatigue." And yet, within a contemporary cultural logic of fast-edit, sound bite, and cross-cutting bricolage, the fluctuation of attention (the infamous shortened attention span of postmodern youth, for instance) is often read as an index of hyperactivity. While the wavering or hesitation I have in mind cannot be completely severed from the ambivalence of mental fluctuation (it is part of its concrete manifestation), my emphasis is chiefly on the possibility of reflection and flexibility that this kind of para-dialectical thinking provides.

17. This is an enormous topic, where Marxism of various kinds brushes against or wars with its post-Marxist declensions. But even as I question some of the elements considered relevant in contemporary discussions of class formation (the dictatorship of the proletariat?), that is far from ejecting the problem of class *tout court*. On the contrary, part of my argument is that a multiculturalism, for instance, that does not take up class and classism is seriously denuded and indeed idealist. To recall Jameson once more, an optionality regarding class remains deficient in accounting for the circulation of capital and social formations of domination on a global scale. Examples of reflexivity in Marx are legion, even in the base/superstructure argument where culture is often read to be only an "effect" of the material base. Of course, what "determines" what depends on the constituent element of materiality and material force.

18. See Karl Marx, *Capital,* vol. 1, trans. Ben Fowkes (London: Penguin, 1976), particularly chapter 19, "The Transformation of the Value (and Respectively the Price) of Labour Power into Wages"; subsequent references to volume 1 of *Capital* will be given in the text and indicated by *C*1, plus the page number. Marx uses the metaphor of oscillation at least seven times in volume 1 to characterize price, wage, labor, business, and supply and demand fluctuations. I am not arguing only that Marx develops the general laws of motion of capital in terms of oscillation (although this is indeed the case) but that the concept of oscillation should be read as immanent to a materialist understanding of these laws.

19. It is interesting that Marx initially accepts the argument for the decennial cycle in the expansion and contraction of capital but in the French edition goes on to note that the globalization of capital will tend to produce greater variation in this periodization, eventually producing an overall shortening of capital's business cycle. Clearly for some locations this is indeed the case today, but in general the multiplicity of interdependent and semiautonomous business cycles defies or inhibits the ability to substantiate the law. The opacity of globalization plays a key role in the instability of capital, but that is not the same as saying that it heralds a more comprehensive set of dysfunctions in its operations. It may explain, however, why the intensity of oscillation appears more felt while yet remaining abstract. And this is a problem that has economic, political, and cultural implications.

20. See Edward Soja, *Postmodern Geographies* (New York: Verso, 1989), 15.

21. Homi Bhabha, *The Location of Culture* (New York: Routledge, 1994) 1.

22. See Robert C. Tucker, ed., *The Marx/Engels Reader* (New York: Norton, 1978), 597.

23. Gianni Vattimo, *The Transparent Society,* trans. David Webb (Baltimore: Johns Hopkins University, 1992), 10; subsequent references will be given in the text. This

work picks up some of the themes developed more fully in his *The End of Modernity*, trans. Jon R. Snyder (Baltimore: Johns Hopkins University Press, 1991).

24. See Walter Benjamin, "The Work of Art in the Age of Mechanical Reproduction" in *Illuminations*, trans. Harry Zohn, ed. Hannah Arendt (New York: Schocken, 1969); and Heidegger's "The Origin of the Work of Art," in *Poetry Language Thought*, trans. A. Hofstadter (New York: Harper and Row, 1971). I will discuss the latter in more detail in chapter 4 in relation to thingness and the fetish.

25. The recent argument for the coauthoring of much of Brecht's drama (in fact, his nonauthoring) lends a significant feminist twist to this reading of modernity. Certainly it urges a reappraisal of Brecht's "originality." For Benjamin's stunning analysis of Brecht, see *Understanding Brecht*, trans. Anna Bostock (London: Verso, 1983). For an indication of the intensity of debates on these and related questions among German thinkers of the time see, Ernst Bloch et al., *Aesthetics and Politics*, trans. and ed. Ronald Taylor (London: Verso, 1980).

26. For instance, I have used Bakhtin's "Author and Hero in Aesthetic Activity" in terms of the Bakhtin Circle's more general materialist critique of the sign as an attempt to elaborate a constitutive logic of oscillation in aesthetic practice in the relationship of I/other. See my "Cultural Materialism and Material Dialogics," *Discours social/Social Discours* 7, no. 3/4 (fall 1995): 197–209; and the review essay, "Bakhtin/'Bakhtin,'" *Discours social/Social Discourse* 5 no. 1/2 (winter/spring 1993): 172–80. My point is that examples of a tremulous renegotiation of subject/object relations in materialism are legion and do not support the alignment that Vattimo attempts.

27. See Jean Baudrillard, *Simulations* (New York: Semiotext[e], 1983), 26. The machine referred to here is Los Angeles, which underlines that the imaginary that Baudrillard construes operates in a spatial economy, if not always a satisfactory political one. Again, as in the Vattimo example, I am interested in seeing to what extent postfoundational polemics also reflect upon an informing condition of oscillation in the modern era. I will return to this general problem in the conclusion.

28. Fredric Jameson, "Postmodernism, or, the Cultural Logic of Late Capitalism," *New Left Review* 146 (July/August 1984): 53–92. For all its faults, some of which I will discuss in chapter 4, this remains the single most important essay on postmodernity in terms of both its breathtaking range and, in particular, its political implications. Marxism has not read postmodernism the same way since.

29. Quoted in David Harvey, *The Condition of Postmodernity* (Oxford: Blackwell, 1989), 62.

30. See Jürgen Habermas, *The Theory of Communicative Action*, trans. Thomas McCarthy (Boston: Beacon Press, 1985). Habermas is a popular target for Vattimo since his approach appears to underestimate the mediatization of the public sphere, one that, by its very agonistic play of difference, preempts the consensual economy of communicative action. The argument is familiar and for many measures the difference between normative notions of modernity (with its dependence on the Enlightenment) and a rhetorical overinvestment in the signifier within postmodernity. As indicated in Jameson, an either-or approach to this problem seriously misrepresents their mutual imbrication. Discourses of reason and rationality can impede oscillation even when they eschew subject-centered reason, as is the case with Habermas, but this is different from saying they stand outside uncertainty or forms of vacillation. In general, however, Habermas identifies oscillation as a weakness in all philosophical discourse.

See, for example, his critique of Marx in lecture 3 and his admonitions of Derrida's "dizziness" in lecture 7 in *The Philosophical Discourses of Modernity,* trans. Frederick Lawrence (Cambridge, Mass.: MIT Press, 1987).

31. Jameson describes postmodernism theory as an attempt to take the temperature of the age without instruments, but then mentions one: "an enormous Claes Oldenburg thermometer, however, as long as a whole city block, might serve as some mysterious symptom of the process" (*Postmodernism, or, the Cultural Logic of Late Capitalism* [Durham, N.C.: Duke University Press, 1991], xi). My "symptom," rather obviously, would be the oscillograph.

32. See Raymond Williams, *Problems in Materialism and Culture* (London: Verso, 1980), 103.

33. I refer, of course, to the collaborative work of Gilles Deleuze and Félix Guattari, particularly *A Thousand Plateaus,* trans. Brian Massumi (Minneapolis: University of Minnesota Press, 1987). Massumi's definition of nomad thought expresses something of this spirit. See Brian Massumi, *A Reader's Guide to Capitalism and Schizophrenia* (Cambridge, Mass.: MIT Press, 1992), 5: " 'Nomad thought' does not lodge itself in the edifice of an ordered interiority; it moves freely in an element of exteriority. It does not repose on identity; it rides difference. It does not respect the artificial division between the three domains of representation, subject, concept, and being; it replaces restrictive analogy with a conductivity that knows no bounds. The concepts it creates do not merely reflect the eternal form of a legislating subject, but are defined by a communicable force in relation to which their subject, to the extent that they can be said to have one, is only secondary. Rather than reflecting the world, they are immersed in a changing state of things."

34. Balibar's work is a continuation, albeit in a different key, of the project of "reading capital" begun with Althusser and others some years earlier. This is not the place to discuss the scandal of Althusser's own contribution to that "reading" (or his admitted lack of reading!), but it is clear at least in Balibar's work that the model of reading initially proposed continues to be a source of inspiration. See Balibar, *Masses, Classes, Ideas;* subsequent references to this work will be given in the text.

35. I have begun to tire of reading dismissive "critiques" of Marxism as "reductionist" that miss this fundamental point. It may well be the litmus test of legitimate arguments against Marx, if not materialism. Of course, abstraction is no safe haven either in understanding the components of materialist critique: the problem of abstract labor itself has precipitated a genre of dissenting interpretation.

36. See Friedrich Engels, *Anti-Dühring,* Moscow: Foreign Language Publishing House, 1971: 135.

37. See Friedrich Engels, "On the History of Early Christianity," in *Collected Works of Marx and Engels,* vol. 27 (New York: International Publishers, 1975), 457.

38. The material on this is extensive, and I can do no more than indicate some of the places where one might productively start. McLellan's book on the subject has a good bibliography and argues from within the Marxist tradition. If one accepts Habermas's point that "ideologies are co-eval with the critique of ideology," then ideology as a concept is at least coextensive with the rise of the bourgeoisie, and McLellan gives a logical explanation for why this might indeed be the case. See David McLellan, *Ideology* (Minneapolis: University of Minnesota Press, 1986). For a more detailed analysis of the development of research on ideologies, see John B.

Thompson, *Studies in the Theory of Ideology* (Berkeley: University of California Press, 1984). Thompson has expanded and deepened his critique of the concept in *Ideology and Modern Culture* (Stanford, Calif.: Stanford University Press, 1990). His general thesis is that "to study ideology is to study the ways in which meaning serves to establish and sustain relations of domination" (56). This must continue to be a primary focus of millennial materialism. The wittiest and most polemical recent analysis of ideology is by Terry Eagleton, to be discussed below.

39. Slavoj Žižek, *Tarrying with the Negative* (Durham, N.C.: Duke University Press, 1993), 1. Žižek's Lacanian turn masks the fact that his basic concept of ideology is as legitimation. This is in general accord with the idea that ideology is not illusionist, but doesn't get us out of the woods regarding the worker "dreams" he elaborates. The function of enjoyment as a political factor, however, may yet spur a reassessment of ideology's aura of legitimation.

40. Ibid., 2.

41. See Judith Butler, *Bodies That Matter* (New York: Routledge, 1993), especially chapter 7.

42. This is only to say that an analysis of ideology must be able to distinguish the hierarchy of power invested in it. The common or garden ubiquity of discourse fails precisely to make distinctions of this kind.

43. The use of the language of nonlinear modeling in science will receive more detailed attention in my conclusion. As I will continue to maintain, there is no simple conduit between the world of chaos, complexity, and strange attractors and the conceptual range of materialism. What is true, however, is that there is a shared interest in the determined conditions of oscillation — even if this cannot be identical for conceptual change.

44. See V. N. Volosinov, *Marxism and the Philosophy of Language*, trans. Ladislav Matejka and I. R. Titunik (Cambridge, Mass.: Harvard University Press, 1986), 9. In this way, ideology cannot be immanent to things but only in their interaction, in their processes of signification.

45. See Raymond Williams, *Marxism and Literature* (Oxford: Oxford University Press, 1976), 66.

46. Terry Eagleton, *Ideology* (London: Verso, 1990), 28.

47. See, in particular, the preface to *A Contribution to the Critique of Political Economy*, excerpted in *The Marx-Engels Reader*, ed. Robert C. Tucker (New York: Norton, 1978).

48. Eagleton, *Ideology*, 45; subsequent references to this work will be given in the text.

49. Terry Eagleton, *The Ideology of the Aesthetic* (London: Blackwell, 1990), 13; subsequent references to this work will be given in the text.

50. Karl Marx, *Economic and Philosophical Manuscripts*, in *Karl Marx: Early Writings* (London: Harmondsworth, 1975), 356.

51. See Michael Taussig, *Mimesis and Alterity* (New York: Routledge, 1993). Where Edward Soja views the repressed capacity in materialism as spatial, Taussig argues for a developed sense of the mimetic faculty. In part, this depends upon a particularly novel reading of Benjamin's exploration of sentience, but it also links to Marx's emphasis (in the *Economic and Philosophical Manuscripts*) on sensuousness, exactly the point that Eagleton uses for his discussion of the aesthetic. After quoting

Marx on the "emancipation of the senses," Taussig asks, "Might not the mimetic faculty and the sensuous knowledge it embodies be precisely this hard-to-imagine state wherein 'the senses therefore become directly in their practise theoreticians'?" Taussig's notion of the mimetic faculty as "second nature" is highly provocative in terms of the metaphoricity of materialism, as if oscillation itself might be a response to the truncation of material sensuousness. Taussig does not develop this particular possibility, but his study does reveal why a "history of the senses" is concomitant with the material "development" of capitalism and two aspects of its representational logic: imperialism and colonialism.

52. See Michael Sprinker, *Imaginary Relations* (London: Verso, 1986).

53. See Benjamin's "Theses on the Philosophy of History," in *Illuminations*.

54. Immanuel Wallerstein, *Geopolitics and Geoculture: Essays on the Changing World System* (Cambridge: Cambridge University Press, 1991), 121.

55. See Immanuel Wallerstein, "Class Conflict in the Capitalist World Economy," in Etienne Balibar and Immanuel Wallerstein, *Race, Nation, Class: Ambiguous Identities* (London: Verso, 1991), 121.

56. Etienne Balibar, "The Vacillation of Ideology," in *Marxism and the Interpretation of Culture;* subsequent references to this work will be given in the text.

57. Etienne Balibar, "The Vacillation of Ideology," in *Masses, Classes, Ideas;* subsequent references to this work will be given in the text.

2. BODIES (OF MATERIALISM)

1. This is a large question for philosophy and one recently enjoined by Jean-Luc Nancy in his *Corpus* (Paris: Éditions A. M. Métailié, 1992). Obviously the slide between body and body of work is not coincidental and must be reinscribed within a history of the senses that Marx can only gesture toward. It is not simply a function of capitalism (since it preexists that economic formation in religious discourse), but it has a precise interpretation within capital that Marx explains in a variety of ways, not least of which is his analysis of alienation and fetishism.

2. See Karl Marx, *Economic and Philosophic Manuscripts of 1844,* in *The Marx/ Engels Reader,* ed. Robert C. Tucker (New York: Norton, 1978), 108; subsequent references to the work will be given in the text.

3. I refer here to Irigaray's argument in "Any Theory of the 'Subject' Has Always Been Appropriated by the Masculine" (in Luce Irigaray, *Speculum of the Other Woman,* trans. Gillian Gill [Ithaca, N.Y.: Cornell University Press, 1985], 133–46). This is not a defense of the role of the mystic in Irigaray's book. I do, however, find some provocation in the attributive role of the feminist mimic she often invokes. As Toril Moi has pointed out, such mimicry is ambivalent, so that, even when Irigaray analogizes from Marx, the specular logic of Marxism seems vindicated. My point would be that this "vindication" cannot leave Marxism as is: its own logic is specularized, turned inside out and upside down. For Moi's critique, see Toril Moi, *Sexual/ Textual Politics* (London: Methuen, 1985), especially chapter 7. For two examples of Irigaray's Marxist analogizing, see Luce Irigaray, *This Sex Which Is Not One,* trans.

Catherine Porter (Ithaca, N.Y.: Cornell University Press, 1985), especially chapters 8 and 9.

4. These could include the following: the emphasis on the body as both productive and reproductive; an understanding of the body as an ambivalent site of consumption and excess — the latter including analysis of how the body exceeds its borders through all kinds of fluids and solids; the reconstruction of the body by taste, style, and cultural overdeterminations in general; the disciplining of the body not just in terms of work but in an economy of normative notions of gender and sexual differentiation. The classical body of Marxism often alludes to such issues but has not made them constitutive of material understanding. The oscillation of the body for materialism begins with precisely these kinds of rearticulation.

5. The script of this video can be found in Laura Kipnis, *Ecstasy Unlimited* (Minneapolis: University of Minnesota Press, 1993). Page numbers will refer to this text. Kipnis's book also contains videotape distribution information for this and other videos she has made.

6. Of course, this does not mean that there is a body beyond othering, which is the condition of its very possibility. What materialism emphasizes, particularly the materialism of Marx, is that a concrete form of othering can come to dominate all others in social modes of interaction. On one level, the otherness of the other is the ground for social being (there would be no need for language if all humans were identical); on another, a regulative form of alienation (say, in capital's extraction of surplus value) can occlude some of the most basic components of self-fulfillment. The latter is the strangeness through which my body belongs to me but is owned by another in capital exchange.

7. A recent special issue of *South Atlantic Quarterly* edited by Toril Moi and Janice Radway offers a critical sense of what materialist feminism might be in the 1990s without unifying its theoretical purview (see *South Atlantic Quarterly* 93, no. 4 [fall 1994]). For a text that historicizes materialist feminism *and* argues for the positive contributions of other contemporary theory to its project (including deconstruction), see Donna Landry and Gerald MacLean, *Materialist Feminisms* (London: Blackwell, 1993). In a similar vein, Rosemary Hennessy offers a possible rapprochement between critical postmodernism and materialist feminism in *Materialist Feminism and the Politics of Discourse* (New York: Routledge, 1993).

8. This is clearly the viewpoint of Teresa Ebert, for whom "post-al(ity)" (a term she shares with Mas'ud Zavarzadeh and members of the *Transformations* editorial collective) means "discourses and practices that erase the relations of production and class struggle from contemporary knowledges" (*Ludic Feminism and After* [Ann Arbor: University of Michigan Press, 1996], 45). How much this view and the general critique of "ludic" theory might apply to the present study readers will decide.

9. Hennessy, *Materialist Feminism*, 5.

10. This is not always successful since Pêcheux's own argument bears the weight of its structuralist inscription in specific theoretical debates of the 1970s. Nevertheless, see Michel Pêcheux, *Language, Semantics, and Ideology*, trans. H. Nagpal (New York: St. Martin's Press, 1982).

11. I have explored this possibility in an unpublished manuscript on theories of women's history. Briefly, like most materialist feminists, Hennessy takes issue with conventional feminist discourses on rights for excising the materiality of knowledge

and the nondiscursive production of oppression. Hers is a materialist feminism as a "reading practice" concerned to rearticulate a systemic conception of the social independent of the humanist subject as a basis for knowledge. No one serious about the project of an insurgent or dissident materialism would quibble with these aspects of Hennessy's intervention. In recognizing the "contradictory allegiance" to a discursively constructed subject and an experiential self that itself is a playing out of the disjuncture between discursive critique and nondiscursive lives, Hennessy offers an understanding of discourse as ideology. Two problems immediately become apparent: first, does such a solution actually mediate the problem of the discursive/nondiscursive, or does it simply err on the side of discursivity (a difference, say, between the early Foucault and the later)? second, if theoretical practice is a discourse and discourse can be understood as ideology, then materialist feminism is an ideology and, as such, cannot adjudicate the question of ideology that it in fact presents. Thus, while Hennessy correctly notes that a concept of theory as ideology "dispels the distinction between narrative and metanarrative," it also blocks the reflexivity that materialism would advocate (i.e., that theories "acknowledge their own historicity" [7]) because *as* ideology such self-knowledge is precluded. A similar problem rests in Hennessy's argument for history as ideology since this would cancel through the truth claims of feminism's significant project to dismantle the historical production of systemic patriarchy that forms the present. Clearly, much of the strength of materialist feminism lies in ideological critique, but this is a very different notion from ideology *as* critique.

12. See Gayatri Chakravorty Spivak, "Scattered Speculations on the Question of Value," *In Other Worlds: Essays in Cultural Politics* (London: Routledge, 1987), 154–75.

13. See Gayatri Chakravorty Spivak, "Limits and Openings of Marx in Derrida," in *Outside in the Teaching Machine* (New York: Routledge, 1993), 113.

14. Hennessy, *Materialist Feminism*, 31.

15. This is one of the underlying theses of my *Dialogics of the Oppressed* (Minneapolis: University of Minnesota Press, 1993). Speaking "to" and "for" imply two radically different forms of political engagement. The latter, it seems to me, indulges in a politics of representation in which the critical voice itself supplants or displaces its object, and thus conspires with a process of epistemic objectification and marginalization. The former is based on a notion of reflexivity that, while overdetermined (and not simply "willed"), positions the critic in a more contradictory and agonistic relationship to the production of knowledge.

16. See Spivak, "Woman in Difference" in *Outside*, 77–95; subsequent references to this essay will be given in the text. See also Spivak's introductory material and conversation with Mahasweta Devi in Mahasweta Devi, *Imaginary Maps*, trans. Gayatri Chakravorty Spivak (New York: Routledge, 1995).

17. See, for instance, Gyan Prakash, *Bonded Histories: Genealogies of Labor Servitude in Colonial India* (New York: Cambridge University Press, 1990). Spivak suggests just such a "resonant" reading in a footnote in *Outside*, 301.

18. This is basically the springboard to chapter 4. Here I should note that Spivak's gesture does not elide the material context of the narrative in Devi's conception — she draws on its implications. To show this would require a fairly detailed engagement with Mahasweta Devi's short story collection, *Imaginary Maps*, translated and

introduced by Spivak. "Douloti the Bountiful" is included in that collection and contributes to a more nuanced sense of what Devi calls "the agony of the tribals." Devi's (and indeed Spivak's) effort is not about information retrieval but in fact speaks to the problem of what Devi calls "a wordsoundless message," a knowledge of the other predicated on an alternative imaginary mode, an "imaginary map" that cannot be drawn with a few footnotes on the plight of the tribal in India. An end to what Dipesh Chakrabarty calls the "asymmetric ignorance" of Euramerica's relationship to the world will require a more sweeping reconceptualization of the map.

19. The relevant text here is Michel Foucault, *Discipline and Punish: The Birth of the Prison*, trans. Alan Sheridan (New York: Pantheon, 1979), but see also *The Foucault Reader*, ed. Paul Rabinow (New York: Pantheon, 1984).

20. Landry and MacLean, *Materialist Feminisms*, 208.

21. On this point at least, I wholeheartedly agree with Ebert's reading of Landry and MacLean in *Ludic Feminism*. I would also reassert, however, that what may be read as a methodological error in Landry and MacLean's materialism does not preclude a deconstructive turn. To read *Capital* in the way that Spivak does is not to indulge in tropology or "ludic semiosis," as Ebert calls it, but is to posit instead a polemical reaccentuation of Marx's theory. Metatheory must come to terms with language because that is what theory is written in. Materialist metatheory goes on to note that *Capital* is language and capital is not. Surely we must grant Spivak the ability to make this distinction.

22. See Moi, *Sexual/Textual Politics*, 150–73.

23. Julia Kristeva, *Desire in Language: A Semiotic Approach to Literature and Art* (New York: Columbia University Press, 1980), 171.

24. Judith Butler connects this to a general "regulation of identificatory practices" (see *Gender Trouble* [London: Routledge, 1990]).

25. Julia Kristeva, "Psychoanalysis and the Polis," trans. Margaret Waller, *Critical Inquiry* 9, no. 1 (1982): 77–92.

26. Spivak, *Outside*, 153.

27. Marx, *Economic and Philosophic Manuscripts of 1844*, 75.

28. Spivak, "Feminism and Critical Theory," in *In Other Worlds*, 79.

29. This is Deleuze and Guattari's acronym. For a relatively clear explanation of their use of this term, see Brian Massumi, *A User's Guide to Capitalism and Schizophrenia* (Cambridge, Mass.: MIT Press, 1992), 70–71.

30. Gilles Deleuze and Félix Guattari, *A Thousand Plateaus*, trans. Brian Massumi (Minneapolis: University of Minnesota Press, 1987), 164.

31. Spivak, *Outside*, 149.

32. Marx, *Economic and Philosophic Manuscripts of 1844*, 73.

33. See Robert Young, *White Mythologies* (London: Routledge, 1990), especially chapter 9.

34. Engels, "The Origin of the Family, Private Property, and State," in *The Marx/Engels Reader*, 744.

35. Gilles Deleuze, *Expressionism in Philosophy: Spinoza*, trans. Martin Joughin (New York: Zone Books, 1992), 218.

36. There are several other ways to counter French feminism's reading of Freud and Lacan, as well as psychoanalytic frameworks in general. One should add, however, that a psychoanalytic approach to feminine/masculine differentiation can itself

find sustenance in the logic of oscillation. See, for instance, Parveen Adams, "Per Os(cillation)," in *Male Trouble*, ed. Constance Penley and Sharon Willis, 3–25 (Minneapolis: University of Minnesota Press, 1993).

37. Judith Butler, *Bodies That Matter* (New York: Routledge, 1993), 2.

38. This is how I would characterize Teresa Ebert's reading of Butler in *Ludic Feminism*. In many respects, we share the same discomfort with the metonymic displacement of materialization by citationality in Butler's work, but I am less convinced that the "ludic" (which is just "playful" enough to remind one of ludicrous) in Butler's thinking is simply a "displacement of fundamental issues" (210) either within feminism or, ironically, within historical materialism. Again, this depends on whether one views historical materialism as a relatively stable body of thought vis-à-vis its perceived dissenters. If one accepts the concept of an originary oscillation and vacillation in materialism, the possibilities of its historical reinscription are greatly enhanced. The difficulty remains how far the paradigm can move before it ceases to function as a paradigm, and here, while my skepticism differs in degree, my reading complements Ebert's. I should add that I came to Ebert's critique too late to make it more active in my own.

39. Ebert, *Ludic Feminism*, 212.

40. See Karl Marx, "Theses on Feuerbach," in *Marx/Engels Reader*, 143.

41. Karl Marx and Friedrich Engels, *The German Ideology*, trans. W. Lough, ed. C. J. Arthur (New York: International Publishers, 1988), 42.

42. See Aijaz Ahmad, *In Theory* (London: Verso, 1993). My point here is to warn against bemoaning unruly political affiliation and instead concentrate on what this might mean for the mode of politics under discussion.

43. Irigaray's reading can be found in Luce Irigaray, *Speculum of the Other Woman*, trans. Gillian Gill (Ithaca, N.Y.: Cornell University Press, 1985). As more than one commentator has noted, the form of Irigaray's argument demonstrates the thesis in terms of the form/matter binary. What is more controversial is whether Irigaray's "miming" reproduces the exclusionary logic that is her argument's object. This is where Butler's sense (via Derrida) of iteration becomes operative. But this also reflects on the form of Butler's position, which, in a similar way, performs the logic of its thesis.

44. See Elizabeth Grosz, *Volatile Bodies* (Bloomington: Indiana University Press, 1994), 194.

45. Typically, Ebert singles out Kipnis's reading of *Hustler* as an "apologia" based on the "ludic politics of pleasure" — one forwarded "at the cost of displacing real and representational violence against women" (306). As my comments on *Marx: The Video* have already suggested, this is the exact opposite of Kipnis's polemic.

46. See Mikhail Bakhtin, *Rabelais and His World*, trans. Hélène Iswolsky (Bloomington: Indiana University Press, 1984); subsequent references to the work will be given in the text.

47. See Achille Mbembe, "The Banality of Power and the Aesthetics of Vulgarity in the Postcolony," *Public Culture* 4, no. 2 (spring 1992): 1–30. A subsequent issue of the journal featured a series of spirited responses to Mbembe's provocation (5, no. 1 [fall 1992]).

48. See Judith Butler, "Mbembe's Extravagant Power," *Public Culture*, 5, no. 1 (fall 1992): 67–74.

49. Peter Hitchcock, "Information in Formation: Williams, Media, 'China,' " in *Cultural Materialism*, ed. Christopher Prendergast, 340–58 (Minneapolis: University of Minnesota Press, 1995).

50. Grosz, *Volatile Bodies*, 72.

51. Marx, *Economic and Philosophic Manuscripts of 1844*, 89.

52. Gregory's book provides a critical introduction to new theories of space within geographical theory as well as a cogently argued polemic on the possibility of geographical imaginations. His critique of Lefebvre is bound by the latter. See Derek Gregory, *Geographical Imaginations* (Oxford: Blackwell, 1994). Given what I have just said about "Liberty," Gregory's chapter on this representation is also illuminating.

53. Henri Lefebvre, *The Survival of Capitalism: Reproduction of the Relations of Production* (London: Allison and Busby, 1974), 89.

3. SPACES (OF THEORY)

This essay was first presented in a much-abbreviated form as a paper entitled "Theory on the Move" at a conference entitled "New Metropolitan Forms" held at Duke University in April 1994. The paper has undergone several mutations since then, including this one, which takes account of its function within the rest of the book.

1. This form of knowledge saturates the cultural very quickly. It certainly seeps through, of course, in Shakespeare: "[H]e does smile his way into more lines than are in the new map with the augmentation of the Indies" (*Twelfth Night* 3.2.86).

2. Oscar Wilde, *The Soul of Man under Socialism* (Chicago: Kerr Publishing, 1984), 28.

3. Of course, this is an extremely complex issue that pitches one headlong into often autonomous debates within science and philosophy. Here I favor paradigms that stress the production of space over, or against, universalist assumptions. Conventional analysts of urbanism will not see an ally in the spatialization of theory offered here, but radical geographers (even if not in agreement) have provided significant inspiration to the present project. For more on relative space, see Neil Smith's *Uneven Development* (Oxford: Blackwell, 1984). Smith notes that "capital can effect a social emancipation from natural space only to the extent that it involves itself in the simultaneous production of relative space" (85). While theory's status is not synonymous with capital's in Smith's argument its function as cultural capital is not incongruous in that regard.

4. Walter Benjamin, *Illuminations*, trans. Harry Zohn, ed. Hannah Arendt (New York: Schocken, 1969), 256.

5. Benjamin's reference is to "time filled by the present of the now" — a mysticism that gains greater purchase in the time/space compression of the epoch.

6. These definitions are provided by the *OED* (2d edition). I am particularly taken with the citation from the "Resolves" (ca. 1620) by the precocious Owen Felltham, who proclaims, "We know not in the flows of our contentedness what we ourselves are." The Atlantic zone of flow is about such an identity crisis since its imperial contentedness is being emptied out. Obviously, that this space "fluctuates" is important to my overall thesis.

7. See Arjun Appadurai, "Disjuncture and Difference in the Global Cultural Economy," in *The Phantom Public Sphere*, ed. Bruce Robbins, 269–95 (Minneapolis: University of Minnesota Press, 1993).

8. See James Clifford, "Traveling Cultures," in *Cultural Studies*, ed. Lawrence Grossberg et al., 100 (London: Routledge, 1992). While not all of Clifford's thoughts on the spatialization of culture mesh with "traveling theory," he does at least suggest a structural relationship at the level of commodity.

9. Paul Gilroy, *The Black Atlantic* (Cambridge, Mass.: Harvard University Press, 1993); idem, "Cultural Studies and Ethnic Absolutism," in *Cultural Studies*, 187–98; and idem, part 3 of *Small Acts* (London: Serpent's Tail, 1993), especially the dialogue with bell hooks. In the latter and the first chapter of the former, Gilroy acknowledges the work of others on the black Atlantic world. I mention this since Gilroy's brilliant spatialization of the racial encoding of the Atlantic will, of necessity, provoke territorial rights.

10. Others have already been inspired by Gilroy's cartographic conscience of space. See, for instance, Joseph Roach's study of "circum-Atlantic" performance and memory in *Cities of the Dead* (New York: Columbia University Press, 1996). The Atlantic zone of flow has, perhaps, a more definitive political project than Roach's effort, but his is nevertheless an object lesson in imaginary mapping.

11. Thus, the production of theory itself must be implicated more forcefully in economic structures of power. This not only fights the mental/manual binary in labor but connects theoretical work to a mode of answerability inscription with the worlds of labor per se. This is one of the themes of chapter 5.

12. See Edward Said, "Traveling Theory," in *The World, the Text, and the Critic* (Cambridge, Mass.: Harvard University Press, 1983), 226–47.

13. For further, more extensive critiques of Said's conception of traveling theory, see the special issue of *New Formations* 3 (winter 1987). The question of Said's ambivalent relationship to Foucauldian critique in "Traveling Theory" has been noted by Ahmad (see *In Theory* [London: Verso, 1993], 199–200). Indeed, as he points out with a quote from *The World, the Text, and the Critic* (from pp. 244–46), much of what Said says about Foucault in his reevaluation could be applied to himself. It is noticeable that in Said's more recent *Culture and Imperialism* (New York: Vintage, 1993), almost every mention of Foucault is in negative terms, particularly when Said links his later thought and that of Lyotard to a general evacuation of the politics of liberation. With the example of their "exhaustion and disappointment," Said then leaps to some startling consequences: "Enter now terrorism and barbarism" (27). A derogation of intellectual responsibility could be argued, perhaps, but not so abruptly.

14. In chapter 1 I have read much of this in terms of materialism, but these tendencies can be examined within other theoretical trajectories. For instance, in more naive versions of poststructuralism there is a propensity to take it on faith that the Enlightenment is all about nasty centered subjectivity, all knowing "I"s, and metaphysical bluster, but this view, or reductionism, can serve poststructuralism's epistemological break as it attempts to detour the Enlightenment's own tradition of autocritique. Thus, while I have not read a Derridean critique that takes up deconstruction without an understanding of Derrida's rigorous negotiation through Nietzsche and Heidegger (to name but two points of reference), it is within the realm of possibility that Derridean critique can attend to Kant without calling on Hume. Of

course, one can revert to chronologism (although for poststructuralism this would be an unconscionable defense), but surely there is ample evidence of skepticism's deconstruction of the *Critique of Pure Reason* in Hume's *Treatise of Human Nature*, which is a youthful work but nevertheless a devastating blow to foundational rationality. Interestingly, by the end of the first book Hume's own theory has self-deconstructed, a disintegration whose allegory (as deferral) now claims greater purchase.

15. See Pierre Macherey, *A Theory of Literary Production*, trans. Geoffrey Wall (London: Routledge, 1978).

16. For more on time/space compression, see David Harvey, *The Condition of Postmodernity* (London: Blackwell, 1989). Again, Said has recently acknowledged the importance of speed in terms of global predicaments, if not necessarily to the circulation of theory. See his references to the work of Paul Virilio in the last section of *Culture and Imperialism*, "Movements and Migrations."

17. The most significant elaboration of cultural capital in this regard is Pierre Bourdieu's *Distinction*, trans. Richard Nice (Cambridge, Mass.: Harvard University Press, 1984). Such capital embodies specific codes, the competence in which designates social positioning of various kinds. For my purposes, the function of cultural capital within institutions of learning is most suggestive and can help to identify the shifting lines power and knowledge in their constellations.

18. I don't want to labor this point, but the speed of retrieval obviously favors those in close proximity to major publishing distribution points, or those with easy access to the same; in short, those of the Western metropole in particular. It also depends on access to "events" in the field, witness my experience at the Modern Language Association meeting in Toronto where two speakers on separate occasions invoked the term "contrapuntal" in the specific sense that Edward Said had used it the day before (and not just as he has used it in his published writings). Again, there are ways in which this point cancels through the present argument, but the aim here, at least, is to provide a "contrapuntal" reading of the moment of this logic.

19. This is part, at least, of the impetus behind Bruce Robbins's erudite intervention *Secular Vocations* (London: Verso, 1993).

20. Even the expansion of NATO can be read in these terms — as a last-ditch alliance not in the face of possible Russian resurgence, but as an integer of what Cornel West has noted as the end of the Age of Europe.

21. See Robert Young, *White Mythologies: Writing History and the West* (London: Routledge, 1990), especially chapter 1.

22. See Marjorie Howes, "Theory, Politics, and Caricature," *Public Culture* 6, no. 1 (1993): 90. This essay is part of a special issue devoted to *In Theory*. The level of hostility to Ahmad's argument is sometimes so intense as to be vitriolic (in this issue his formulations are, at one point, described as "puerile," and his literary histories are dismissed as "potted"). There are serious problems with Ahmad's polemic, as my own points attest, but the rapacious reflex of the American theorati suggests that, even at the level of generalization, his characterizations of literary theory have some credence to them.

23. Quoted in Harvey, *Condition*, 237.

24. See Pierre Bourdieu, *The Field of Cultural Production* (New York: Columbia University Press, 1993). What counts as theory and as movement depends upon belief systems and their relative antagonism as well as pleasant exchanges.

25. Randal Johnson's introduction to *The Field of Cultural Production* notes that many of Bourdieu's terms, like "symbolic power," "symbolic violence," "symbolic capital," and so on, have shown up in new historicist argumentation. Given the new historicist tendency to use economistic terms metaphorically, the favorable disposition to terms that are already "symbolic" should not be surprising.

26. See Erica Carter, James Donald, and Judith Squires, eds., *Space and Place* (London: Lawrence and Wishart, 1993), xii.

27. Of course, schizoanalysis is about particular processes of decoding and deterritorialization, not the clinical instance of the schizoid. The relevant tomes on "capitalism and schizophrenia" are Gilles Deleuze and Félix Guattari, *Anti-Oedipus*, trans. Robert Hurley, Mark Seem, and Helen R. Lane (Minneapolis: University of Minnesota Press, 1983), and *A Thousand Plateaus*, trans. Brian Massumi (Minneapolis: University of Minnesota Press, 1987). The most insightful (and "schizo") analysis of their nomadism is Brian Massumi, *A User's Guide to Capitalism and Schizophrenia* (Cambridge, Mass.: MIT Press: 1992).

28. Of course, the zone of flow is a gendered space, as other parts of this chapter will indicate. I would hope that my work elsewhere on Nawal el Saadawi and Assia Djebar would supplement, in a complicated and contradictory way, the spatial transcoding at issue. Here, however, the writing of Françoise Lionnet provides a strong sense of the engendered border zone. In an essay on contemporary Francophone women writers she argues, "The global mongrelization or métissage of cultural forms creates hybrid identities, and interrelated, if not overlapping, spaces. In those spaces, struggles for the control of means of representation and self-identification are mediated by a single and immensely powerful symbolic system: the colonial language, and the variations to which it is subjected by writers who enrich, transform, and creolize it." While Lionnet is writing about feminist fiction rather than theory, she does provide a persuasive conceptual understanding for the despacing of patriarchal theoretical "exchange." See Françoise Lionnet, "'Logiques métisses': Cultural Appropriation and Postcolonial Representations," *College Literature* 19, no. 3 (October 1992): 100–120.

29. Evidence for this lies in the work of the Montreal group, CIADEST, and its journal *Discours social/Social Discourse*, although recently both have apparently expired.

30. The example of what happens to cultural materialism when it crosses the Atlantic (and becomes, in recent history, new historicism) is beyond summary here. A comparative analysis of the work of Williams and Greenblatt itself would require detailed exegesis (one that I have attempted in an unpublished manuscript). Here, I will restrict myself to the implications of this spatial transformation in theory for materialism. Briefly, materialism on the move replicates in fairly conventional ways the problems of the hegemonic flow in the Atlantic zone, but clearly it is not an embodiment of those restrictions. Indeed, the logic of the dissemination of materialism is counterhegemonic to the extent that materialism seeks to implode the geopolitical dominance of the northern economic axis. When one looks at specific examples of the spacing, despacing, and respacing of materialist critique, however, contextual sensitivity quickly problematizes what might be held as immanent to a materialist approach, as if the space in which materialism is taken up continually deontologizes the integrity of its aims and questions the logical consistency of its historicity. This has to do both with its oscillatory potential, its conceptual flexibility in the face of new prob-

lems, and with the sort of porous predilection that reconfigures theory from without, from outside the terms of theory itself. This is particularly the case with cultural materialism, whose somewhat abbreviated history suggests a journey from Budapest to Berkeley but whose spatial problematic represents much more complex geographical and historical trajectories (for instance, in the crisscrossing to and from Konigsberg, or the Kantian compulsion) that converge and diverge in the United States at a moment of palpable self-doubt: the "end" of the American century. While the discussion here will not focus on that problem, I do want to maintain the sense that materialism on the move is not just about the dissolution of a certain theory but also about a specific dissolution of the space in which it is elaborated.

31. Gilroy, *Black Atlantic,* 29.

32. I do not exempt the present study from that criticism, but the attempt, at least, is to oscillate the logic of that inevitability.

33. See Jean-Loup Amselle, *Logiques métisses: Anthropologie de l'identité en Afrique et ailleurs* (Paris: Payot, 1990).

34. Ahmad's approach does not exhaust or "end the debate" of this issue. Jameson's use of "Third World," which precipitated much of Ahmad's response, has been defended by Santiago Colas as an integral paradox to an understanding of postmodernity and late capitalism (see "The Third World in Jameson's *Postmodernism, or, the Cultural Logic of Late Capitalism,*" *Social Text* 31/32 [1992]: 258–70). In the same issue Madhava Prasad argues that in Jameson's work "the signifier 'Third World'... receives a new signified" that, although problematic, is not in itself unproductive. Prasad sees Ahmad personalizing Jameson's label rather than testing its deployment in a more systematic way. Jameson, meanwhile, ends up with a "left literary anthropology" that I am not sure is any less obfuscatory than the term for which Jameson is taken to task (see Prasad's "On the Question of a Theory of [Third World] Literature," 57–83). My support for Ahmad on this point is that he urges an understanding that "we" live in one world, not three. For the materialist, if not for the humanist, this means facing up to the fragmentation on a world scale (to paraphrase Jameson) that is the very sign for our real or imagined unities (as peoples, nations) under or through capitalist globalization. Even if "Third World" functioned as an interruption to that process, it is unclear now that it could possibly serve that purpose.

35. I refer here to several works, including: Brathwaite's provocative essay "History of the Voice," first presented at Carifesta 76 in Jamaica and subsequently expanded and revised as a lecture given at Harvard University, August 1979. The full text with bibliography has been published as Edward Kamau Brathwaite, *History of the Voice* (London: New Beacon Books, 1984); Sistren, *Lionheart Gal* (London: Women's Press, 1985); and Jean Bernabé, Patrick Chamoiseau, and Raphael Confiant, *Éloge de la Créolité* (Paris: Gallimard, 1989), trans. M. B. Taleb-Khyar as "In Praise of Creoleness," *Callaloo* 13 (1990): 886–909. The French/English versions of *Éloge* are now available in a single volume published by Gallimard in 1993.

36. See Edouard Glissant, *Caribbean Discourse,* trans. Michael Dash (Charlottesville: University of Virginia Press, 1989); and Antonio Benítez-Rojo, *The Repeating Island,* trans. James E. Maraniss (Durham, N.C.: Duke University Press, 1992); subsequent references to these works will be given in the text.

37. See Edouard Glissant, *Le discours antillais* (Paris: Éditions du Seuil, 1981). To

be fair, Dash only meant his translation to be a representative collection drawn from the original, not a complete version. Still, until the latter is available readers should, when possible, cross-reference the English version with the French. For more on Glissant's notion of "Caribbeanness," see my "Antillanité and the Art of Resistance," *Research in African Literatures* 27, no. 2 (summer 1996).

38. Given the vast amount of material on oscillation's relationship to nonlinear models in science, I will have more to say about the relevance of chaos to millennial materialism in my conclusion.

39. See Christopher Miller, *Theories of Africans: Francophone Literature and Anthropology in Africa* (Chicago: University of Chicago Press, 1990), and Neil Lazarus, "Disavowing Decolonization: Fanon, Nationalism, and the Problematic of Representation in Current Theories of Colonial Discourse," *Research in African Literatures* 24, no. 4 (1993): 69–98. One of the themes of Miller's book is the continuing formation of African countries on Eurocentric models of the nation-state, with all the elision of underlying disunities and the subsequent sociopolitical problems that can create. Part of Lazarus's response is that national liberation movements do not univocally mime the paradigms of the colonizing moment, but neither can they simply purge themselves of such detritus. The argument cannot be resolved here, but one should note that theory can, in specific moments and places, theorize out the contaminants that might otherwise still constitute the living tissue that forms its object. This, of course, is apposite with the present theoretical discussion.

40. I should add that Lazarus himself is not uncritical of Fanon's narrative of colonialism that tends, as Lazarus points out, to confuse dominance with hegemony ("Disavowing," 77) and therefore leads Fanon to assume the obliteration of traditional culture. In addition, Miller's book has much to recommend it beyond the dispute that Lazarus raises. In many ways *Theories of Africans* is a practical lesson in dialogism, particularly with regard to Western cultural anthropology's erstwhile (and continuing) unequal relationship to the "subjects" of Africa. Miller does not assume the sublation of that powerful hierarchization but carefully negotiates the construction of observer and observed in his investigation while conceding that "to make use of anthropology is to borrow trouble." His analysis of Camara Laye's work as well as his use of Ahmadou Kourouma's *Les soleils des indépendances* and the chapter on Senegalese women writers raise a plethora of significant issues of which I mention three that are pertinent to the present discussion: Laye's articulation of mythical space as the scene for an ironic commentary on the politics of knowledge; Kourouma's "Africanizing" of French as an internal distanciation of the colonial mind-set (this theme will be explicitly engaged in my later critique of Glissant); and the engendering of African space (often a phantasm of Western ethnocentrism but also an emergent discourse on how "woman" as a cultural and political problematic is redrawing African cartography).

41. See Kwame Anthony Appiah, *In My Father's House: Africa in the Philosophy of Culture* (New York: Oxford University Press, 1992).

42. Appiah discusses these issues under the headings of "nativism" and "ethnophilosophy." The works he has in mind include Cheikh Anta Diop, *The African Origin of Civilization* (New York: Lawrence Hill, 1974), and Chinweizu, Onwuchekwa Jemie, and Ihechukwu Madubuike, *Toward the Decolonization of African Literature* (Enugu: Fourth Dimension, 1980). Interestingly, although acknowledging the plausibility of Diop's argument about the dubious claims of Greek originality, Appiah

prefers Martin Bernal's version of the debate because "he is simply concerned to set the record straight" (202). Whatever the individual merit of the scholarship, this carries the unintended but nevertheless questionable implication that one author is politically impassioned while the other is intellectually dedicated.

43. See Faith Smith, "A Conversation with V. Y. Mudimbe," *Callaloo* 14, no. 4 (1991): 969–86.

44. V. Y. Mudimbe, *The Invention of Africa* (Bloomington: Indiana University Press, 1988).

45. In Smith, "Conversation," 981.

46. Michel de Certeau, *The Practice of Everyday Life*, trans. Steven F. Rendall (Berkeley: University of California Press, 1984), 117.

47. See Ahmad, *In Theory*. The controversies produced by this book are beyond summary here, but without doubt Ahmad has touched a nerve in postcolonial consciousness. The special issue of *Public Culture* 6, no. 1 (1993) devoted to Ahmad's book testifies to such edginess, which is often displaced onto knee-jerk reactions to Ahmad's Marxism. Arif Dirlik's essay entitled the "The Postcolonial Aura" in *Critical Inquiry* also complicates our sense of the postcolonial reconceptualization of the zone of flow, for equally controversial reasons (Arif Dirlik, "The Postcolonial Aura," *Critical Inquiry* 20 [winter 1994]: 328–56).

48. See Kamala Visweswaran, *Fictions of Feminist Ethnography* (Minneapolis: University of Minnesota Press, 1994), 110.

49. See Janet Wolff, "On the Road Again: Metaphors of Travel in Cultural Criticism," *Cultural Studies* 7, no. 2 (May 1993): 235.

50. I will make more of this internationalism elsewhere in this work. See Gayatri Chakravorty Spivak, "French Feminism Revisited," in her *Outside in the Teaching Machine* (London: Routledge, 1993).

51. This is one of the key lessons of the "reification" chapter in Georg Lukács, *History and Class Consciousness*, trans. Rodney Livingstone (Cambridge, Mass.: MIT Press, 1971).

52. Robbins first explored the term in an essay for *Social Text* 25/26 (1992) then elaborated on it for his *Secular Vocations* (London: Verso, 1993). Robbins suggests that comparative cosmopolitanism better describes "our sensibility" than multiculturalism, but terminological substitution is only half the gambit here. What I would argue is that comparativism itself must wrest multiculturalism away from liberal humanist or incorporatist agendas not because the term will do, but because the term is already doing: that is, it occupies a contestable space in bureaucratic consciousness. The Atlantic zone of flow is an intervention in another field of terminological engagement.

4. FETISHISM (OF SHOES)

1. Etienne Balibar, *The Philosophy of Marx* (New York: Verso, 1995), 56. As Balibar suggests, the general idea of commodity fetishism is not difficult, but the actual process of its effects is extremely complex — the more so for its apparent ubiquity. The case study that is developed in this chapter is an attempt to critique commodity fetishism in the moment of globalization.

2. Gilles Deleuze and Félix Guattari, *What Is Philosophy?* trans. Hugh Tomlinson and Graham Burchell (New York: Columbia University Press, 1994), 35.

3. Alfonso M. Iacono, *Le Fétichisme: Histoire d'un concept* (Paris: Press Universitaires de France, 1992), 126.

4. See W. J. T. Mitchell, *Iconology* (Chicago: University of Chicago Press, 1986), especially chapter 6. Mitchell follows a long tradition that has accused Marx or Marxism of fetishizing the fetish, yet his reminder that we attend to the historical specificity of ideology and fetishism reads as an articulate riposte to a tendency to hypostatize these terms of analysis.

5. While some still read the mainstreaming of fetishism as destabilizing public approbation, it could just as well be read as the symptom of a more thoroughly commodified cultural arena in which the last vestiges of desire are paraded as exchangeable objects. Here in New York there is even a "mardi gras" for fetishists with, unbelievably, a dress code! No doubt the ordering of such desire should be appropriately masochistic ("Tell me what to wear — and make me pay for the privilege" [the tickets are $50]), but whether the spectacle is disaffection or affirmation no longer seems to matter. This mystifying optionality or inconsequentiality is perfect for the fashion industry, which regularly sells fetishistic styles according to the logic of the fashion season. Again, however, the logic of fetishism is a good deal more complicated than its "glossy surfaces" (perhaps even that image is an indication of the fact). See Valerie Steele, *Fetish: Fashion, Sex, and Power* (Oxford: Oxford University Press, 1996).

6. Jacques Lacan and Wladimir Granoff, "Fetishism: The Symbolic, the Imaginary, and the Real," in *Perversions: Psychodynamics and Therapy*, ed. Sandor Lorand and Michael Balint (New York: Random House, 1956). They suggest that "if the strength of the repression (of the affect) is to be found in the interest for the successor of the feminine phallus, it is the denegation of its absence which will have constructed the memorial. The fetish will become the vehicle both of denying and asseverating the castration. It is this oscillation which constitutes the very nature of the critical moment" (273). The sexual division and undecidability of fetishism will be considered in more detail below.

7. Karl Marx, *Capital*, vol. 1, trans. Ben Fowkes (London: Penguin, 1976), 163.

8. The main reason for this is primarily the shoe's contradictory status within and between commodity fetishism and its psychosocial cognates. This is a huge and separate debate in its own right, and one that dances among the lines that follow. For a wide-ranging and suggestive collection in this regard, see Emily Apter and William Pietz, eds., *Fetishism as Cultural Discourse* (Ithaca, N.Y.: Cornell University Press, 1993). Appropriately, the cover of this book features a pair of shoes bound tightly together — it's an illustration from a work by Mary Kelly entitled *Supplication*.

9. Here I simultaneously allude to Derrida's reading of Heidegger, "Restitutions of the Truth in Pointing," in *The Truth in Painting*, trans. Geoffrey Bennington and Ian McCleod (Chicago: University of Chicago, 1987) and Kumar's image of the worker locked underfoot. The confluence of these images will be explained below. In general, I use Lacan's interpretation of Jones on aphanisis to underline the difference between the meaning that is ascribed to the commodity and the "disappearance" of the labor that marks its very possibility. The "fading" of the worker as subject is a function of her relationship to the commodity form under capitalism.

10. The geopolitical imagination eschews the totalizing impulse of the dialectic at the same time as it resists the aestheticizing tendencies of the dialogic. If this imagination is indeed representable, the commodity under transnational capitalism is its most prescient instance.

11. Part of this reevaluation is manifest in the work of William Pietz, particularly in a series of articles published in *Res: A Journal of Aesthetics and Anthropology* and in his contributing essay, "Fetishism and Materialism," for the anthology he edited with Emily Apter. I must say, however, that Pietz's general rejection of what he characterizes as "semiological" readings of Marx on fetishism seriously underestimates the significance of the imagination and the imaginary in commodity desire. The affective responsibility I explore is predicated on a materialist approach to semiosis.

12. This, of course, is not how Bakhtin uses "responsibility," which, in his early essays at least, is a means to foreground an ethical responsibility in aesthetics that is often antagonistic to the neo-Kantian Marburg school from which Bakhtin nevertheless drew sustenance. For Bakhtin's sense of responsibility ("answerability"), see Mikhail Bakhtin, *Art and Answerability*, trans. Vadim Liapunov, ed. Michael Holquist and Vadim Liapunov (Austin: University of Texas Press, 1990). What I will attempt to do with both Bakhtinian answerability and chronotope is reinscribe them within an economy of difference that does not resolve itself in an aesthetic "ought." The globalization of commodity culture answers traditional notions of authoring with the magic of the fetish: it "speaks" to them. But it also marks out new territories of practical engagement for the academic, for whom responsibility cannot remain an "academic" inquiry. For this sense of responsibility, see, for instance, Gayatri Chakravorty Spivak, "Responsibility," *boundary 2* (fall 1994): 19–64.

13. See Mikhail Bakhtin, "Forms of Time and of the Chronotope in the Novel: Notes towards a Historical Poetics," in *The Dialogic Imagination*, trans. Caryl Emerson and Michael Holquist, ed. Michael Holquist (Austin: University of Texas Press, 1981), 84–258. The chronotope has engendered intense disputes among Bakhtinians. My effort here is to accentuate its spatial possibilities in the critique of the commodity form.

14. See Michael Holquist, *Dialogism: Bakhtin and His World* (London: Routledge, 1990), 108–25.

15. Bakhtin, "Forms," 253.

16. See Katerina Clark and Michael Holquist, *Mikhail Bakhtin* (Cambridge, Mass.: Harvard University Press, 1984), 278.

17. Bakhtin, "Forms," 280.

18. The culture of sport is very big business in the United States: in 1992 it represented a market of over $60 billion.

19. Donald Katz, *Just Do It: The Nike Spirit in the Corporate World* (New York: Random House, 1994), 9.

20. Nike's share of the athletic shoe market has hovered around 33 percent for several years now, and between 1987 and 1993 its profits rose 900 percent. For more on transnationalism in particular and its relationship to colonialism, see Masao Miyoshi, "A Borderless World? From Colonialism to Transnationalism and the Decline of the Nation State," *Critical Inquiry* 19 (summer 1993): 726–51.

21. In 1996, revenue reached $6.47 billion, and profits rose to $553.2 million. As an example of brand power, in 1992 Nike's shop in Chicago (the shop is called "Nike

Town") was the most popular tourist attraction in the city. For more on the Nike Town concept, see Kerry Hannon, "The 1992 Store of the Year," *Money* (December 1991): 156–60.

22. In addition to the book by Katz, Nike has been eulogized and criticized in J. B. Strasser and Laurie Becklund, *Swoosh: The Unauthorized Story of Nike and the Men Who Played There* (New York: Harper, 1993). The "swoosh" is Nike's trademark — vaguely reminiscent of the goddess's wing but more evocative of a secret diacritic. Such is the brand recognition of Nike that it can market all manner of shoes and clothing merely by adding the "swoosh." Branding and iconography are, of course, not new, but it takes a tremendous amount of marketing for a brand to enter the pantheon of a global symbolic.

23. While late capitalism does not share the identical cultural codes of the age of European imperialism, the objectification of Asia as a market is not far removed from such an ideology. Interestingly, Phil Knight, the CEO of Nike, is something of a collector of "oriental" objets d'art, and his office is designed and decked out in traditional Japanese style.

24. See Fredric Jameson, *The Geopolitical Aesthetic: Cinema and Space in the World System* (Bloomington: Indiana University Press, 1992), 2; subsequent references to this work will be given in the text.

25. For instance, a Bakhtinian reading of the postmodern might find virtual reality an electronic adventure time, what Bakhtin calls a "pure digression from the normal course of life," which is "characterized by a technical, abstract connection between space and time, by the reversibility of moments in a temporal sequence, and by this interchangeability of space" (*Dialogic Imagination*, 90, 100). Again, this is another way to read Bakhtinian chronotope beyond the confines of his own examples at the same time as it highlights the transhistorical impulse it fosters.

26. This, therefore, is not a humanist response to the inhumanity of the commodity for the worker. In *Capital* (volume 1), Marx is quite explicit about the twofold character of embodied labor in the commodity and its connection to the socialization of consciousness. The issue of embodied labor must be kept separate from that of the worker as commodity, or as an exploitable cost of production.

27. Nike also makes athletic shoes in South Korea, Taiwan, China, and, more recently, Vietnam. These countries may be interchangeable for transnational capital, but they are not for this argument.

28. See Aijaz Ahmad, *In Theory* (London: Verso, 1992), 97. A further problem, as Ahmad well knows, is that even if one focuses one's critique in relation to a national paradigm, the necessary expertise calls into question the globalism of the critique itself, and not just the blithe country-hopping of the TNC. The answerability of theory is bound by a cognitive shortfall, one that prescribes and denatures even the most ardent openness to global others.

29. The CIA's role in this is still hotly debated (it was clearly involved in the civil war of the 1950s), as are the consequences for American foreign policy in the aftermath of the genocide that swept Indonesia at that time (the estimates of murdered PKI members, sympathizers, and anti-Suharto supporters of all persuasions range from 250,000 to 1,000,000). By 1967 Sukarno's power was effectively nullified, and opposition to Suharto had either "disappeared" or was languishing in prison (in the late 1960s Indonesia could boast of over one hundred thousand political prison-

ers). A critical account of the coup is provided in Benedict R. O'G. Anderson and R. T. McVey, *A Preliminary Analysis of the October 1, 1965, Coup in Indonesia* (Ithaca, N.Y.: Cornell University Press, 1971). A useful, if general, reading of the period can be found in Robert Cribb and Colin Brown, *Modern Indonesia* (London: Longman, 1995).

30. To borrow from Benedict Anderson's famous formulation, the Pancasila are about as good an example of how communities get "imagined" as one could find (the principles are belief in God, national unity, humanitarianism, people's sovereignty, and social justice and prosperity). Sukarno kept them sufficiently vague to smooth over the obvious divisions that racked the Indonesian archipelago in the aftermath of colonization. If the geopolitical imagination merely replays the deficiencies of the imagined community epitomized in the Pancasila, then it must fail as an adequate critical apparatus.

31. See, for instance, D. Cherchichovsky and O. E. Meesook, *Poverty in Indonesia: A Profile* (Washington, D.C., 1984), and C. Iluch, *Indonesia: Wages and Employment* (Washington, D.C., 1985).

32. Consider the World Bank monograph, *Indonesia: Strategy for a Sustained Reduction in Poverty* (Washington, D.C., 1990). The Bank reports that in 1987 thirty million Indonesians lived in poverty (17 percent of the population at that time). Indonesia had one of the lowest per-capita income levels, lowest life expectancy, and lowest number of doctors per capita in the world (1 doctor for 9,460 people). The Bank recommends that, because of the limited feasibility of expanding Indonesia's rice farming, the country embark on a course of light-industrial, labor-intensive manufacturing. Several years (and millions of Nike shoes) later, the Bank reports in *Indonesia: Environment and Development* (Washington, D.C., 1994) that the problem is overindustrialization from the expansion and inclusion of the workforce in manufacturing (by the end of the 1990s, this will represent 45 percent of Indonesia's GDP). The Bank asks where Indonesia is going to get the foreign capital to sustain such an industrial workforce and wonders at the same time whether the severe pollution (particularly on Java) is a catastrophe waiting to happen. Income, life expectancy, and the number of doctors have all improved, but these reports reveal that the World Bank, foreign governments, and foreign corporations have all played a part in exacerbating underlying systemic problems in Indonesia. The effects of greater pollution, for instance, and indeed of industrialization in general, may well lower life expectancy in the years to come. While there is little rigidity to developmental models in Asia, the experience of urban centers like Jakarta and Taibei might give the Bank some pause about the prospects of Beijing, or Shanghai.

33. Unless the selling of a representation itself is at stake. While there is no space here to detail the intricacies of "cultural diplomacy," it is clear that the Indonesian government has attempted in the past to sell an image of the nation that provides a cultural compensation for its otherwise authoritarian operations — and that foreign governments and corporations are entirely complicit with this process (since to overlook a massacre or two might garner economic preferences). See, for instance, Clifford Geertz's trenchant assessment of the "Festival of Indonesia" in the United States in 1991, "The Year of Living Culturally," *New Republic* (October 21, 1991): 30–36; and Brian Wallis, "Selling Nations," *Art in America* 79 (September 1991): 85–91.

34. One of the best English-language studies is provided by Benedict R. O'G. An-

derson, *Language and Power: Exploring Political Cultures in Indonesia* (Ithaca, N.Y.: Cornell University Press, 1990). See also J. D. Legge, *Indonesia* (Sydney: Prentice-Hall, 1980), and Leslie Palmier, ed., *Understanding Indonesia* (Aldershot: Gower, 1985).

35. For instance, the infamous *Cultuurstelsel,* or Forced Cultivation System (which basically paid for the Netherlands' debts, costs of war, and public works programs *in Holland* from 1830 to 1869), is an object lesson in colonial excess *and* modes of labor exploitation in Indonesia.

36. Sigmund Freud, "Fetishism," trans. Joan Riviere, in *The Standard Edition of the Complete Psychological Works of Sigmund Freud* (London: Hogarth, 1961), 21:154.

37. Most of the innovative work in this area does not just take issue with the normative function that Freud provides for this "minor perversion" but unpicks the model of masculinity it seems to imply. This includes feminist appropriations and renegotiations that, while not necessarily complementary, have "feminized the fetish" in significant ways. See, for instance, Donald Kuspit, "The Modern Fetish," *Artforum* (October 1988): 132–40, in which he argues that some contemporary women artists fetishistically mimic the phallic mother in order to attach the power of birth to the creation of their objects. Researching the *aliénistes* (as the nineteenth-century French psychiatrists often called themselves), Jann Matlock reinterprets the phenomenon of women as clothing fetishists in "Delirious Disguises, Perverse Masquerades, and the Ghostly Female Fetishist," *Grand Street* (summer 1995): 157–71. In a highly original reading of fetishism's economic and psychic interrelations, Linda Williams explores how ambivalent phallocentrism can structure even the conventional masculinist narratives of hard-core pornography in "Fetishism and the Visual Pleasure of Hard Core: Marx, Freud, and the 'Money Shot,'" *Quarterly Review of Film and Video* 11, no. 2 (1989): 23–42.

38. Emily Apter, *Feminizing the Fetish* (Ithaca, N.Y.: Cornell University Press, 1991), 2.

39. And these are many, especially as they slide into and contradict Marx's metaphors for ideology. As noted, for a provocative reading of the function of metaphor for Marx's concepts, see W. J. T. Mitchell, *Iconography: Image, Text, Ideology* (Chicago: University of Chicago, 1986). While not subscribing to a Marxist position, Mitchell is careful to distinguish the tactical, historical deployment of metaphors in Marx's arguments. What can and cannot be seen in the commodity fetish remains vital to the present polemic but as an indication of a continuing dissymmetry between visualization and imagination.

40. Frederic Jameson, *Postmodernism, or, the Cultural Logic of Late Capitalism* (Durham, N.C.: Duke University Press, 1991); subsequent references to the work will be given in the text.

41. See "The Origin of the Work of Art" ("Der Ursprung des Kunstwerkes"), trans. Albert Hofstadter, in Martin Heidegger, *Basic Writings,* ed. David Farrell Krell (New York: Harper Collins, 1993), 143–212.

42. See, for instance, Haynes Horne, "Jameson's Strategies of Containment," in *Postmodernism/Jameson/Critique,* ed. Douglas Kellner, 268–300 (Washington, D.C.: Maisonneuve Press, 1989).

43. See Jacques Derrida, "Restitutions of the Truth in Pointing," 256; subsequent references to this essay will be given in the text.

44. Marx, *Capital*, 1:163.

45. It seems to me that "pointing" underestimates the sexual economy of the shoe in comparison to "pricking." True, a prick was an early form of the knitting needle, and pricking also once referred to embroidery of certain kinds, but there is more evidence in English for an excess of signification than perhaps the French word allows. Pricking, for instance, might describe the process by which leather is stitched (the result is called a "prick stitch"), but it is also a mental operation, not just in pricking one's conscience, but also in the infliction of mental pain. Similarly, a prick is a dot or metrical mark in literature and music, but also a less writerly puncture in the sole of the foot of a horse. Just in case this seem too far removed from the principle of the chronotope, one should add that a prick is both a point of space, a geometrical point, and the smallest portion of time — an instant. Indeed, in one of its meanings, prick is the precise instant at which anything happens: it is the critical moment. In the sixteenth century, prick was a vulgar term of endearment, but in the twentieth it became a particular term of abuse for a man. Finally, in the seventeenth century one could test if a woman were a witch by pricking her until one found a spot that did not bleed, but more recently pricking could mean the magical act of writing itself. Of this surplus of signification shoes indeed might be made. See the *OED* (2d edition).

46. It is highly appropriate in this regard that young males, the primary consumers of athletic shoes, face a wall of single shoes when exercising their consumer choice. True, this is a general feature of the mass consumption of shoes (to display pairs invites shoplifting), but this will have a particular valence for the consumer of athletic shoes, as a later example will accentuate.

47. I will make more of this translucence in a moment. The function of Cinderella's foot in a phallic economy of presence continues to garner critical attention. See Susanne Sara Thomas, "'Cinderella' and the Phallic Foot: The Symbolic Significance of the Tale's Slipper Motif," *Southern Folklore* 52, no. 1 (1995): 19–51.

48. Indeed, the proletarianization of Asian women emphasizes either dexterity or eyesight and often both. For a keen analysis of the treatment of women workers under transnational capitalism, see Annette Fuentes and Barbara Ehrenreich, *Women in the Global Factory* (Boston: South End Press, 1983).

49. Katz, *Just Do It*, 185.

50. Quoted in ibid., 172. The disciplinary zeal of the managers is reinforced by the ideological underpinnings of the Pancasila, which encourage dutiful submission and *ibuism*, the belief that a woman should primarily act as a mother without demanding power or prestige in return. Clearly, women workers have resisted every element of this desire, despite the threat of wage cuts or dismissal.

51. Yet the higher Nike's profile, the more vocal the resistance against such business practices has become. For capitalist investors, however, Nike is an exemplary organization. In 1993, *Money* magazine included Nike in a list of six American companies who offered investors returns of up to 47 percent per annum. See Ellen Stark, "Making Money on America's Top Money," *Money* (June 1993): 114–17.

52. The conservative reinterpretation of the Pancasila as a document that supports patriarchy is detailed in Cribb and Brown, *Modern Indonesia*. For an important essay on the enlistment of young peasant women into the Indonesian industrial workforce, see Diane L. Wolf, "Linking Women's Labor with the Global Economy: Factory Workers and Their Families in Rural Java," in *Women Workers and Global Restruc-*

turing, ed. Kathryn Ward, 25–47 (Ithaca, N.Y., 1990). Wolf has written one of the most extensive and detailed analyses of the effect of globalization on Javanese women workers. See Diane L. Wolf, *Factory Daughters* (Berkeley: University of California Press, 1992). For some pertinent discussion of the cultural representations of the effects of the Pancasila for women, see Tineke Hellwig, *In the Shadow of Change: Images of Women in Indonesian Literature*, (Berkeley: University of California Press, 1994).

53. See Jeffrey Ballinger, "The New Free Trade Heel," *Harper's Magazine* (August 1992): 46–47. In 1993, Ballinger appeared in a special edition of *Street Stories* on CBS that focused on Nike's operations in Indonesia. Ironically, the main factory featured was about the cleanest shoe manufacturing plant on the planet. Nevertheless, the program reported that a strike at another Indonesian plant had resulted in twenty-two workers being "suspended," and it did document the practice of confining the women workers to the plant dormitories. Katz provides plenty of details on this and other evidence of Nike's misdeeds in Asia, but his critique remains a long way from condemnation.

54. Quoted in Strasser and Becklund, *Swoosh*, 501.

55. It also reminds the business community of Nike's economic vulnerability. Michael Janofsky, for instance, recalls the misfortune of Quincy Watt, the American runner whose Nike shoes came apart during a race at the world track and field championships in Stuttgart in August 1993. Watt, an Olympic champion, finished fourth. Janofsky uses this as an occasion to discuss a quarter in which Nike's earnings dropped. He suggests that "Just Do It" be amended to "Just Glue It." See Michael Janofsky, "Market Place," *New York Times*, September 24, 1993, D6.

56. For more on the cult-like campus at Beaverton, see James Servin, "Camp Nike: It's Not a Job, It's a Lifestyle," *Harper's Bazaar* (June 1994): 46–48. In another odd twist in economic history, a psychology professor suggests that the model for the Nike World Campus was the athletic sports camps provided in Eastern Europe under communism!

57. Katz, *Just Do It*, 49.

58. See Kate Bednarski, "Convincing Male Managers to Target Women Customers," *Working Woman* (June 1993): 23–24, 28. Not surprisingly, the language of this article is generally in step with capitalist consciousness. There is no recognition, for instance, that Nike had been "targeting" women workers for quite some time. In effect, the women managers disavow the women workers just like their male counterparts, although that is not the same as saying that a woman's identification with the shoe is simply the equivalent of male fetishism; it is to acknowledge, however, that male fetishism is hegemonic.

59. Katz describes a process of invention at Nike World Campus that is indistinguishable from artistic reverie and is nurtured "in a general ambiance of youthful, free-associative creativity that is invariably tempered by some flavor of sophisticated wit" (see Katz, *Just Do It*, 130).

60. On this point, labor is the deciding factor: "No matter how inspired a new technical design, style statement, or marketing campaign, the entire industry's productive processes were still based on how fast the women in Pusan, South Korea, and Indonesia could glue together by hand up to twenty-five pieces of a single shoe" (Katz, *Just Do It*, 174).

61. Katz, *Just Do It*, 151; subsequent references to the work, abbreviated *J*, will be given in the text.

62. Vietnam has become the next in line.

63. Nike's hiring of Andrew Young, the former mayor of Atlanta and United Nations representative, is a crass attempt to reinforce this view. Young's consulting company, Goodworks International (!), is busily retooling Nike's international good work, or at least the image thereof, but thus far the scandal of Nike's transnational labor practices has not abated.

64. The use of factory dormitories is a widespread phenomenon, but this has been a particular feature of Nike's Chinese operations. The retort has been that this is for "security reasons" and has nothing to do with the fear that the workers might become romantically involved, want to start families, or even choose another line of work.

65. In another version of this essay I intend to shift the question of imaginative response more extensively to Indonesia, where narratives of capitalist discipline and nationalist dogma are confounded in innovative ways. Here, obviously, the emphasis has been on the affective responsibility of global critique from the position of a Bakhtinian critic of globality — me. I cannot erase this emphasis, but intend instead to build it into the promise of disruption in other logics of imagination. Both approaches, both angles of address, are, I hope, dialogic, although the individual critic cannot adjudicate this process. For Ong's analysis of spirit possession as resistance among Malaysian women factory workers, see Aihwa Ong, *Spirits of Resistance and Capitalist Discipline* (Albany: State University of New York Press, 1987).

66. See Mark Clifford, "Spring in Their Step," *Far Eastern Economic Review* (November 5, 1992): 56–57. The title refers to Nike's practice of hopping from one Asian country to the next in search of cheap labor.

67. For more on the culture of killing for sportswear, see Rick Telander, "Senseless," *Sports Illustrated*, 72, no. 20 (May 14, 1990): 36–49. See also *J* 268–70. On Tuesday, December 19, 1995, in New York, a man went berserk in a shoe store after being told that the Nike high-tops he had ordered had not yet arrived. He pulled out a 9mm pistol and shot dead five people. The man had been previously diagnosed as a schizophrenic. While Nike cannot be blamed for individual acts of madness like this, a culture of active responsibility does not resolve itself in the mere fact of diagnosis.

68. See, for instance, Wiley M. Woodward, "It's More Than Just the Shoes," *Black Enterprise* (November 1990): 17.

69. Heidegger claims the Van Gogh painting "spoke" the Being of the thing, the product-being in the shoes. Jameson's comment that Warhol's *Diamond Dust Shoes* "doesn't speak to us at all" implies that Van Gogh's effort does. And Derrida's entire investigation is about how the truth "speaks" in painting. Derrida suggests that Heidegger makes the peasant shoes "speak" — once they are painted, "these shoes talk." My point is that these figures of speech are written into the product-being of commodity fetishism.

70. Indeed, the rise in popularity of rugged "outdoor" shoes and boots has already redrawn the athletic shoe market. Nike, of course, has switched production accordingly and has also expanded its market "penetration" into other sports and sporting goods. The swoosh is becoming ubiquitous.

71. As noted above, an alternative version of this piece will link Indonesia much more forcefully to the imaginative plane, including the imaginary state symbolized by the contradictory logic of the athletic shoe within global capital.

72. Bakhtin, "Forms," 84.

5. (   ) OF GHOSTS

1. See Jacques Derrida, *Specters of Marx*, trans. Peggy Kamuf (New York: Routledge, 1994), 100; subsequent references will be given in the text as *SOM* followed by page number; references to the French text will be noted within the text as *SDM* followed by page number (*Spectres de Marx* [Paris: Galilée, 1993]).

2. This is a philosophical and political knot of some complexity that I will attempt to untangle below. The standard argument says that the actual existence of socialism was predicated on a promissory note on which the state could not deliver. But this is not just because of the contradictions of socialism in one country or the globalization of capitalist social and economic relations. It is also a function of the way "actual existence" was posed. Think, for a moment, of Althusser's appeals to determination "in the last instance." The advantage of this move is that it offers an analytical framework that remains open to the processes of material change. The disadvantage lies in the advantage: that is to say, the proposition tends to prescribe a material reality to which another "instance" may not be reducible. The relative autonomy of other "instances" (like ideology) becomes something of a magical key leaving Althusser to opine famously that "the lonely hour of the 'last instance' never comes." The first problem of "actual existence" is its contradictory philosophical proposition. Without a serious rethinking of the logic of becoming in materialism one is left with a neat but dystopian Althusserian gesture: the lonely hour of "actual existence" never comes.

3. Etienne Balibar, *The Philosophy of Marx*, trans. Chris Turner (New York: Verso, 1995), 1. On occasion, I will also use the French version, *La philosophie de Marx* (Paris: Éditions La Découverte, 1993); different page numbers will be noted accordingly within the text preceded by *POM* or *PDM*.

4. Bern Magnus and Stephen Cullenberg, eds., *Whither Marxism? Global Crises in International Perspective* (New York: Routledge, 1995).

5. I refer, of course, to Michael Ryan, *Marxism and Deconstruction: A Critical Articulation* (Baltimore: Johns Hopkins University Press, 1982). Most of the groundwork for Ryan's book was worked out, as he indicates in his preface, in the arguments of the 1970s — another moment when "Whither Marxism?" gained prescience, this time in the wake of the failures of '68 in France.

6. See, in particular, chapter 4 of Ryan's book, which focuses on *Capital*. The example of the table, with its "wooden brain" and "grotesque ideas," comes from the fetishism section of chapter 1 of *Capital* (volume 1) on "the commodity." The dancing table is Marx's metaphor for fetishism, and spiritualism in particular. For his part, Derrida usefully connects the "thingness" of the thing to the ghostliness of the "thing" in *Hamlet*, but he seems to lose track of the reality of the thing for the worker in capitalist relations of production. The ghost in the commodity form is always already the trace of the worker's embodied labor paradoxically revealed in the absence of that body.

7. Etienne Balibar, "From Class Struggle to Classless Struggle?" in Etienne Balibar and Immanuel Wallerstein, *Race, Nation, Class: Ambiguous Identities*, trans. Chris Turner (New York: Verso, 1991), 153–84.

8. See Gilles Deleuze and Félix Guattari, *What Is Philosophy?* trans. Hugh Tomlinson and Graham Burchell (New York: Columbia University Press, 1994), especially chapter 4. Deleuze and Guattari here link geophilosophy to their notion of deterri-

torialization; in other words, they align their philosophical concept with actual spatial coordinates — Why does philosophy develop in Greece? and so on. Becoming, as a concept, is geographical rather than historical according to this scheme, but a little more of the temporal could specify the spatiality at issue. Geophilosophy is also a trajectory of theory and might benefit from the details of its movement.

9. See Jean-Luc Nancy, *The Experience of Freedom*, trans. Bridget McDonald (Stanford, Calif.: Stanford University Press, 1993). Nancy reads experience back into the thought of the imagination while questioning its status as a dream of empiricism. Thinking the ghost may seem to replay Nancy's exposition of the impasse in thinking freedom, but it is also part of his solution in that the "ground" of the ghost cannot be thought except as a function of the imagination. This is the way that the uncanny, for instance, haunts what is known. But there is another version of "haunting" in Nancy's reading of Kant, which we may call the ghost of moral consciousness. What Kant's categorical imperative appears to do is disregard "fact" in the service of a consciousness that legislates itself. Facts, therefore, haunt the consciousness that would deny them. Obviously, Nancy's target remains the brutality of the ground itself, "the positivity of wickedness," rather than the logic of shifting grounds that is my main concern. The logical trap of positing grounds has a certain inevitability to it, but the critique of, say, positivism does not in itself secure the experience of freedom. If your freedom is insecure, then perhaps we are all free already to the extent that insecurity is a topos of the present — which is only to say that the revolution in thinking necessary for the experience of freedom is currently (determinately) almost unimaginable. And the "almost" is where materialism comes back.

10. Balibar, "Class," 154; subsequent references to this work will be given in the text as "Class," plus the page number.

11. See Jacques Derrida, *Positions*, trans. Alan Bass (London: Athlone Press, 1972).

12. This argument was originally presented at Cerisy-la-Salle as "Représentation et les travailleurs" (August 1995), forthcoming in André Collinot and Clive Thomson, eds., *Mikhail Bakhtine et la pensée dialogique* (London, Ont.: Mestengo Press). The following month a conference on "ghosts" took place in Cardiff. Ernesto Laclau's keynote speech, "The Time Is Out of Joint," has since been published in *Diacritics* and his *Emanicpation(s)* (London: Verso, 1996). Although my effort here is not directly influenced by Laclau's, it may complement it in certain ways.

13. Karl Marx, *Capital*, vol. 1, trans. Ben Fowkes (London: Penguin, 1976), 98.

14. This is part of what Derrida challenges in *Specters of Marx*. His section on Fukuyama's "end of history" thesis is, however, a curiously hurried reading that yet manages to grant Fukuyama a perspicacity his central idea does not deserve.

15. For an idea of the critical difference between "Marx beyond Marx" and "Marxism beyond Marxism" the reader might usefully consult Negri's book *Marx beyond Marx* in relation to his contribution to the volume of collected essays, *Marxism beyond Marxism*. The former includes a close reading of the *Grundrisse* in which Negri considers the possibility of the subject and subjectivity in the path to communism as an integer of the crises in the law of value with which Marx's notebooks seem to grapple. The autonomous subject is the subject of "Autonomia," the independent Leftist movement in Italy in the 1970s. By the 1950s, Negri has broken with the progressivist implication in the classical texts of historical materialism that reads a subsumption of labor under capital. The philosophy of Marx, according to this interpretation, is more

properly periodized in the sense that the law of value for Marx was predicated on a critique of industrial capital. In essence, the ghosting of Marxism is achieved by the intervention of periodicity (given to Negri in the present by forms of Post-Fordism). And this, of course, animates the ghost of Marx recalled in Negri's "Twenty Theses." See Antonio Negri, *Marx beyond Marx*, trans. Harry Cleaver, Michael Ryan, and Maurizio Viano (South Hadley, Mass.: Bergin and Garvey, 1984); and idem, "Twenty Theses on Marx," in *Marxism beyond Marxism*, ed. Saree Makdisi, Cesare Casarino, and Rebecca Karl, 149–80 (New York: Routledge, 1996).

16. *In Theory* is the kind of book that precipitates discussion on so many levels that it is destined to provide grist for materialist critique for some time (its half-life as a whipping post will be considerably shorter). Although he provides a useful gloss on the predicaments of the world system today, Ahmad tends to limit the oscillatory range of the principles he deploys. This purism can be devastating where liberal humanism is concerned, but it is less patient with the problematic internal dynamics of Marxist theory itself. See Aijaz Ahmad, *In Theory* (New York: Verso, 1993).

17. In this respect, Magnus and Cullenberg are overly generous in their introduction to Derrida's text where they suggest four ways in which *Specters of Marx* speaks to (or is "in direct conversation with") the contributors to *Whither Marxism?* Whether the conversation exists in either direction is not the point, but whether Derrida's procedures "suspend" the conversation at the moment where their logic is challenged by the "conditions" of the Marx made possible.

18. It would be interesting to explore the number of times and under what conditions the various prefaces to the *Manifesto* were left out of its editions even when, as Marx does in 1872, the general principles are reaffirmed. The various translations of the *Manifesto* also make for informative (and entertaining) reading. The first English translation of the *Manifesto* appeared in a journal called the *Red Republican* in 1850 and began: "A frightful hobgoblin stalks through Europe"! Personally, I think this perfectly captures the spirit of Marx's caricature of the ruling orders' fear.

19. Paradoxically, the condition of the former — the specter — can be "represented" by the materiality of the latter — an empty space. The empty parentheses of my chapter title are meant to signify this philosophical and political conundrum. The difference, I would argue, is an example of an undecidable, or what Derrida terms "a determinate oscillation."

20. Balibar, *Masses, Classes, Ideas*, trans. James Swenson (New York: Routledge, 1994), xx; subsequent references to this work will be given in the text; Balibar and Wallerstein, *Race, Nation, Class*, 179.

21. In this I agree to a great extent with Callari and Ruccio. They argue that the peculiar motor-of-history argument used to promote the primacy of the working class depended on a homogenization of the economic sphere. It is against this conservative determinism that a more open or "aleatory" materialism must be brought to bear. See the introduction to Antonio Callari and David F. Ruccio, eds., *Postmodern Materialism and the Future of Marxist Theory* (Hanover, N.H.: Wesleyan University Press, 1996).

22. Fowkes renders this translation as "insubstantial semblance." In the edited 1887 and 1890 4th edition, the *Gespenst* is more pronounced.

23. Jean-Marie Vincent, *Critique du travail: Le faire et l'agir* (Paris: Presses Universitaires de France, 1987); available in English as *Abstract Labor: A Critique*, trans. Jim Cohen (New York: St. Martin's Press, 1991). The latter contains a useful critical intro-

duction by Stanley Aronowitz and an additional preface by Vincent framed in reference to the recent collapse of "actually existing socialism." Vincent suggests that "thought needs interrogations . . . for it must live in a constant state of tension" (xxix). This, I believe, is further evidence of the homeostasis of materialist theory in the present.

24. The negative consequence is that the "double-nature" can nevertheless be read off in a univocal and unilinear way. Again, the paradox is that the material reality of labor can be hypostatized as its only form, negating its "unsubstantial ghost" in favor of a "fetish of labor" (*le fétiche travail*) itself. The condition of the commodity becomes labor's articulation in theory, and, as Vincent demonstrates, a dynamism in identity is reinscribed as a monism.

25. In addition to the work by Ryan already mentioned, see Gayatri Chakravorty Spivak, "Scattered Speculations of the Question of Value," in *In Other Worlds* (London: Methuen, 1987), 154–75; and idem, "Marginality in the Teaching Machine," in *Outside in the Teaching Machine* (New York: Routledge, 1993), 61–64. See also Thomas Keenan, "The Point Is to (Ex)Change It: Reading *Capital*, Rhetorically," and Jack Amariglio and Antonio Callari, "Marxian Value Theory and the Problem of the Subject," in *Fetishism as Cultural Discourse*, ed. Emily Apter and William Pietz (Ithaca, N.Y.: Cornell University Press, 1993), 152–85 and 186–216 respectively.

26. Or rather, should we be surprised *now*? It is the collapse of those systems that attempted to suppress this founding ambivalence that now allows theory to consider this exploded contradiction. History's contingencies allow such "ghosts" to return.

27. "Whither Marxism?" is not the "putting into question" of Marxism *tout court* according to this interpretation. Instead, it is the *mise en scene* of a specific materialist problem for which philosophy facilitates an explanation. The fear of such philosophy is justified (there is always *a politics* of deferral), but the nature of the problem cannot be addressed simply by dismissing the contingent.

28. See Jean-Christophe Bailly and Jean-Luc Nancy, *La comparution: Politique à venir* (Paris: Christian Bourgois Editeur, 1991), 62. Nancy's contribution to this volume examines the theoretical space between the existence of communism and the community of existence. While I maintain a sharp difference with Nancy's interpretation of community in the latter, his transcription of communism to mean a specific attenuation of the "presence" of capital — the real movement, as he borrows from Marx, of that which destroys the existing state of things — is in keeping with the allusions and illusions of "actual existence" explored here.

29. Of course, the "worlds of labor" that Hobsbawm explores under this rubric do not correspond to labor in the world as such. Hobsbawm is concerned to examine in some detail the labor history of Western societies, in which a different sense of globality is at issue. Nevertheless, the experience of globalism itself is now giving new prescience to the plurality of labor that Hobsbawm's title invokes. That is to say, there are now many more worlds in which the history of labor becomes manifest. See Eric Hobsbawm, *Worlds of Labour* (London: Weidenfeld and Nicolson, 1984).

30. See Balibar, *Masses, Classes, Ideas*, 107.

31. Jean-Luc Nancy, *Le sens du monde* (Paris: Galilée, 1993), 126. To be sure, some of the difficulties of Nancy's formulations on sense rest in the sense of the question for philosophy, and not just the playful extremities of the French language, to which Nancy also pays obeisance. But one could also view his analysis as part of a more general coming to terms with alternative modes of worldliness after the age of "high"

imperialism. A geopolitical aesthetic, in Jameson's conception, is made possible by a restructuring of the cognitive according to specific material conditions. Although these are different for Nancy, his reading of Balibar on *égaliberté* (or a mutual dependence and impasse in equality and liberty in democracy) emphasizes the political implications of a different sense of the world.

32. These phrases are taken from *The Eighteenth Brumaire,* in *Surveys from Exile,* ed. and introduced by David Fernbach, trans. Ben Fowkes et al. (London: Harmondsworth, 1973).

33. See Douglas Kellner, "The Obsolescence of Marxism?" in *Whither,* 3–27.

34. Gayatri Chakravorty Spivak, "Supplementing Marxism," in *Whither,* 109–19.

35. Bhaskar is easily the most difficult theorist of materialism currently available in English, but the following works are recommended, particularly the last: *A Realist Theory of Science* (Leeds: Leeds Books, 1975); *Scientific Realism and Human Emancipation* (London: Verso, 1986); *Reclaiming Reality* (London: Verso, 1989); and *Dialectic: The Pulse of Freedom* (London: Verso, 1993). For a review essay that places Bhaskar within a tradition of Marxist philosophies of science, see Michael Sprinker, "The Royal Road: Marxism and the Philosophy of Science," *New Left Review* 191 (January/February 1992): 122–44.

36. Eric Hobsbawm, *The Age of Empire* (New York: Pantheon, 1987), 336.

CONCLUSION

1. Aware of the pitfalls of neologism, particularly in light of other names available — multicultural materialism, postmodern materialism, fin de siècle socialism, cultural materialism, and so on — I would say that "millennial materialism" as a term is more prospective than denotative. What it accentuates is the historical consonance between the prospect of the new century and more sweeping changes in the way we think about materialist critique.

2. Of course, there is an argument that would argue that the "random" psychologism and the fragment of modernism are contrived. The chaos that appears to constitute the surface of modernist culture often belies the overarching mythical structure that in fact organizes individual works. That version of the "center" did hold for a good part of the twentieth century. If the fragmentation appears more pronounced in the present (and defies even those myths of last resort), then this is a question of scale rather than a more general aesthetic or epistemic transformation. To invoke modernism here is to register its continuities and differences within the moment of globalization. For an elaboration of the centripetal inclinations of modernism, see James McFarlane, "The Mind of Modernism," in *Modernism,* ed. Malcolm Bradbury and James McFarlane, 71–79 (London: Penguin, 1976).

3. See Virginia Woolf, "Modern Novels," in *The Essays of Virginia Woolf* (vol. 3, 1919–24), ed. Andrew McNeillie, 33–34 (New York: Harcourt, 1988).

4. See Thomas Mann, *Death in Venice,* trans. David Luke (New York: Bantam, 1988), especially chapter 3.

5. Balibar suggests that Althusser began with an epistemological interpretation of structural causality and moved, within the context of a crisis in Marxist theory, to a reconsideration of the issue in terms of a social and historical ontology. That sense of

"becoming" in Being certainly underlies the present discussion. See Etienne Balibar, "Structural Causality, Overdetermination, and Antagonism," in *Postmodern Materialism and the Future of Marxist Theory*, ed. Antonio Callari and David F. Ruccio, 109–19 (Hanover, N.H.: Wesleyan University Press, 1996).

6. See Teresa Ebert, *Ludic Feminism and After* (Ann Arbor: University of Michigan Press, 1996), especially chapter 1. I will have more to say about the ludic implications of oscillation below.

7. A recent example is from Paul Gross and Norman Levitt, *Higher Superstition: The Academic Left and Its Quarrels with Science* (Baltimore: Johns Hopkins University Press, 1994). The book is well within the established genre of policing the boundaries in scientific analysis, especially where a demonized "Left" is concerned. Despite their entertaining debunking of many a pseudoscientist their argument begs the question about how scientific discourses structure their modes of objectification. Even if the scientist refused to use language in her or his theoretical framework (a dubious proposition in any event), one would still have to come to terms with the "utterance context" for such labor. To deny the cultural (as well as economic and social) conditions of science may reaffirm a specialist knowledge, but does nothing to elaborate the knowledge of itself or a knowledge with which even a nonspecialist might share. The most notorious example is actually one that occurs within the Left: the "Sokal Affair." I will not flog this particular dead horse, which is actually more about academic honesty than the status of science for culture. I would urge, however, that when the dust of sensationalism has settled a more systematic consideration of this event's politics be read into the peculiar and specific history of the American Left.

8. See Henri Poincaré, *Les oscillations électriques* (Paris: Georges Carre, 1894). This book contains lectures that Poincaré had given in the previous two years.

9. James Gleick, *Chaos: Making a New Science* (New York: Viking, 1987), 46. Gleick's book was one of the first to make some of the principles of chaos theory accessible to a wider audience. What I will do in the pages that follow is link this phenomenon at the end of the twentieth century to the discoveries that prepared it.

10. This forms the epigraph to the first chapter of Peter Coveney and Roger Highfield, eds., *Frontiers of Complexity: The Search for Order in a Chaotic World* (New York: Fawcett Columbine, 1995). This is one of a large number of books that have appeared in recent years that uses the Gleickian mode of crossover. Using the motto "Simplicity is the mother of complexity," the authors explore some of the latest experiments in complex mathematical modeling. Looking at, for instance, their discussion of the mixed-mode oscillations of the "crosscatalator" this reader is unsure whether they have understood what Kant might mean by "perfect world system" in his formulation.

11. Immanuel Wallerstein, *Geopolitics and Geoculture* (Cambridge: Cambridge University Press, 1991); subsequent references will be given in the text.

12. Gayatri Chakravorty Spivak, "Limits and Openings of Marx in Derrida," in *Outside in the Teaching Machine* (New York: Routledge, 1993), 115.

13. Obviously my own efforts are not outside this tendency. I should add that there have been some very provocative contributions to this particular arena. See, for instance, N. Katherine Hayles, *Chaos Bound: Orderly Disorder in Contemporary Literature and Science* (Ithaca, N.Y.: Cornell University Press, 1990); idem, ed., *Chaos and Order: Complex Dynamics in Literature and Science* (Chicago: University of Chicago Press, 1991); and Harriet Hawkins, *Strange Attractors: Literature, Culture, and Chaos*

Theory (New York: Prentice Hall, 1995). For a general review of literature that oscillates between culture and the new science, see Steven Johnson, "Strange Attraction," *Lingua Franca* (April 1996): 42–50.

14. Karl Marx, *Economic and Philosophical Manuscripts,* in *The Marx/Engels Reader,* ed. Robert C. Tucker (New York: Norton, 1978), 87.

15. In addition to the film documentary (and, of course, the music and films in which the Theremin has been used), the following reviews are recommended: Anthony Henk, "Sublime Theremin," *New Scientist* 148 (November 1995): 76; "Theremin: The Man, Music, and Mystery, and Now the Movie," *New York Times,* late New York edition, August 24, 1993, C13+; Susan Stark, "The Buzz," *Detroit News,* January 19, 1996, D3; Desson Howe, "'Theremin': Good Vibrations," *Washington Post,* January 26, 1996, WW38; Hal Hinson, "'Theremin' Strikes a Chord," *Washington Post,* January 26, 1996, F6; Michael Wilmington, "'Theremin': Truth Is Stranger Than Fiction," *Chicago Tribune,* December 15, 1995, 7J; Peter Stack, "Strange Man, Strange Music," *San Francisco Chronicle,* November 3, 1995, C10; Edward Guthmann, "The Wizard of Weird Vibes," *San Francisco Chronicle,* October 19, 1995, DAT42; C. M. Wetzler, "Little Black Box Put Electronic Music on Map," *New York Times,* October 29, 1995, WC16; Jay Carr, "'Theremin': A Love Story with Electricity," *Boston Globe,* September 29, 1995, 49. For more on the recent revival of the Theremin in music, see Alex Bellos, "Here a Woo, There a Woo, Everywhere a Woo-woo," *Guardian,* July 24, 1995, 2:4, and idem, "Pop Goes Mad for the Electronic Sound of the Twenties," *Guardian,* February 20, 1995, 1:4; Sarra Manning, "Live! Lydia Kavina," *Melody Maker,* 72, no. 41 (October 14, 1995): 20; Tony Horkins, "The X-mas Files: Longwave Pocket Theremin," *Melody Maker,* 72, no. 51 (December 23, 1995): 79–80; "The Talk of the Town: Theremin, Theremin," *New Yorker,* 66, no. 31 (September 17, 1990): 34–36. In addition, a Theremin home page can be found on the World Wide Web with information for both general readers and "techies." There are several manuals now available on how to build your own Theremin, as well as companies in the States and Europe that will build a Theremin for you. Steven M. Martin is also a collector of Theremins. The prize, in this regard, is one of the three hundred Theremins built by RCA in the 1920s. Theremins are part of the permanent collections of several museums; indeed, in the documentary we see Theremin himself "tuning" one such museum piece in Moscow. While the articles above register something of the Theremin phenomenon, my principal interest is in highlighting and integrating the lesson of the Theremin in the history of sense perception. And the "love story with electricity" is integral to the force and relations of production in the modern era. Incidentally, the original cover for this book was a morphed image of Marx playing the Theremin, but this wild oscillation was vanquished by something a little less oscillatory: the production schedule.

16. See Michael Taussig, *Mimesis and Alterity* (New York: Routledge, 1993), xv. Taussig's reading of Benjamin stands in sharp contrast to the cognitive criteria deployed in Vattimo's argument. His elaboration of the mimetic faculty is a careful exegesis of what the commodity form does to sense perception and includes important lessons drawn from noncapitalist (and sometimes anticapitalist) modes of fetishism.

17. Gilles Deleuze and Félix Guattari, *What Is Philosophy?* trans. Hugh Tomlinson and Graham Burchell (New York: Columbia University Press, 1994), 202–3.

SELECTED BIBLIOGRAPHY

Adams, Parveen. "Per Os(cillation)." In *Male Trouble*. Edited by Constance Penley and Sharon Willis, 3–25. Minneapolis: University of Minnesota Press, 1993.

Adorno, T. W. *Aesthetic Theory*. Edited by Gretel Adorno and Rolf Tiedemann. Translated by C. Lenhardt. London: Routledge, 1984.

Ahmad, Aijaz. *In Theory*. London: Verso, 1993.

———. "The Third World in Jameson's *Postmodernism, or, the Cultural Logic of Late Capitalism*." *Social Text* 31/32 (1992): 258–70.

Amariglio, Jack, and Antonio Callari. "Marxian Value Theory and the Problem of the Subject." In *Fetishism as Cultural Discourse*. Edited by Emily Apter and William Pietz, 186–216. Ithaca, N.Y.: Cornell University Press, 1993.

Amselle, Jean-Loup. *Logiques métisses: Anthropologie de l'identité en Afrique et ailleurs*. Paris: Payot, 1990.

Anderson, Benedict R. O'G. *Language and Power: Exploring Political Cultures in Indonesia*. Ithaca, N.Y.: Cornell University Press, 1990.

Anderson, Benedict R. O'G, and R. T. McVey. *A Preliminary Analysis of the October 1, 1965, Coup in Indonesia*. Ithaca, N.Y.: Cornell University Press, 1971.

Anderson, Perry. "The Antimonies of Antonio Gramsci." *New Left Review* 100 (November–January 1976–77): 5–78.

———. *Considerations on Western Marxism*. London: Verso, 1976.

———. *A Zone of Engagement*. London: Verso, 1992.

Appadurai, Arjun. "Disjuncture and Difference in the Global Cultural Economy." In *The Phantom Public Sphere*. Edited by Bruce Robbins, 269–95. Minneapolis: University of Minnesota Press, 1993.

Appiah, Kwame Anthony. *In My Father's House: Africa in the Philosophy of Culture*. New York: Oxford University Press, 1992.

Apter, Emily. *Feminizing the Fetish*. Ithaca, N.Y.: Cornell University Press, 1991.

Apter, Emily, and William Pietz, eds. *Fetishism as Cultural Discourse*. Ithaca, N.Y.: Cornell University Press, 1993.

Bailly, Jean-Christophe, and Jean-Luc Nancy. *La comparution: Politique à venir*. Paris: Christian Bourgois Editeur, 1991.

Bakhtin, Mikhail. *Art and Answerability*. Translated by Vadim Liapunov. Edited by Michael Holquist and Vadim Liapunov. Austin: University of Texas Press, 1990.

———. *The Dialogic Imagination*. Translated by Caryl Emerson and Michael Holquist. Edited by Michael Holquist. Austin: University of Texas Press, 1981.

———. *Rabelais and His World*. Translated by Hélène Iswolsky. Bloomington: Indiana University Press, 1984.

Balibar, Etienne. "From Class Struggle to Classless Struggle?" In Etienne Balibar and Immanuel Wallerstein, *Race, Nation, Class: Ambiguous Identities*. Translated by Chris Turner, 153–84. New York: Verso, 1991.

————. *Masses, Classes, Ideas.* Translated by James Swenson. New York: Routledge, 1994.

————. *The Philosophy of Marx.* Translated by Chris Turner. New York: Verso, 1995.

Balibar, Etienne, and Immanuel Wallerstein. *Race, Nation, Class: Ambiguous Identities.* London: Verso, 1991.

Ballinger, Jeffrey. "The New Free Trade Heel." *Harper's Magazine* (August 1992): 46–47.

Baudrillard, Jean. *Simulations.* New York: Semiotext[e], 1983.

Bednarski, Kate. "Convincing Male Managers to Target Women Customers." *Working Woman* (June 1993): 23–24, 28.

Benítez-Rojo, Antonio. *The Repeating Island.* Translated by James E. Maraniss. Durham, N.C.: Duke University Press, 1992.

Benjamin, Walter. *Illuminations.* Translated by Harry Zohn. Edited by Hannah Arendt. New York: Schocken, 1969.

————. *Understanding Brecht.* Translated by Anna Bostock. London: Verso, 1983.

Benton, Ted. *The Rise and Fall of Structural Marxism.* London: Macmillan, 1984.

Bernabé, Jean, Patrick Chamoiseau, and Raphael Confiant. *Éloge de la Créolité.* Paris: Gallimard, 1989.

Bhabha, Homi. *The Location of Culture.* New York: Routledge, 1994.

Bhaskar, Roy. *Dialectic: The Pulse of Freedom.* London: Verso, 1993.

————. *A Realist Theory of Science.* Leeds: Leeds Books, 1975.

————. *Reclaiming Reality.* London: Verso, 1989.

————. *Scientific Realism and Human Emancipation.* London: Verso, 1986.

Bloch, Ernst, et al. *Aesthetics and Politics.* Translation editor Ronald Taylor. London: Verso, 1980.

Bourdieu, Pierre. *Distinction.* Translated by Richard Nice. Cambridge, Mass.: Harvard University Press, 1984.

————. *The Field of Cultural Production.* New York: Columbia University Press, 1993.

Brathwaite, Edward Kamau. *History of the Voice.* London: New Beacon Books, 1984.

Butler, Judith. *Bodies That Matter.* New York: Routledge, 1993.

————. *Gender Trouble.* London: Routledge, 1990.

————. "Mbembe's Extravagant Power." *Public Culture* 5, no. 1 (fall 1992): 67–74.

Callari, Antonio, and David F. Ruccio, eds. *Postmodern Materialism and the Future of Marxist Theory.* Hanover, N.H.: Wesleyan University Press, 1996.

Carter, Erica, James Donald, and Judith Squires, eds. *Space and Place.* London: Lawrence and Wishart, 1993.

Certeau, Michel de. *The Practice of Everyday Life.* Translated by Steven F. Rendall. Berkeley: University of California Press, 1984.

Cherchichovsky, D., and O. E. Meesook. *Poverty in Indonesia: A Profile.* Washington, D.C., 1984.

Chinweizu, Onwuchekwa Jemie, and Ihechukwu Madubuike. *Toward the Decolonization of African Literature.* Enugu: Fourth Dimension, 1980.

Clark, Katerina, and Michael Holquist. *Mikhail Bakhtin.* Cambridge, Mass.: Harvard University Press, 1984.

Clifford, James. "Traveling Cultures." In *Cultural Studies.* Edited by Lawrence Grossberg et al. London: Routledge, 1992.

Clifford, Mark. "Spring in Their Step." *Far Eastern Economic Review* (November 5, 1992): 56–57.

Coveney, Peter, and Roger Highfield, eds. *Frontiers of Complexity: The Search for Order in a Chaotic World.* New York: Fawcett Columbine, 1995.

Cribb, Robert, and Colin Brown. *Modern Indonesia.* London: Longman, 1995.

Deleuze, Gilles. *Expressionism in Philosophy: Spinoza.* Translated by Martin Joughin. New York: Zone Books, 1992.

Deleuze, Gilles, and Félix Guattari. *Anti-Oedipus.* Translated by Robert Hurley, Mark Seem, and Helen R. Lane. Minneapolis: University of Minnesota Press, 1983.

———. *A Thousand Plateaus.* Translated by Brian Massumi. Minneapolis: University of Minnesota Press, 1987.

———. *What Is Philosophy?* Translated by Hugh Tomlinson and Graham Burchell. New York: Columbia University Press, 1994.

Derrida, Jacques. *Limited Inc.* Translated by Samuel Weber. Evanston, Ill.: Northwestern University Press, 1988.

———. *Positions.* Translated by Alan Bass. London: Athlone Press, 1972.

———. *Specters of Marx.* Translated by Peggy Kamuf. New York: Routledge, 1994.

———. *The Truth in Painting.* Translated by Geoffrey Bennington and Ian McCleod. Chicago: University of Chicago, 1987.

Devi, Mahasweta. *Imaginary Maps.* Translated by Gayatri Chakravorty Spivak. New York: Routledge, 1995.

Diawara, Manthia. "Black Studies, Cultural Studies, Performative Acts." *Border/lines* 29/30 (1993): 21–26.

Diop, Cheikh Anta. *The African Origin of Civilization.* New York: Lawrence Hill, 1974.

Dirlik, Arif. "The Postcolonial Aura: Third World Criticism in the Age of Global Capitalism." *Critical Inquiry* 20 (winter 1994): 328–56.

Eagleton, Terry. *Ideology.* London: Verso, 1990.

———. *The Ideology of the Aesthetic.* London: Blackwell, 1990.

———. *The Illusions of Postmodernism.* Oxford: Blackwell, 1996.

Ebert, Teresa. *Ludic Feminism and After.* Ann Arbor: University of Michigan Press, 1996.

Elliot, Gregory, ed. *Althusser: A Critical Reader.* Oxford: Blackwell, 1994.

Engels, Friedrich. *Anti-Dühring.* London: Lawrence and Wishart, 1955.

———. "On the History of Early Christianity." In *Collected Works of Marx and Engels.* Vol. 27. New York: International Publishers, 1975.

Foucault, Michel. *Discipline and Punish: The Birth of the Prison.* Translated by Alan Sheridan. New York: Pantheon, 1979.

Freud, Sigmund. "Fetishism." Translated by Joan Riviere. In *The Standard Edition of the Complete Psychological Works of Sigmund Freud.* Vol. 21. London: Hogarth, 1961.

Fuentes, Annette, and Barbara Ehrenreich. *Women in the Global Factory.* Boston: South End Press, 1983.

Geertz, Clifford. "The Year of Living Culturally." *New Republic* (October 21, 1991): 30–36.

Gilroy, Paul. *The Black Atlantic.* Cambridge, Mass.: Harvard University Press, 1993.

———. "Cultural Studies and Ethnic Absolutism." In *Cultural Studies.* Edited by Lawrence Grossberg et al., 187–98. London: Routledge, 1992.

———. *Small Acts.* London: Serpent's Tail, 1993.

Gleick, James. *Chaos: Making a New Science.* New York: Viking, 1987.

Glissant, Edouard. *Le discours antillais.* Paris: Éditions du Seuil, 1981. Translated as *Caribbean Discourse.* Translated by Michael Dash. Charlottesville: University of Virginia Press, 1989.

Gregory, Derek. *Geographical Imaginations.* Oxford: Blackwell, 1994.

Gross, Paul, and Norman Levitt. *Higher Superstition: The Academic Left and Its Quarrels with Science.* Baltimore: Johns Hopkins University Press, 1994.

Grosz, Elizabeth. *Volatile Bodies.* Bloomington: Indiana University Press, 1994.

Habermas, Jürgen. *The Philosophical Discourses of Modernity.* Translated by Frederick Lawrence. Cambridge, Mass.: MIT Press, 1987.

———. *The Theory of Communicative Action.* Translated by Thomas McCarthy. Boston: Beacon Press, 1985.

Hannon, Kerry. "The 1992 Store of the Year." *Money* (December 1991): 156–60.

Harvey, David. *The Condition of Postmodernity.* Oxford: Blackwell, 1989.

Hawkins, Harriet. *Strange Attractors: Literature, Culture, and Chaos Theory.* New York: Prentice Hall, 1995.

Hayles, N. Katherine. *Chaos Bound: Orderly Disorder in Contemporary Literature and Science.* Ithaca, N.Y.: Cornell University Press, 1990.

———, ed. *Chaos and Order: Complex Dynamics in Literature and Science.* Chicago: University of Chicago Press, 1991.

Heidegger, Martin. *Language Thought.* Translated by A. Hofstadter. New York: Harper and Row, 1971.

———. "The Origin of the Work of Art" ("Der Ursprung des Kunstwerkes"). Translated by Albert Hofstadter. In Martin Heidegger, *Basic Writings.* Edited by David Farrell Krell, 143–212. New York: Harper Collins, 1993.

Hellwig, Tineke. *In the Shadow of Change: Images of Women in Indonesian Literature.* Berkeley: University of California Press, 1994.

Henk, Anthony. "Sublime Theremin." *New Scientist* 148 (November 1995): 76.

Hennessy, Rosemary. *Materialist Feminism and the Politics of Discourse.* New York: Routledge, 1993.

Hitchcock, Peter. "Antillanité and the Art of Resistance." *Research in African Literatures* 27, no. 2 (summer 1996): 33–50.

———. "Bakhtin/'Bakhtin.'" *Discours social/Social Discourse* 5, no. 1/2 (winter/spring 1993): 172–80.

———. "Cultural Materialism and Material Dialogics." *Discours social/Social Discourse* 7, no. 3/4 (fall 1995): 197–209.

———. "Cultural Studies and the Prospect for a Multicultural Materialism." *Rethinking Marxism* 5, no. 1 (spring 1992).

———. *Dialogics of the Oppressed.* Minneapolis: University of Minnesota Press, 1993.

———. "Information in Formation: Williams, Media, 'China.'" In *Cultural Materialism: Essays on Raymond Williams.* Edited by Christopher Prendergast. Minneapolis: University of Minnesota Press, 1995.

Hobsbawm, Eric J. *The Age of Empire.* New York: Pantheon, 1987.

———. *The Age of Extremes.* London: Abacus, 1995.

———. *Worlds of Labour.* London: Weidenfeld and Nicolson, 1984.

Holquist, Michael. *Dialogism: Bakhtin and His World.* London: Routledge, 1990.

Horkheimer, Max, and Theodor Adorno. *Dialectic of Enlightenment.* Translated by John Cumming. New York: Herder and Herder, 1972.

Horne, Haynes. "Jameson's Strategies of Containment." In *Postmodernism/Jameson/ Critique*. Edited by Douglas Kellner, 268–300. Washington, D.C.: Maisonneuve Press, 1989.

Howes, Marjorie. "Theory, Politics, and Caricature." *Public Culture* 6, no. 1 (1993): 83–95.

Iacono, Alfonso M. *Le fétichisme: Histoire d'un concept*. Paris: Press Universitaires de France, 1992.

Iluch, C. *Indonesia: Wages and Employment*. Washington, D.C.: 1985.

Irigaray, Luce. *Speculum of the Other Woman*. Translated by Gillian Gill. Ithaca, N.Y.: Cornell University Press, 1985.

———. *This Sex Which Is Not One*. Translated by Catherine Porter. Ithaca, N.Y.: Cornell University Press, 1985.

Jameson, Fredric. *The Geopolitical Aesthetic: Cinema and Space in the World System*. Bloomington: Indiana University Press, 1992.

———. *Late Marxism: Adorno, or the Persistence of the Dialectic*. London: Verso, 1990.

———. *Postmodernism, or, the Cultural Logic of Late Capitalism*. Durham, N.C.: Duke University Press, 1991.

———. "Postmodernism, or, the Cultural Logic of Late Capitalism." *New Left Review* 146 (July/August 1984): 53–92.

Janofsky, Michael. "Market Place." *New York Times*, September 24, 1993, D6.

Jay, Martin. *Adorno*. Cambridge, Mass.: Harvard University Press, 1984.

———. *Force Fields*. New York: Routledge, 1993.

Johnson, Steve. "Strange Attraction." *Lingua Franca* (April 1996): 42–50.

Kaplan, E., Ann and Michael Sprinker, eds. *The Althusserian Legacy*. New York: Verso, 1993.

Katz, Donald. *Just Do It: The Nike Spirit in the Corporate World*. New York: Random House, 1994.

Keenan, Thomas. "The Point Is to (Ex)Change It: Reading *Capital*, Rhetorically." In *Fetishism as Cultural Discourse*. Edited by Emily Apter and William Pietz, 152–85. Ithaca, N.Y.: Cornell University Press, 1993.

Kellner, Douglas. "The Obsolescence of Marxism?" In *Whither Marxism? Global Crises in International Perspective*. Edited by Bern Magnus and Stephen Cullenberg, 3–27. New York: Routledge, 1995.

Kipnis, Laura. *Ecstasy Unlimited*. Minneapolis: University of Minnesota Press, 1993.

Kristeva, Julia. "Psychoanalysis and the Polis." Translated by Margaret Waller. *Critical Inquiry* 9, no. 1 (1982): 77–92.

Kuspit, Donald. "The Modern Fetish." *Artforum* (October 1988): 132–40.

Lacan, Jacques, and Wladimir Granoff. "Fetishism: The Symbolic, the Imaginary, and the Real." In *Perversions: Psychodynamics and Therapy*. Edited by Sandor Lorand and Michael Balint. New York: Random House, 1956.

Laclau, Ernesto. *Emancipation(s)*. London: Verso, 1996.

Landry, Donna, and Gerald MacLean. *Materialist Feminisms*. London: Blackwell, 1993.

Lazarus, Neil. "Disavowing Decolonization: Fanon, Nationalism, and the Problematic of Representation in Current Theories of Colonial Discourse." *Research in African Literatures* 24, no. 4 (1993): 69–98.

Lefebvre, Henri. *The Production of Space*. Translated by Donald Nicholson-Smith. Oxford: Blackwell, 1991.

———. *The Survival of Capitalism: Reproduction of the Relations of Production*. London: Allison and Busby, 1974.

Lionnet, Françoise. "'Logiques métisses': Cultural Appropriation and Postcolonial Representations." *College Literature* 19, no. 3 (October 1992): 100–120.

Lowe, Donald M. *The Body in Late-Capitalist USA*. Durham, N.C.: Duke University Press, 1995.

Lukács, Georg. *History and Class Consciousness*. Translated by Rodney Livingstone. Cambridge, Mass.: MIT Press, 1971.

Macherey, Pierre. *A Theory of Literary Production*. Translated by Geoffrey Wall. London: Routledge, 1978.

Magnus, Bern, and Stephen Cullenberg, eds. *Whither Marxism? Global Crises in International Perspective*. New York: Routledge, 1995.

Makdisi, Saree, Cesare Casarino, and Rebecca E. Karl, eds. *Marxism beyond Marxism*. New York: Routledge, 1996.

Mann, Thomas. *Death in Venice*. Translated by David Luke. New York: Bantam, 1988.

Marx, Karl. *Capital*. Vol. 1. Translated by Ben Fowkes. London: Penguin, 1976.

———. *The Eighteenth Brumaire*. In *Surveys from Exile*. Translated by Ben Fowkes et al. Edited and introduced by David Fernbach. London: Harmondsworth, 1973.

———. *Karl Marx: Early Writings*. London: Harmondsworth, 1975.

Marx, Karl, and Friedrich Engels. *The German Ideology*. Translated by W. Lough. Edited by C. J. Arthur. New York: International Publishers, 1988.

Marxism beyond Marxism? Special issue of *Polygraph* 6/7 (1993).

Massumi, Brian. *A Reader's Guide to Capitalism and Schizophrenia*. Cambridge, Mass.: MIT Press, 1992.

Matlock, Jann. "Delirious Disguises, Perverse Masquerades, and the Ghostly Female Fetishist." *Grand Street* (summer 1995): 157–71.

Mbembe, Achille. "The Banality of Power and the Aesthetics of Vulgarity in the Postcolony." *Public Culture* 4, no. 2 (spring 1992): 1–30.

McFarlane, James. "The Mind of Modernism." In *Modernism*. Edited by Malcolm Bradbury and James McFarlane, 71–79. London: Penguin, 1976.

McLellan, David. *Ideology*. Minneapolis: University of Minnesota Press, 1986.

Miller, Christopher. *Theories of Africans: Francophone Literature and Anthropology in Africa*. Chicago: University of Chicago Press, 1990.

Mitchell, W. J. T. *Iconology*. Chicago: University of Chicago Press, 1986.

Miyoshi, Masao. "A Borderless World? From Colonialism to Transnationalism and the Decline of the Nation State." *Critical Inquiry* 19 (summer 1993): 726–51.

Moi, Toril. *Sexual/Textual Politics*. London: Methuen, 1985.

Moi, Toril, and Janice Radway, eds. *Materialist Feminism*. Special Issue of *South Atlantic Quarterly* 93, no. 4 (fall 1994).

Mudimbe, V. Y. *The Invention of Africa*. Bloomington: Indiana University Press, 1988.

Nancy, Jean-Luc. *Corpus*. Paris: Éditions A. M. Métailié, 1992.

———. *The Experience of Freedom*. Translated by Bridget McDonald. Stanford, Calif.: Stanford University Press, 1993.

———. *The Sense of the World*. Translated with a foreword by Jeffrey S. Librett. Minneapolis: University of Minnesota Press, 1997.

Negri, Antonio. *Marx beyond Marx*. Translated by Harry Cleaver, Michael Ryan, and Maurizio Viano. South Hadley, Mass.: Bergin and Garvey, 1984.

Ong, Aihwa. *Spirits of Resistance and Capitalist Discipline.* Albany: State University of New York Press, 1987.

Pêcheux, Michel. *Language, Semantics, and Ideology.* Translated by H. Nagpal. New York: St. Martin's Press, 1982.

Pfeil, Fred. "Postmodernism as a 'Structure of Feeling.'" In *Marxism and the Interpretation of Culture.* Edited by Cary Nelson and Lawrence Grossberg, 381–403. Urbana: University of Illinois Press, 1988.

Poincaré, Henri. *Les oscillations electriques.* Paris: Georges Carré, 1894.

Prakash, Gyan. *Bonded Histories: Genealogies of Labor Servitude in Colonial India.* New York: Cambridge University Press, 1990.

Prasad, Madhava. "On the Question of a Theory of (Third World) Literature." *Social Text* 31/32 (1992): 57–83.

Prigogine, Ilya, and Isabelle Stengers. *Order out of Chaos.* New York: Bantam, 1984.

Rabinow, Paul, ed. *The Foucault Reader.* New York: Pantheon, 1984.

Roach, Joseph. *Cities of the Dead.* New York: Columbia University Press, 1996.

Robbins, Bruce. *Secular Vocations.* New York: Verso, 1993.

Ryan, Michael. *Marxism and Deconstruction: A Critical Articulation.* Baltimore: Johns Hopkins University Press, 1982.

Said, Edward. *Culture and Imperialism.* New York: Vintage, 1993.

———. "Traveling Theory." In *The World, the Text, and the Critic,* 226–47. Cambridge, Mass.: Harvard University Press, 1983.

Servin, James. "Camp Nike: It's Not a Job, It's a Lifestyle." *Harper's Bazaar* (June 1994): 46–48.

Simpson, David, ed. *Subject to History.* Ithaca, N.Y.: Cornell University Press, 1991.

Sinfield, Alan. *Faultlines: Cultural Materialism and the Politics of Dissident Reading.* Berkeley: University of California Press, 1992.

Sistren. *Lionheart Gal.* London: Women's Press, 1985.

Smith, Faith. "A Conversation with V. Y. Mudimbe." *Callaloo* 14, no. 4 (1991): 969–86.

Smith, Neil. *Uneven Development.* Oxford: Blackwell, 1984.

Soja, Edward. *Postmodern Geographies.* New York: Verso, 1989.

Spivak, Gayatri Chakravorty. *In Other Worlds: Essays in Cultural Politics.* London: Routledge, 1987.

———. *Outside in the Teaching Machine.* New York: Routledge, 1993.

———. "Responsibility." *boundary 2* (fall 1994): 19–64.

———. "Supplementing Marxism." In *Whither Marxism? Global Crises in International Perspective.* Edited by Bern Magnus and Stephen Cullenberg, 109–19. New York: Routledge, 1995.

Sprinker, Michael. *Imaginary Relations.* London: Verso, 1986.

———. "The Royal Road: Marxism and the Philosophy of Science." *New Left Review* 191 (January/February 1992): 122–44.

Stark, Ellen. "Making Money on America's Top Money." *Money* (June 1993): 114–17.

Steele, Valerie. *Fetish: Fashion, Sex, and Power.* Oxford: Oxford University Press, 1996.

Strasser, J. B., and Laurie Becklund. *Swoosh: The Unauthorized Story of Nike and the Men Who Played There.* New York: Harper, 1993.

Taussig, Michael. *Mimesis and Alterity.* New York: Routledge, 1993.

Telander, Rick. "Senseless." *Sports Illustrated* 72, no. 20 (May 14, 1990): 36–49.

Thompson, John B. *Ideology and Modern Culture.* Stanford, Calif.: Stanford University Press, 1990.

———. *Studies in the Theory of Ideology.* Berkeley: University of California Press, 1984.

Timpanaro, Sebastiano. *On Materialism.* Translated by Lawrence Garner. London: Verso, 1975.

Tucker, Robert C., ed. *The Marx/Engels Reader.* New York: Norton, 1978.

Vattimo, Gianni. *The End of Modernity.* Translated by Jon R. Snyder. Baltimore: Johns Hopkins University Press, 1991.

———. *The Transparent Society.* Translated by David Webb. Baltimore: Johns Hopkins University Press, 1992.

Vincent, Jean-Marie. *Critique du travail: Le faire et l'agir.* Paris: Presses Universitaires de France, 1987. Translated as *Abstract Labor: A Critique.* Translated by Jim Cohen. New York: St. Martin's Press, 1991.

Visweswaran, Kamala. *Fictions of Feminist Ethnography.* Minneapolis: University of Minnesota Press, 1994.

Volosinov, V. N. *Marxism and the Philosophy of Language.* Translated by Ladislav Matejka and I. R. Titunik. Cambridge, Mass.: Harvard University Press, 1986.

Wallerstein, Immanuel. *Geopolitics and Geoculture: Essays on the Changing World System.* Cambridge: Cambridge University Press, 1991.

Wallis, Brian. "Selling Nations." *Art in America* 79 (September 1991): 85–91.

Wilde, Oscar. *The Soul of Man under Socialism.* Chicago: Kerr Publishing, 1984.

Williams, Linda. "Fetishism and the Visual Pleasure of Hard Core: Marx, Freud, and the 'Money Shot.'" *Quarterly Review of Film and Video* 11, no. 2 (1989): 23–42.

Williams, Raymond. *Marxism and Literature.* Oxford: Oxford University Press, 1976.

———. *Problems in Materialism and Culture.* London: Verso, 1980.

Wolf, Diane L. *Factory Daughters.* Berkeley: University of California Press, 1992.

———. "Linking Women's Labor with the Global Economy: Factory Workers and Their Families in Rural Java." In *Women Workers and Global Restructuring.* Edited by Kathryn Ward, 25–47. Ithaca, N.Y.: Cornell University Press, 1990.

Wolff, Janet. "On the Road Again: Metaphors of Travel in Cultural Criticism." *Cultural Studies* 7, no. 2 (May 1993): 224–39.

Woodward, Wiley M. "It's More Than Just the Shoes." *Black Enterprise* (November 1990): 17.

Woolf, Virginia. "Modern Novels." In *The Essays of Virginia Woolf* (vol. 3, 1919–24). Edited by Andrew McNeillie. New York: Harcourt, 1988.

World Bank. *Indonesia: Environment and Development.* Washington, D.C.: 1994.

———. *Indonesia: Strategy for a Sustained Reduction in Poverty.* Washington, D.C., 1990.

Young, Robert. *White Mythologies.* London: Routledge, 1990.

Žižek, Slavoj. *Tarrying with the Negative.* Durham, N.C.: Duke University Press, 1993.

INDEX

233

Peter Hitchcock is currently professor of literary and cultural studies at Baruch College and the Graduate School and University Center of the City University of New York. He is author of *Working-Class Fiction in Theory and Practice* and *Dialogics of the Oppressed* (Minnesota, 1993), as well as the forthcoming *Imaginary States: Studies in Cultural Transnationalism.* Hitchcock has also published numerous articles on materialist, postcolonial, and feminist theory and is the editor of a special issue of *South Atlantic Quarterly* on Bakhtin.

Stephen E. Cullenberg is chair of the Department of Economics at the University of California, Riverside. He is coeditor of *Rethinking Marxism* and (with Jack Amariglio and David Ruccio) coeditor of the forthcoming *Postmodernism, Economics, and Knowledge.*